A LITTLE BIT

Wicked

(LIFE, LOVE, AND FAITH IN STAGES)

KRISTIN CHENOWETH

with Joni Rodgers

A TOUCHSTONE BOOK
PUBLISHED BY SIMON & SCHUSTER
NEW YORK   LONDON   TORONTO   SYDNEY

Touchstone
A Division of Simon & Schuster, Inc.
1230 Avenue of the Americas
New York, NY 10020

First Touchstone trade paperback edition April 2010

TOUCHSTONE and colophon are registered trademarks of Simon & Schuster, Inc.

For information about special discounts for bulk purchases, please contact Simon &
Schuster Special Sales at 1-866-506-1949 or business@simonandschuster.com

The Simon & Schuster Speakers Bureau can bring authors to your live event. For
more information or to book an event contact the Simon & Schuster Speakers
Bureau at 1-866-248-3049 or visit our website at www.simonspeakers.com.

Designed by Mary Austin Speaker

Manufactured in the United States of America

10 9 8 7 6 5 4

The Library of Congress has cataloged the hardcover edition as follows:
Chenoweth, Kristin.
    A little bit wicked : life, love, and faith in stages / by Kristin Chenoweth with Joni
Rodgers.
        p.   cm.
    1. Chenoweth, Kristin.   2. Actresses—United States—Biography.   3. Singers—
United States—Biography.   I. Rodgers, Joni, 1962–   II. Title.
    PN2287.C532A3   2009
    792.02'8092—dc22
    [B]
                                                                        2008045875

ISBN 978-1-4165-8055-3
ISBN 978-1-4165-8056-0 (pbk)
ISBN 978-1-4391-0067-7 (ebook)

To Mom and Dad
for giving me faith, self-esteem,
and unconditional love.

contents

overture

Los Angeles, California
February 8, 2008

I face myself in the full-length mirror, stability in one hand, sex in the other.

The white Armani gown is the dress every little girl dreams of. A lot of big girls, too. A line of blushing attendants, all picture-pretty, clutch their bouquets of roses and baby's breath, each on the arm of a dashing, tuxedoed counterpart. My best always-a-bridesmaid buddy Denny Downs is looking at me with wide, moist eyes, telling me how perfect it all is . . . but suddenly I'm not sure.

A moment ago, I was ready to commit myself to the faithful friend who's supported and stood by me all these years. Then Jimmy showed up, and everything became a question. Now, here I am at the eleventh hour, wondering what might happen, who will I be, if I allow my passion to be swayed by this dangerous bad boy. Crystallized moments like this one arise in every woman's life. Moments of truth in which she makes the choices that guide her destiny. Moments that ultimately write the story of her.

Sugar or spice? I agonize. Naughty or nice?

Sensible angels whisper in my ear, but the runaway bride in me is getting restless. I am a type A "leap and a net will appear" risk-taker, and if I trust that God made me this way for a reason, then I have to believe that the risk will be worth it in the long run. Experience has taught me that we all stumble and fall; faith assures me that He'll be there to catch me when I do. My heart speaks, and I listen.

I chose Jimmy.

Jimmy Choo, that is. A fabulous pair of four-inch platform sling-backs. Setting aside the safe-and-sane character shoes I was planning to wear onstage tonight, I cast my lot with the bad boy. Oh, I know what you're thinking, and, yeah, it's not exactly *Sophie's Choice*. But this is Oscar night. I'm about to step out onstage in front of thousands of people—friends, colleagues, peers, people I hope and dream of working with—plus my parents and everyone else watching the live broadcast on television.

People keep reminding me that billions—with a *b* as in *bombastic* and *boy howdy!*—yes, *billions* of people all over the world will be tuned in. Even in the coziest venues, performers can and do get hurt onstage all the time. There's a broken toe for every light on Broadway. But I'm not as concerned for myself as I am for the burgeoning cast of backup dancers. This is a huge shot of résumé adrenaline for most of these kids; I don't want it to turn into some tragicomic YouTube video labeled "Cheno Falls on Ass." On the other hand, when you're four feet eleven inches you get pretty comfortable in heels.

"A nice pair of Jimmy Choos never hurt anyone," I tell my friend Denny, but I take the precaution of having the soles rubbered for slip-resistance. (Faith is fine, but the Lord helps those who help themselves, right?)

I'll be performing "That's How You Know," one of three Oscar-nominated songs written by Alan Menken and Stephen Schwartz for Disney's frothy fairy tale *Enchanted*. As Tilda Swinton collects the Best Supporting Actress Oscar for *Michael Clayton,* the backstage cavern turns into an anthill of scurrying crew members preparing for my number, which is being staged in full-on Broadway showstopper style. Joining me on the sweeping two-story set is a village-size cast including half a dozen dancing brides niftily accessorized with dancing grooms, quick-stepping waiters, acrobatically inclined construction workers, happy townies, multiculti mariachis, and (putting us indisputably over the top) a marching band. Against a miniature backdrop of Manhattan, a battalion of gorgeous guys will form sort of a hunk-powered elevator and pass me bodily off an ornate, ten-foot-tall bridge.

A great song. A magical night. Gown by Armani and travel by hunk-o-vator. I am in grave danger of thinking it doesn't get any better than this when someone tells me, "George Clooney is on the front row." I don't ask who else is on the front row. *Is* there anyone else?

George Clooney needs to know that he and I are perfect for each other. We would be instantly matched on eHarmony.com. I can already see us in that ad campaign, oozing adorable, giddily telling the story of our first kiss. Happily ever after, cue Chaka Khan, roll credits. He is my Mr. Right. The problem is, I'm still in love with Mr. Writer, a man who is more likely to show up in a "Falls on Ass" video than an "Everlasting Love" commercial. Truth be told, eHarmony would not encourage me to share so much as a cab uptown with this guy. But of course this is precisely what makes him irresistible.

Never for a moment did I even fantasize that Aaron Sorkin was Mr. Right. From the day we met, he was Mr. Sets My Brain on Fire, then he evolved for a long, lovely spell into Mr. Makes Me Sing REO Speedwagon in the Shower, but there was always an undercurrent of Mr. You Are Seriously Pushing Your Luck Here, and I eventually found myself doing the ol' step-ball-change with Mr. Why Am I

Banging My Head Against This Wall? Instead of coming up with a cutesy Hollywood powercouple name for us—"Sorkoweth" or "Chenorkin"—the tabloids wearily call us "on again/off again," which means we periodically put each other through a wrenching spate of separation, but I keep reinstating him as Mr. Might Actually Be Worth the Trouble. We are now "off again," and it's painful to not share this amazing moment with him. I love the man, and whatever happens or doesn't happen between us in the long run, I always will.

"It's in God's hands," I tell my father whenever he shakes his head about it.

The only thing I can say with utter certainty is that come what may, my feelings for George Clooney will remain unsullied. Whatever curtains rise and fall, the "Kristlooney" dream lives on.

Hosting the Oscars tonight is Jon Stewart, who's been onstage riffing about the bitter writers' strike that was recently resolved. His wry, wisenheimer humor is good medicine for our cruel but tenderhearted community.

"Welcome to the makeup sex," he said at the start of the show, and I felt a twinge of knowing exactly what he was talking about.

Aside from my periodic reunions with Mr. If Loving You Is Wrong, I Don't Wanna Be Right, I've been holding my breath through the strike, terrified for the fate of *Pushing Daisies,* this beautiful baby bird of a TV show I've been doing. With the strike ended, we are all breathing again and anxious to get back to work this summer. Before I resume shooting the show, I'll spend the spring in New York, shoot a movie in Minneapolis, squeeze in some family time with my far-flung loved ones in Texas, Denver, and Oklahoma, do a concert with the Chicago Symphony, and give a special benefit performance for a friend in Manhattan—all of which keeps me pleasantly occupied and comfortably distanced from L.A. with all its potential complications and painful reminders.

I make my way backstage in my Jimmy Choos. I'm getting nervous. This doesn't happen to me much anymore. Like everyone around me, I'm a seasoned pro. Stage fright is a thing of the past. But tonight, as I prepare to step onstage, a hollow, little ice cube of doubt forms in the pit of my touchy stomach. I close my eyes. *Heavenly Father . . .*

I don't have to say anything else. He knows.

Adding one last dash of adorable to the *Enchanted* number is Vanessa Williams's little daughter Sasha, so Vanessa is here, helping her get ready. She gives me a good-luck scrunch and tells me, "Sasha's going to be right there when you look at her."

It's good to have another Broadway girl backstage. There's no unnerving a woman who's conquered the pageant circuit and delivered eight shows a week. She's a glam-cat paragon of strength and calm. Sasha's learning early what it took me years to understand.

Crew hands hustle out the set pieces. The hunks and I brace ourselves for places.

Deep breath.

Jon Stewart catches my eye.

"You're going to knock it out of the park," he assures me.

"I feel like I could pee my pants."

Jon smiles at me without a trace of wisenheimer. "Just get out there and do what you do."

꿍

chapter one

LITTLE JAZZ BABY, THAT'S ME

"Spread your legs," the beautiful girl says softly, and I do.

She waves the metal-detection baton between my knees and up and down over my torso while another TSA agent rifles through my bag.

Am I the only one who feels vaguely invaded every time this happens? My heart sinks when I hear that call for "female assist." It seems to happen every time I fly, and I fly a lot. I don't feel that I'm entitled to special treatment, but is there really some valid concern that Broadway performers are plotting to take over the world? People, we don't get up that early. I promise. You have nothing to fear from us aside from the occasional eruption of "He's Just My Bill" while we stand in line at Starbucks.

"I can't believe how tiny you are in person," the TSA agent exclaims. "I mean, you're like *small*."

"Yup. I've heard that." I raise my arms to crucifixion posture.

"You don't look that little on TV. I saw you on the Oscars last month." She smiles, and I smile back at her. "That must be so awesome. The red carpet and all those movie stars and the parties—oh, my gosh. You were at a party with George Clooney, weren't you? I bet you went to like a million parties and like partied with movie stars until dawn."

In truth, I went straight home because I was in the middle of shooting a movie, *Four Christmases*, and I had to be on the set at five forty-five the next morning looking like someone who sleeps occasionally. But partying till dawn with a million movie stars—it sounds so lovely, I don't want to ruin it for her.

"Wouldn't be Oscar night without the parties," I say gamely.

"I like you on *Pushing Daisies*," gains the young man going through my underwear. "And I saw you in that, um . . . that magazine. You know."

"Yes." I can tell by the color in his cheeks that he's talking about my itsy-bitsy bikini layout in an issue of *FHM* that is probably still tucked between the mattress and box spring of many a corn-fed all-American boy.

"I got the calendar. It's *awesome*," he says earnestly.

"Well, thank you so much. You're so sweet." I shine him a Miss February smile because I see him eyeing my fancy-schmancy hair gel. "That's as close as I could get to travel size. It's only half an ounce over. Do you suppose . . . just this once . . ."

He takes my hair gel, which cost $28, which is worth it if you have flea-fine hair like mine. He takes my tweezers, and I *need* my tweezers. Why, why, *why* do they always commandeer my dang tweezers?

Let me just say right now and for the record that I, Kristi Dawn Chenoweth, do solemnly swear that I will never hack through a Kevlar door and stab a pilot in the neck with my tweezers. I will never seek, nor have I ever sought, to overthrow the government of the United

States of America by force of tweezer. Anyone who knew me back in the eighties can tell you, I am far more dangerous *without* my tweezers. Jimmy Kimmel once whipped out a photo of me from my pageant days, and I thought those eyebrows were going to leap right off the matte finish like a couple of centipedes. I had a whole lotta Brooke Shields going on, except Brooke somehow manages to carry it off, all of which is to say *I need my dang tweezers.*

"Miss Chenoweth, could I please get a picture with you?" asks the female assist sister. "My little girls listen to the *Wicked* sound track like ten times a day. They'll go crazy when they hear I actually got to wand down Glinda the Good Witch." She laughs. I laugh. We all laugh. Wand? Witch? Get it? I glance nervously at my watch.

"It'll only take a second, I swear," she swears. She whips out her cell phone and shows me photos. They are adorable. Two little peanut-butter-and-jelly princesses.

"Sure. No problem."

I pose with her, and it only takes a second. And a few seconds more to pose with the young man who loves me on *Pushing Daisies,* and a few more for the passengers behind me in line, who aren't exactly sure who I am but assume, because the other security people are now asking for my autograph, that I'm famous.

"Y'all are so sweet," I keep saying. "I really need to get to my gate, though."

"Ma'am, you have to be at the gate thirty minutes early for first class," the gate agent tells me when I get there. "We gave your seat away."

"But . . . but it was paid for. My father checked me in online. And I was here but—"

"There should be a seat in coach." She studies her computer monitor with a look of deep disapproval. "Just get on and take whatever seat is available."

"Oh . . . okay." I weigh the time constraint against the possibility that arguing will get me anywhere. Heavy sigh. "Then you'll refund the difference for the first-class seat?"

"There's no refund," she says curtly. "It's up to you to get here on time."

She shoots a no-nonsense glance toward the Jetway, and I dutifully drag my bag on board, passing through the first-class cabin with my eyes forward. It crosses my mind briefly that I could pipe up and ask the dapper businessmen which of them is sitting in the seat I paid for, but I don't want to come off all *Don't you know who I think I am?* so I go to a seat facing the wall just on the other side of the magic curtain.

"You need to take your seat, miss," says the frazzled flight attendant.

"Could you help me with this bag, please?" I indicate the overhead storage miles above my head.

"There's no room in the overheads. You should have been here earlier."

"Yes, we've established that. I made a mistake. I apologize. But if you could—"

"If that doesn't fit under the seat, it'll have to be checked."

"No. Really. I can't check it. There's medication in it, and somehow my checked bags never end up landing the same place I do."

"Well, here's a tip. Don't put medication in your checked bags."

"I didn't."

"You'll have to check it."

"I'm not checking it."

"There's no room."

"I'll find room."

Her lips go thin as a snapping turtle's. My grip tightens on the handle of my Louis Vuitton trolley bag. We stand there giving each other the bitch-eye.

"Ms. Noodle?" A voice from the seat behind me blossoms like a tiny crocus and rises to a shriek. The little girl is spazzing with joy, refusing to be hushed by her embarrassed mother. *"Ms. Noodle! Ms. Noodle! From 'Elmo'!"*

"Hey there, cutie." I smile at her without giving up one degree of grip on my bag.

"I'm sorry to bother you," says the mom. "Are you the *Sesame Street* girl?"

The flight attendant looks at me suspiciously, wondering if I'm someone, and quickly letting me know I'm not. "Miss. Please check the bag and take your seat."

"Ms. Noodle! Ms. Noodle!"

"Could she maybe get your autograph?" asks the mom. "When you get settled?"

"Miss? You need. To take. Your seat. Please."

"Ms. Chenoweth?" There's a hand on my elbow. The flight attendant from first class has joined the fray. "I'll find room for your bag up front."

I nod. At least Louis will travel in style. "I appreciate that. Thank you."

"Sorry for the inconvenience," she says kindly.

Turtle Lips turns on her heel and stalks down the aisle. My bag disappears into the Emerald City up front. Making Miss Noodle faces for the little girl behind me, I sign my name in a Hello Kitty notebook, then sink into my seat, swallowing tears that burn uncomfortably close to the surface. It's no one's fault. The TSA agents, the gate dominatrix, the frazzled flight attendant—they're undoubtedly nice people who would have been gentler had they known I was traveling to a funeral. *A death in the family.* That's one of those conversational trump cards that makes everyone around the table lower their eyes, but I'm not one to play those cards. Not how I was raised.

My BlackBerry vibrates in my pocket. A message from Aaron. He's being very sweet. Shortly after the Oscars, he e-mailed me a whole lot

of *words*, and I ended up going to Mexico with him. Cabo is a place
we go to find each other. Long story short, Chenorkin is on again.

"That needs to be off," Turtle Lips snaps on her way past.

"Tell me about it."

I power down the BlackBerry and close my eyes. I hate flying. My
travel karma sucks. Even when everyone is nice—and people usually
are—my flights get mysteriously delayed, my bags inexplicably turn
up in Toledo instead of Toronto, my heel breaks as I dash down the
concourse. It's always something, and I'm only half joking when I say
this might be genetic.

I don't know much about my biological mother. Only that she was
twenty-one when I was born, a flight attendant who got pregnant by
a pilot who had a wife and children. That's the story anyway, and
while I'm a curious person by nature, I feel a surprising lack of curiosity about whether it's true.

My real mom is Junie Smith Chenoweth. Her name is a bright wink
to her birthday, the first of June, and she is the best mom in the world.
(I'm sorry if you were under the mistaken impression that your mom is
the best mom in the world or that there might be moms in Portugal or
Wisconsin who come close. That's not the case.) My mom is this wonderful dichotomy: her breezy, athletic style blends a jeans-and-sneakers
spirit with skirt-and-pumps grace. She's one of six tall sisters, each of
whom is uniquely fabulous. When I was little, Mom's dark, curly hair
was sassed up with Frost & Tip and pulled back sometimes in a casually
twisted headscarf like Jackie O. She has gorgeous blue eyes and bone
structure that works beautifully with her well-chosen glasses. Not everyone's face works with glasses. Mom pulls it off.

Best of all, there's not a hint of stage mama about her. She knew
nothing about showbiz and cared even less. The home she made for us
was all about happiness, the value of a hearty breakfast, the impor-
tance of doing what's right. Instead of pushing me to perform, she
taught me to pray, and that made her the perfect mother for me.

Dad also wears glasses. (Come to think of it, I'm the only one in the family who doesn't.) His thick brown hair has gently grayed over the years, but when I look at his face now, I see the same quiet strength I saw when I was barely big enough to climb up into his lap. I've always seen him as the gatekeeper. One of those Rock of Gibraltar men who stands on faith and lives by principle. He's balanced and calm, a suit man until about five minutes after he gets home from work; then it's Bermuda shorts and shirts, which Mom has to help him match because he's color-blind. My earliest memories are of my father chasing me around the coffee table, teasing, "I'm gonna get you! I'm gonna get you!" but always letting me get away so I could feel like I won. (In many ways, we're still playing that game.) We don't always agree, but he's the first one I turn to for advice about business and life.

Some people say we pick our parents, but God had to play some jazz to get me to the family where I was supposed to be. If I ever need evidence of the Lord's hand on me, proof of His plan for my little strand in His tightly woven tapestry, all I have to do is look across the dining room table at Junie and Jerry Chenoweth.

∞

No one ever made a secret of the fact that I was a bonus baby who drifted quite miraculously into the family when I was five days old. Mom was only twenty-four and facing a heartbreaking hysterectomy three years after the birth of my brother, Mark. She and Dad desperately wanted another child. They were prepared to wade through the paperwork and spend years on the adoption waiting lists, but they didn't have to.

Mom confided in the ob-gyn who was going to do her surgery that more than anything, she wanted a little girl. That's understandable, right? Join the national average, balance out the Christmas card, *tea for two and two for tea,* and all that. But I think it was more than this for Mom. She and I have always had a unique connection, and I wonder if, somehow, some part of her spirit knew that I was out there, that I belonged to her, and she needed to find me.

Cue the Mile High Club.

When my flight-attendant birth mama turned up pregnant by a married man, her wealthy family shipped her off to Oklahoma (or so I'm told), and arrangements were made for the expected baby to be placed with a nice Catholic family who were next in line on the long list. But just before I was born, the adopting mother-to-be turned up pregnant herself and offered to allow another family to have this baby girl. She told the ob-gyn, and he immediately thought of my mother. It bugs me when people assume that this woman passed me along because she figured having her own baby was better. I'm certain that this was not only an incredibly selfless thing to do, but also a huge act of faith; a lot can happen in the course of a pregnancy, especially for a woman who's struggled through years of infertility. Perhaps some part of her spirit knew that I didn't belong to her. It also bugs me when I hear about "Angelina's adopted son" or "Rosie's adopted children"—as if that word will always separate them instead of binding them together. Angelina's son and Rosie's kids and I should get a regular apostrophe-plus-*s* like everybody else. I'm "Junie's girl," plain and simple, whatever serendipity and string-pulling went into the magic bubble ride that took me from forbidden love to the Chenoweth home in Broken Arrow, Oklahoma.

"I felt like I had you," my mom always told me. "I had the surgery, and we came home from the hospital together. It felt just like that newborn recovery period when I had Mark."

I can't imagine what my father was going through in the meantime. Sorting through logistics and legalities. Waiting on pins and needles. Mom says they could hardly breathe during the one-year waiting period in which the biological mother could have changed her mind. But the moment of truth came and went, and I was their baby. Signed, sealed, and delivered. Not necessarily in that order.

I am deeply grateful to the three women who brought me into my world: one loving enough to reach out for me, two loving enough to let me go. However, since the question always gets asked, no, I have no interest in contacting or being contacted by my biological mother. I've never felt the slightest frisson of something missing in my life, and the whole medical-records thing doesn't concern me much. I'm vigilant about my health. (In my profession, you're either vigilant about your health or you're Janis Joplin.) I do vaguely wonder if my biological mother suffers from Ménière's disease like I do.

If you're unfamiliar with the joy of Ménière's (and I hope you are), imagine a floor-warping, ceiling-spinning, brain-churning, think-you're-gonna-die-and-afraid-you-might-not hangover and multiply that times the aftermath of a power outage at the all-you-can-eat Chinese buffet. That's Ménière's. Saying it's "an inner ear disturbance that causes vertigo" sounds so *Bless my petticoats, Miss Petunia is having a spell*. This is more than that. This SOB is seriously debilitating at times. So I sleep on an incline (even though hotel housekeeping people look at me as if I were requesting handcuffs and a swing above the bed), I limit sodium and several other factors that bring on episodes, and I take my don't-fall-over-and-throw-up drugs when I fly or experience a climate change. And I pray. A lot. I've tried everything short of the handcuffs and swing in an effort to control it. Bottom line: Ménière's disease sucks a big fat corncob. Knowing if some biological family member also has it wouldn't really make a difference. I mean, what are we supposed to say to each other about it?

"Howdy, stranger. Throw up much?"

"Yup. Tough to be us sometimes, huh?"

"Yup. Have a nice day."

"You, too. Try not to fall over."

The light haze of curiosity isn't enough for me to risk disrupting my life or the life of the woman who gave me up for adoption. She made a difficult choice, and I have profound respect for that. In 1968, abortion was still illegal in the United States, but she apparently had the money (and the flight bennies) to go wherever she needed to go to get it done. She chose to have me instead, and *thank you* does not begin to cover how I feel. But that's all I've ever really wanted to say to her.

There was one strange little incident back in my pageant days. While I was the reigning Miss Oklahoma City University, I was invited to sing at an event honoring then vice president Dan Quayle, who was visiting Tulsa. At this sort of event, I was always accompanied by my handler, Kathleen McCracken, the pageant Rambo who steered me to wherever I was supposed to go and made sure I looked like a beauty queen when I got there. You get to be like sisters with your pageant handler (which makes me an aunt to her daughter, who's now a Broadway babe). Who else can you trust to let you know if your roots are showing or there's a scrap of toilet tissue trailing from the hem of your gown?

A huge crowd had turned out to greet the vice president. After I sang, speeches were made, I sang again, and then I was wrangled off to a table to sign autographs. A strange assortment of folks show up to get Miss OCU's autograph: lots of little girls and I don't know whom else. Some people in Oklahoma don't get out much, I guess. I don't allow myself to wonder if there's an autographed eight-by-ten glossy of me attached to the head of an inflatable doll in some guy's basement up in Okfuskee County. I prefer to think we were all caught up in the festive occasion, and people wanted something to remember it by. It's not like I was famous; the whole autograph thing was probably more thrilling for me than it was for them.

"I've been watching your career."

The voice was choked with emotion. I glanced up to find a small blond woman with luminous green eyes.

"I just wanted to say . . . I'm so proud of you."

"Well, thank you so much," I said with my pageant-perfected smile. "That's so sweet."

Oklahomans are proud of their own, but she seemed particularly overwhelmed. Her eyes welled. She bit her lip and thrust a wrinkled program forward, unable to say anything more. I didn't find this terribly odd; I'd sung "God Bless the USA," and a lot of people get choked up about that song. It's not unusual for one song or another to strike a deeply personal chord, and I'm grateful when people let me know that they were moved. It's a privilege. I signed her program and thanked her again. As she retreated into the crowd, Kathleen gripped my arm.

"What . . ."

"Kristi, that woman—she looked exactly like you."

"What . . ."

"I think that might have been—I mean—do you think she's—"

I bolted from behind the table, not to stop the woman, only to catch another glimpse of her, to see if the resemblance was as striking as Kathleen thought. I craned and gandered after her, but like me, she stood head and shoulders shorter than most of the people in the crowd. It was like trying to spot a daffodil in a cornfield. Only a few seconds had passed, but she was already lost in the throng.

I'll never know for sure, but if that really was the landed flight attendant, that young girl from old money who made the choice to bring me into the world and cared enough for me to give me a good home, I love her all the more for walking away. Perhaps she has a happy family of her own now. (Please, God, let her have a happy family of her own now.) And perhaps she's chosen not to tell them about her difficult past. I wouldn't dream of intruding on this woman's privacy, and naturally I'm uncomfortable with the idea of strangers intruding on mine, but it makes me happy to think that she knows about the blessings that have rained down on this life she knitted. If she was aware of the Miss OCU pageant, she must know about *Wicked, Candide,* and *Pushing Daisies.* She must have watched me collect a Tony and sing at the Oscars. She's reading this book right now. It's the loveliest thing she could have said: *I've been watching your ca-*

reer. There's no bragging rights attached to that statement, no attempt to reestablish a territory. There's only gladness in the most unselfish package possible.

Remember the Bible story about wise King Solomon? Two women came to him with one baby, each claiming to be the infant's mother.

"Bring me a sword," he said. "Cut the child in two, and give each woman half."

The first woman instantly cried, "No! Please! Give the baby to my sister."

Meanwhile, the other chick shrugged. "Go ahead. Neither of us will have him."

How brilliant was that? The ultimate test of a mother's love. King Solomon immediately knew that the first woman was the baby's mother because love is not about doggedly clinging to what belongs to you; it's about finding it in yourself to let go, even when letting go breaks your heart.

I remember Judy Garland singing "Over the Rainbow," the smell of the mosquito-spray trucks that slowly rolled down our street at night, dozing against my mother's shoulder in church on Sunday morning, playing with my brother, Mark, on this huge grassy mound (at least it seemed huge as we scrambled up and over it) in the yard outside our pleasant ranch-style house in Broken Arrow, a little town just outside Tulsa. I don't remember this happening, but Mom says she came out one day and found me posing on that mound with a stick in my mouth. Several feet away, Mark had positioned himself with this bull-whip that Dad had made when he was a teenager. In one of those classic "Someone could put an eye out!" shenanigans, Mark was winding up to whip that stick out of my mouth like a lion tamer, and I was standing there with all the faith in the world that he could do it.

That's how it was, is, and ever shall be with me and my big brother.

I'd follow him to the ends of the earth, and though that isn't a great example of it, he was always my champion and protector. One summer, we went on a family road trip that sort of Chevy Chased out of control. At one point, poor Dad was struggling to jack up the car to change a flat when a semi roared by and the car came down with a *kafwumph*. Dad started cussing a blue streak—the first time I'd ever heard any such language—and I must have gotten wide-eyed because Mark scootched over and slid his arm around me, telling me it was okay. A while later, we felt the car bouncing up and down and peeked over the seat back to see Dad hurling himself on the trunk, trying to get it closed. Then we just busted out in giggle fits.

When I was in sixth grade, Mark met Betsye. Blond, adorable, and such a terrifically *good* young woman. Anything she did, I wanted to do—cheerleading, summer camp, you name it. We were girlie girls together. If I got clothes for Christmas or my birthday, I laid them all out on my bed and made her come and look through them the second she walked through the door. She made Mark happy and never treated me like the annoying little sis. She became my sister, plain and simple. (For me, family has never been restricted by genetics or paperwork.) When Betsye was in ninth grade and Mark in tenth, he broke up with her briefly, and I was devastated.

"Mark!" I sobbed. "How can you do this to me? You have to get back together."

In a week or two, she was part of the family again and hasn't missed a beat since.

I thought Mark was the smartest kid around. He even looked smart with his smart-kid glasses, which didn't diminish the Greg Brady brand of cool he achieved with his sharp blue eyes, longish hair, and groovy stovepipe cords. In many ways, Mark was a chip off the ol' block, very much like my dad (who achieved his own brand of cool with one of those *Magnum, P.I.* mustaches), and Dad, in turn, was an apple who didn't fall far from the tree. His own father had the same quiet strength. My grandfather Roy Chenoweth was a gatekeeper, too, a salt-of-the-earth Christian and devoted family man, married to his beloved Mildred Alice for seventy years.

Grandpa was humble and hardworking, easygoing as an Oklahoma evening. Grandma, on the other hand, ran a pretty tight ship. She was a Southern Baptist who played canasta with the Methodists and dominoes with the Church of Christers, which kinda says it all. She believed by the Book, but embraced socially liberal ideals.

"I'll always be a Democrat," she told me when I was old enough to know what that meant but still young enough to think it made a difference. "Jesus cared for the poor. He was for the people, and I gotta stick with him."

She thought Jimmy Carter was the greatest man who ever lived, which made my conservative Republican father groan and invoke the name of his patron saint, Ronald Reagan. Needless to say, this made things interesting when everybody got to talking late in the evening, and I learned two things from all that lawn-chair filibustering:

1. It is possible to discuss differences of opinion in a friendly, respectful way.

2. There are good people of every political stripe, all with good reasons for believing the way they do.

I'm a swinger when it comes to voting. Not even interested in a monogamous relationship with one party or another. Following Grandma Chenoweth's example, I subject everything to the Jesus smell test. He was an issues guy who staunchly refused to dish out or swallow spoon-fed answers. He told people to search the Scriptures and think for themselves, so that's what I try to do. But following Grandpa Chenoweth's example, I mostly keep my politics to myself. A good barber must also be a master of diplomacy. Being right was never as important to him as being kind.

Conversation in Grandpa's shop revolved around the weather, family gatherings, local harvests, high school football scores. (Southern towns are all about the Friday-night lights.) There was the usual busybody stuff, but no malicious gossip. All the local curmudgeons gathered for morning coffee and a shave. If it was too hot for coffee, they went to the old Coke machine in the back, where you could plug in your money and pull out a bottle of 7UP, Dr Pepper, Orange Crush, Strawberry Crush, or my personal favorite, Grape Crush. Sometimes, Grandpa would let my cousin Kimbo and me sweep the floor in exchange for whatever pocket change he had on him so we could walk up the street and buy candy from Red Bud Grocery or Hobbs Drug, with its genuine heart-shaped soda fountain right out of the 1930s.

I always saved up my allowance to buy my mom and dad a present every summer. Grandma worked up the street in a ladies' shop, so finding a knickknack or a charm bracelet or tennis-racquet brooch for Mom was always easy, but I never knew what to get for Dad, so Grandpa always fixed me up with a bottle of this particular green hair gel, which he assured me Dad couldn't do without. Dad was always delighted and thanked me profusely when he opened it, but just before I left for college, I was looking for something in the dark reaches of my parents' bathroom closet and came upon a dozen bottles of that green hair gel. He'd never used a single squirt. Maybe that was Grandpa's silent revenge for the Reagan administration, I don't know, but I love that simply because it was a gift from me, Dad couldn't bring himself to throw it away.

In a funny way, that green hair gel tells you everything there is to know about how my parents raised me. The choices I've made haven't necessarily been what they hoped for. Sensible? Not always. Utilitarian? Not hardly. But they were delighted with just about anything I presented to them. Ballerina? Give it a whirl. Songbird? Lovely. They saw value in each endeavor, purely because it came from me. Looking back, I'm sure at times they weren't quite sure what to do with me. My physical appearance and realm of interests were noticeably different from those of everyone else in my family, but I always felt that I fit in because they have always loved me exactly as I am. They never expected or even asked me to be anything else. That's the kind of family we are.

It hit Grandpa hard when Grandma died. I was in the middle of shooting a Christmas movie called *Deck the Halls,* and it took some scrambling, but the director, John Whitesell, was kind enough to shuffle the schedule for me to fly down just in time for the funeral. Mark and I stayed with Grandpa afterward, and late that night I found Grandpa standing in Grandma's closet, drifting his hands over her empty dresses and coats.

"Grandpa? Are you okay?"

He looked at me, his face full of loss. "What am I supposed to do now?"

"You keep on keepin' on," I said. Because that's what Grandma always said.

He told me I should take anything of hers that I wanted, but I wasn't ready to do that. Long after he left, I sat looking through her things. Her Bible was in a quilted cover with handles, and every margin of every page was written completely full of notes, prayers, and questions. You can tell a lot about a person from the way she interacts with her Bible. Grandma's Bible was a living thing, a running dialogue between her and God. She knew her Scripture up, down, and sideways, well enough to be comfortable with both her faith and her doubts. When I first started feeling uncertain about some of the teachings I was raised on, I went straight to her.

"Grandma, do you think maybe they're wrong about—I mean—in my heart, I just don't think being gay is a sin."

"I don't know," she said. "But Jesus told us to love everybody without judging, so I try to do that."

I never really knew how many friends she had until her funeral. Lots of ladies from lots of faiths, each bearing a gift of lemon bars, shoofly pie, or Tater Tots hotdish because Jesus told us to feed each other, too. (The one delicacy not available on the Upper West Side: church-lady cuisine.)

Over the next year or so, I tried to pay extra attention to Grandpa, tried to call more often and visit whenever I could. Mark and I chipped in with our cousins Kim and Karla and hooked him up with a new plasma TV so he could watch *As the World Turns,* Red Skelton reruns, golf, and me on *Pushing Daisies.* When I called him, he was marvel-struck about it.

"I can't believe there's a flat TV now," he said. But over the next several weeks, each time I spoke to him, there seemed to be a little less wind in his sails. Not long ago, he told me, "My bags are packed, Kristi. I miss my girl."

"Grandpa . . ." I hated hearing him talk like that, so I said the worst possible thing in response: "Don't say that."

"I love you, Kristi."

"I love you, too, Grandpa. And I'll be down next month to visit, okay?"

"If I don't see you, you know I love you."

A few days later, as Aaron and I sat stranded on a plane on the tarmac in Mexico—our flight delayed, luggage lost, ticket bollixed, and him finally convinced that I really and truly am cursed with terrible travel karma—I coaxed a last glimmer of life from my BlackBerry and saw that Mark had tried several times to call me.

"Oh, no . . ."

I looked up at Aaron, trying to hold on to the feeling of the sun on my skin, the much needed rest and quiet conversation, laughing, being lovers. That little oasis of days with him had been so sweet, lifted out of our day-to-day hassles like a perfect star lifted from an expanse of rolled-out cookie dough.

"I have to call," I said, and Aaron nodded.

He squeezed my hand while Mark gave me the news. I clicked off the phone and tried to breathe, but there was no air in this empty closet of loss. Aaron pulled me into his arms as best he could with the whole armrest/drink-tray operation between us, and I wept ungracefully, bunching a wad of his shirt in my fist, trying hard to keep quiet, not because I cared what anyone thought but because fresh grief is so intensely private. He brushed his mouth across my temple, holding me without hushing or shushing or offering platitudes.

Aaron gives good comfort. He's that sort. Leaning into his body, I experienced pure, oxygenated gratitude. Oh, what a gift to have someone hold you so dearly in a moment when you so dearly need to be held. But somehow the blessing of his being there made his coming absence cut all the deeper. I thought about Mark, voice husky, eyes red-rimmed at Grandma's funeral. He wasn't crying for himself or even for her; he was looking at Grandpa, wondering how a man goes on without his mate, his wife, the love of his life. If Mark didn't love his own wife with such depth, perhaps he could have looked away.

That's just not the way we do things here in the *Devil Wears Prada* generation. It's a relationship stink bomb for a woman to admit that she wants to be married; it sounds old-fashioned at best and at worst, desperate. (Frankly, it would help matters if they'd allow gay marriage because anything gays do is automatically chic.) I don't make judgments about what's right or wrong for other people, but for me, the idea of living together without being married feels very *leave the gun, take the cannoli*. I don't care if it sounds old-fashioned. Or desperate. Or desperately old-fashioned. I'm saying right now and for the record, I believe in marriage as a social institution, a business deal, and a holy sacrament. I'm not jaded about it because long before I witnessed the bitchy divorces of Beverly Hills, I watched the long, rich marriages of my parents, my grandparents, and Mark and Betsye, still high school sweethearts after all these years.

When I felt the nearness of this man I love, his strong hand on my back, his warm breath on my wet face, I wanted my husband to be holding me, and the thought of that never happening was far more heartbreaking than the thought of my grandfather fixing to spend eternity in the arms of the wife who loved him. I didn't want to suffocate or scare Mr. Writer, but I was suddenly certain I could no longer settle for—

"Peanuts?"

The turtle-lipped flight attendant stands over me. Mexico was yesterday. Now I'm on this airplane. In this time zone. Alone and on my way to Grandpa's funeral and getting glared at by this broad who hates me because she hates short people or hates TV people or whatever it is up her butt. She proffers a sad little foil pouch.

"No, thanks," I tell her quietly.

She walks away, and I retreat into my headphones until we land. Everyone is instantly on their feet, jostling and jockeying for position in the aisle, dragging elephants, anvils, and grand pianos down over my head. Craning to see through the forest of shoulders and elbows, I wave my hand to catch the attention of my missionary from first class, but she's busy with whoever sat in my seat. I'm forced to enlist the help of vitriol-shaped-like-a-flight-attendant.

"Excuse me? Could you please help me locate my bag?"

"No," she says flatly.

"If you could just tell me where—"

"It's not my problem," she snaps.

"Really? I mean . . . because . . . really?" I am genuinely baffled. Why would she choose this? Purely from the standpoint of character study, I wonder, how does a bouncing baby girl grow up so pissed off at the world? "You must be very unhappy in your job."

"Well, that's none of your business."

I quietly ask her for her name.

"That's none of your business either."

She looks down on me from an upright and locked position. I can tell by the way she taps her foot that she knows all about me. How I cut her off on the freeway in my kazillion-dollar car and light gold-leafed cigars with the tattered dreams of my upstairs maid. I'm acutely aware of the little girl behind me and how it would feel to her if she saw Miss Noodle go off all cranky pants on some flight attendant. But even Miss Noodle has her limits.

"Your name. Please."

"Why?"

"I'd like to pray for you."

"I don't need your prayers."

"Oh, honey," I tell her truthfully, "we all need prayers. And I'm fixin' to talk to God about you specifically."

chapter two

WHAT WOULD A BUNNY DO?

Mark meets me at the airport. He and Betsye live in Denver now, the eternally patient parents of two vibrant teenagers. He was a late bloomer, but sometime during high school, he sprouted up over six feet. Gone is the Greg Brady shag, replaced by a *hoo rah* flattop. Though he usually wears Wranglers and a polo to work, he's done out in a somber grief-appropriate suit today, tall, lanky, and handsome. We're the first to arrive at Grandpa and Grandma's church, First Baptist in Hinton (not to be confused with First Baptist in Broken Arrow, First Baptist in Noble, or First Baptist in New York City). I link my arm through his as we approach Grandpa's open casket.

How can anyone who's seen a dead body question the existence of the soul? The difference between the living and the dead so clearly goes beyond temperature and movement. There's an energy that's there.

Until it isn't. Human beings—and let me just interject here that I love being part of a species whose name is a verb—human *beings* have an innate fascination with the idea of afterlife, a close cousin of our fascination with death. We're forever trying to build bridges, find peepholes. It's a major theme in theatre, music, literature, and art. Everything from Dante's *Inferno* to—well, take *Pushing Daisies* for example.

What if (proposed the delightfully quirky mind of Bryan Fuller) a man could bring the dead back to life with a single touch. Interesting premise, but a bit of a free lunch unless you build in a few complications. Another touch and the resurrected one is dead again. And if that second touch doesn't happen in sixty seconds or less, someone else dies. (Another human fixation: the bargain that is salvation. We need things to balance out. If you get a little this, you gotta give a little that.) Of course, capitalism kicks in, and the man decides to use this extraordinary gift to solve murders and collect the rewards. It's a complicated scenario; the protagonist is playing an almost impossible daily game of Twister that has us holding our breath and hopefully being a little more mindful of life, death, and the power of touch.

It's good TV (and, no, that is not an oxymoron) with excellent writing and an amazing ensemble of terrific actors. To see it strangled in its infancy by ratings or the writers' strike would have broken my heart. I learned just how quickly circumstances can kill a worthy show when I did My Huge Hit Sitcom *Kristin* on NBC. (Huge hit. Puccini high-note huge. Ask either of the people who saw it.)

Obviously, *Pushing Daisies* is a great gig, but when it came up, I'd already made a semifirm commitment to do Mel Brooks's *Young Frankenstein* on Broadway. The Madeline Khan role. And I worship Madeline Khan—even named my little dog Maddie in homage. That was hard to turn away from. And now that I think about it, *Frankenstein* is another piece concerning the bridge between life and death, another examination of what truly constitutes life. Electricity? Chemistry? Or is animation without a soul . . . monstrous?

As firmly as I believe in the existence of my left ankle, I believe in the existence of my soul. Einstein said energy can't be created or destroyed, only changed. The Bible says God breathed life into Adam. Do the math. Standing beside my brother at the front of the church, I feel my grandfather in the room, but I know he's not in this box.

Mark puts his arm around my shoulder, and we gaze at this man who was so important to us both. But after a moment, our sniffling gives way to frozen silence. We exchange furtive *Are you lookin' at what I'm lookin' at?* glances.

"What's with his hand?" I whisper.

"I don't know," Mark whispers back. "Seems like it's sort of . . . floating."

And it is. The hands are positioned to cross over Grandpa's abdomen, as you would expect, but the right hand is hovering stiffly a good three inches above the left.

"That's freaky," Mark says.

He reaches out and gingerly presses down on the back of Grandpa's wrist. The entire arm toggles like a diving board. As soon as Mark takes his finger away, the thing springs back up. If anything, the gap is wider.

"Dang," says my brother.

"Oh, my gosh, Mark, why is it doing that?"

"How do I know? You're the one who's fascinated with forensics. All I know is we can't have this arm flailing all over when Dad gets here." Mark hooks a finger inside his necktie, giving himself room to swallow. "Okay. I got it. Here we go."

He gently takes Grandpa's right hand and carefully shuffles it under the left, but when he lets go, both arms pop up, hands hovering over the fly of Grandpa's Sunday pants.

"*Crap!* Mark. That's not good."

"Oh, ya think?" he hisses. "We need somebody from the funeral home."

"Yes. Yes," I agree enthusiastically, envisioning a man in black. He'll know what to do. He'll speak furtively into his cuff link. *We've got a floater, Eames. Get over here with a torque wrench and some glutaraldehyde.*

An undignified giggle snorts from my sinuses.

"Kristi."

"I'm sorry. I'm sorry. It's not funny. I'm—I'm not laughing."

"Me neither," Mark says tightly.

The next moment, we both explode into hysterics, practically strangling each other in an effort to stop laughing. It is the most low-brow, slapstick form of amusement. I'm ashamed to tell you about it. I won't even try to spin it with some kind of "Oh, Grandpa would have loved that" horse crap because, *c'mon,* this is not what anyone envisions when they prepay thousands of dollars for that final fluff 'n' fold. But for Mark and me, it's such a relief. It's like Truvy says in the play *Steel Magnolias:* "Laughter through tears is my favorite emotion." Laughter is life-giving. It makes you breathe.

We finally pull ourselves together, and I hug Mark hard. Mark reshuffles Grandpa's hand so the one that wants to stay down stays down, and the one that doesn't want to cooperate is hovering again. Mark tufts the handkerchief from his own breast pocket and arranges it to fill the gap between the two. Close enough for country, as the saying goes.

Folks begin to arrive. Scattered family. Many friends. Everyone says how nice Grandpa looks. And how nice it is that I'm going to sing. I wish I shared their confidence. As we file into the pews, sitting shoulder to shoulder, I'm not at all sure what sort of sound is going to come out when I open my mouth, but I'm afraid *nice* isn't going to be the word for it. It'll sound about as nice as a dead man looks, I guess.

Keep on keepin' on, I tell myself as we take our seats. *Keep on keepin' on.*

There's a greeting and a prayer, a hymn, the usual things. Then my cousin Karla gets up to read a poem she wrote for Grandpa's retirement party, when he closed the doors of his barbershop after forty-five years of shaves and haircuts. Standing at the podium, she adjusts the goosenecked microphone and clears her throat.

" 'The Very Patient Barber.' " Her voice wavers only a little. " 'Every Tuesday through Saturday, one could find . . . A very patient barber, a one of a kind.' "

Grandpa and Grandma Chenoweth's church is one of the first places I performed, when I was seven or eight years old. I marched up to the front, fully prepared to belt out my favorite Evie Tornquist song, "I'm Only Four Foot Eleven, but I'm Going to Heaven, and It Makes Me Feel Ten Feet Tall." But I was still a long way from my full height of four feet eleven inches (as the song prophesied), so when I got up to the podium, I disappeared completely behind it. I peeked around, stepped to the side, got a big laugh, and proceeded to blow the doors off the place. Evie would have been proud. Grandpa practically burst his buttons.

But singing was not my first grand passion. When I was four, I saw a ballet on PBS and told my mom, "I want to do that." It seemed like an odd but basically healthy pastime, so Mom inquired around and came up with the Runyon School of Ballet, which wasn't far from our house. I vaguely remember my first recital. I was a tulip. I had to pee. One of the other tulips did pee. I immediately realized that this was not a good choice. (Moral of that story: far less embarrassing to learn from the mistakes of others. Feel free to apply this in your own life as needed.)

By the time I was in second grade, I was eating, sleeping, and breathing ballet. I adored my ballet teacher, Miss Jane. She was as strict as a wooden yardstick, with posture to match. She took ballet very, very seriously, and so did I. Not all the girls did. A lot of girls skipped class occasionally, traded Skittles in the corner, complained about the heat, while my friend Sally and I hung on Miss Jane's every word. In addition to the technical steps and forms of dance, she talked about giving oneself to the emotion of the music to create a character. Miss Jane encouraged me to audition for the Tulsa Ballet production of *The Nutcracker,* and I did, but I was fully prepared to be told I was too little. "Too little" was something I heard a lot. I didn't want to be taller just for the sake of being the same as everyone else, I was just tired of looking at butts all the time. Sometimes it seemed as if life in general had a MUST BE THIS TALL TO RIDE sign posted, and I never quite measured up. I was thrilled to flinders when Mom showed me the cast letter listing my name in the "Bunnies" column.

During one performance, I saw a bit of greenery—a piece of garland or something from the set dressing—lying in the middle of the floor just before the company dancers were to make their entrance. All Miss Jane's warnings about stray bobby pins and ribbons on the classroom floor sprang into my mind. Think "Someone could put an eye out!" only with broken ankles and subluxated joints. I knew I had to save them. But wait! I couldn't break character. *What would a bunny do?* I thought. And not just any bunny. A Tchaikovsky bunny. A Victorian Tchaikovsky bunny. On Christmas Eve. With Stanislavsky devotion to my role, I hopped across the stage, took the stray greenery in my mouth, deposited it safely off to the side, and hopped back to my place. After the show, our director, Moscelyne Larkin—an Oklahoma dance legend and veteran of the original Ballets Russes—came backstage and called out over the noise and postshow bustle, "Where's my clever bunny?"

Fearing she wouldn't see me in the forest of long legs, I jumped and waved.

"Me! It was me!"

"Ah! Brava!" she said, and I felt six inches taller than however tall you have to be to ride.

As I got older, I worked hard to perfect my ballerina form and my ballerina body. I focused a lot of attention on my turnout, careful to do everything from riding my bike to climbing the stairs in a way that encouraged the long, lean muscles of a dancer, instead of the tough stems of an athlete. I watched *Great Performances* on PBS anytime they featured dance and read everything I could find about the great ballerinas, including Maria Tallchief, who was not only an Oklahoman, but also part Native American, just like me. Paging through those books, looking at the pictures of stages, lights, and roses, I felt sad for Miss Jane. I thought, *She didn't make it.* And I wondered if maybe that was why she tried so hard to get us girls to take it seriously. Of course, it's possible that she was doing exactly what she wanted to do and it was teaching she took seriously. Either way, I soaked up every ounce, striving to rise to her level of self-discipline.

Dancing was work. Singing came naturally.

Church was a big part of my life, and singing was a big part of church. Mark and I were both in youth choir, and I lived for it, but one evening, riding home with a friend, I saw Mark hanging out at the 7-Eleven. He'd played hooky from *choir*. Sacrilege! But Mom was surprisingly cool about it.

"Music isn't his gift," she shrugged.

And it really isn't. Mark should not be allowed to sing. Ever. Mom quickly recognized this and let him off the choir hook, supporting his unique talents the same way she supported mine. He was a brain, which made my school life about as much fun as his choir life. Every year on the first day of class, teachers would sing the familiar strain: "Oh, you're Mark Chenoweth's little sister!" They always leaped to the conclusion that algebra was in my blood. Disillusionment invariably followed. Mark was a whiz with numbers, who couldn't understand my mathematical tone deafness. Pressed into service as my tutor, he'd laboriously explain the integer over the squared root of blah blah blah, and I tried, truly, I did, but it always ended in frustration.

"Aaugh, Kris! How can you not get it? I told you ten times. Mom?"

Mom would rotate in, make a valiant attempt, eventually calling, "Jerry? Help?"

Then Dad would come in, calm everyone down, and basically do my homework for me.

Poor Mom had to wait for the sports gene to skip a generation; both Mark's kids are athletic. (Heck, my dog, Maddie, is athletic compared to me and my brother.) When bookish Mark and artsy me were little, Mom was still playing tennis, and she was *good*. She competed in a nonpro championship the year I was in third grade. I was invited to a roller-skating party that day. One of the events was a race, and as the only girl who stepped up to participate, I was determined to beat those boys. Unfortunately, halfway through the event, I fell and broke my arm just below the elbow.

"It was the darnedest thing," the party mom told my mom, who arrived breathless and still in her little white tennis dress. "She just got up and kept going. Came in second."

I asked Mom later if she was mad about having to leave the tournament when she was doing so well.

"Of course not!" she said, looking at me as if I'd suggested she might pull the oven out of the wall and reinstall it upside down. "That's not how it is when you love someone, Kristi."

One of the first solos I sang at our church was "Jesus, I Heard You Had a Big House"—a Bill and Gloria Gaither song about the completely welcoming warmth of Heaven. *Jesus, I heard you had a big house where I could have a room of my own. And, Jesus, I heard you had a big yard, big enough to let a kid roam.* And if I do say so myself, I sang the livin' you-know-what outta that song. Someone at a church in Tulsa heard about it and asked if I'd like to come and sing it for them, and naturally I liked that a lot. Another church across town asked me to come, and then another and another, and pretty soon churches across the state were asking me to sing, and it eventually became sort of a family hobby. Dad bought a little sound system for me because sometimes we'd arrive and the church's system was lacking, and he saw how much it bothered me if I couldn't do well. Evie, Sandi Patty, and Amy Grant were quite popular then; the so-called Christian contemporary genre had made it onto the radio and was gaining some serious mass audience. Of course, we didn't know anything about demographics. We just thought it was great that folks invited us over, and they thought it was great that here was this little girl with a big voice.

My aunt Roselan heard there was going to be an all-out national talent search for a little girl to play Little Orphan Annie in the movie version of the Broadway musical and declared that I could sing as well as anyone else they were going to dig up. She and Mom took me to Oklahoma City to audition, and I got called back and actually advanced all the way to the screen test with just a few other girls. I think what sank me was when they asked me if I was familiar with the comic strip, and my answer sounded something like "Ah don't know innything about it, but Ah kin larn it."

Mom tried to coach me on the dialect, but that was the blonde leading the blonde.

"Think about that Barbra Streisand song," she said, affecting a spavined Brooklynese. *"Sam, yuz made the pants too long."*

Mom should not be allowed to sing either. All that did was give us something to crack up laughing about all the way home after I didn't get the part. Of course, I loved the idea of getting to be in a realio-trulio movie with Carol Burnett, whom I worshiped and wanted to *be*, but none of us seriously expected that to happen. The excursion began and ended as something fun to do, so there was no disappointment. Fun was had. Mission accomplished. Mom and I were entirely taken aback when we saw the way some people treated it like guerrilla warfare. Armed with professional headshots and résumés, they drilled and agonized and clearly regarded every other soul in the room as an enemy. Same with the little Oklahoma Kids talent competition I participated in. There were some rabid stage mothers in that greenroom,

let me tell ya, and for their kids, the experience neither began nor
ended as fun. How sad is that for a little child? On the off, off, off,
off—and did I mention *off*?—chance that such a thing would lead to
a big break in showbiz, how likely is it that the person would enjoy a
single moment of his or her working life?

My mom and dad didn't know about professional headshots or
any of that stuff. They didn't even know what they didn't know. They
felt their job was to encourage me in whatever direction made me
happy. I was a *kid;* happiness was the object of the game. Looking
back, I see how this just-for-fun approach benefited me throughout
my career. I've had to make some tough choices: a regular spot on *The
West Wing* or a new musical called *Wicked,* a role in the solidly successful Broadway hit *Annie Get Your Gun* or a completely experimental
character in *You're a Good Man, Charlie Brown.* That's just two. There
have been many others, including the recent *Frankenstein* or *Daisies*
jawbreaker. I never make decisions that angle for advance or grab for
money; it's always about the fun factor, the challenge, the joy of working with people I like and respect.

A room of my own. A big yard to roam.

Literally and figuratively, that's what my parents gave me.

∽∞∾

" 'As the clock was now half past the hour of noon' " Karla's poem
continues, sweet and unaffected, " 'he knew he'd better get home very
soon.' "

It's almost time for me to sing. I'm supposed to do "Amazing
Grace." A cappella. Which seemed like a good idea at the time I said I
would do it. Now not s'much.

Keep on keepin' on, I tell myself, nails to my palm. *Keep on
keepin' on.*

"Just look at the clock," whispers my cousin Kim. "You'll be fine."

Kimbo's always been a regular font of folk wisdom. When we were little, she told me the best way to see if a cow pie was fresh or dry was to stick my foot in it. This worked especially well with my brand-new Holly Hobbies socks. Another time she told me, "A man and a woman go into the woods and get naked, the woman gets on the man's shoulders, and they pray to God about what kind of baby they want, and that's where babies come from."

Something about this just didn't ring right to me.

"Mom?" I said when I got home. "When people go naked in the woods, and the woman is on the man's shoulders, and God gives them the baby—what if they get a baby with no arm? Do some people ask for a baby with no arm? Or do you have to ask specifically for a baby with two arms?"

Mom looked at me for a long moment, then turned her head toward the dining room door and called, *"Jerry!"* Dad came in, got a whiff of what the conversation was about, and experienced a burning desire to mow the lawn. Immediately. As the conversation continued, it became sadly clear to me that Mom knew nothing about the real facts of where babies came from. (She thought it had something to do with a *penis,* the poor dear.)

Karla keeps it together admirably, but I'm a mess by the time she gets to the end.

" 'But this last Sunday afternoon, they were reunited in Heaven, with so many other kin. But I'm sure Grandma was awaitin' and wonderin' where had he been? She probably met him and said, *What took you so long? For you always knew you were my very best friend.'* "

We hug each other as she's on her way back to her seat and I'm on my way up to the podium, which I am now tall enough to see over. Just barely. I peek around it, step to the side. That gets a good laugh. But now my heart fills up. My larynx doesn't feel right. Instead of looking at the clock, I look at my freshly orphaned father, and I'm crying. Sitting next to Dad is his sister Judy. She smiles at me, carefully forming silent words, just moving her lips.

You don't have to, she tells me.

After Grandma died, I brought Judy up to New York to see me do *The Apple Tree* and a concert at the Met, and while she was there, she gave me my grandmother's diamond-and-opal ring.

"Here," she said, pressing it into my hand. "I want you to have this."

"Aunt Judy, no. I can't. You should keep it."

"It's too tiny to fit anyone but you," she laughed. "Wear it when you sing. That way your grandma will be with you."

Aunt Judy and I have always been close, but it seems as if she's been more expressive of her feelings since she came down with breast cancer. She's a farm wife who also works a job in town, and she's worked steadily through her chemo, scheduling treatments on Fridays so she could be sick over the weekend. She keeps on keepin' on. How can I not put one foot in front of the other when I have women like this in my life to show me how it's done?

I sing "Amazing Grace." It sounds like I swallowed tacks.

"I'm sorry," I tell Aunt Judy in the limo on the way to the cemetery. "That was awful."

She takes my hand and says, "Kristi. This wasn't a performance. It was perfect."

"No one else can ask me to sing at their funeral. I'm never doing this again."

"What? You're certainly going to sing at my funeral," says my mother.

I look at her as if she did actually reinstall the oven upside down. "Mom. Are you high?"

That gets a good laugh.

∞

chapter three

SING FROM YOUR HOO HOO

People don't believe me when I tell them about Hum Dum Ditty. It sounds too folksy to be true, but I assure you, it's as real as Southern Comfort. Writers found the name so charming, they decided to use it in an episode of My Huge Hit Sitcom *Kristin* on NBC. (Huge hit. We're talkin' Zsa Zsa Gabor doghouse huge. Ask anyone in my extended family.) People called BS on it and said I was too nice to be true. That's an image problem I've been aware of since eighth grade, when a girl named Jill cornered me in the girls' bathroom and said, "Why are you so freakin' *happy* all the time? It makes me want to beat you up."

Half her size and truly astonished, I stammered, "But—but look at me. I'm not even worth the punch."

Substitute the word *critic* for *Jill* and you have a scenario that has played out several times during my career, and it never ceases to astonish me.

Anyway. Elvis had his fried peanut-butter, bacon, and banana sandwich; I've got my Hum Dum Ditty, a spectacular conglomeration of ground meat, corn, tomatoes, and some kind of gravy. Dip a biscuit in there, and you've got yourself a garage sale of gastronomic delight, a veritable trailer park for the palate. I can't share the exact formula for Hum Dum Ditty because I think it partly depends on what's in the "dented and expired" clearance cart next to the door at the supermarket, but I will share the recipe for my personal specialty, without which your life is a pale imitation of what it could be:

The Top Secret Recipe for Kristi Dawn's No Calorie Left Behind Butterfinger Pie

- Crunch up six king-size Butterfinger bars. Smash them up in a plastic bag or beat them with a rolling pin while they're still in the wrapper. Exercise your aggressions. Very therapeutic.
- Take a twelve-ounce deal of Cool Whip and mix it up with the candy-bar shrapnel.
- Plop all that into one of those graham-cracker crusts. (Just get over yourself and buy the premade kind. Don't be all Barefoot Contessa about it.)
- Freeze! No, not you, the pie. I mean freeze in the freezer, not in the theatrical sense. This is important. If you skip this step, people will assume it's French onion dip and stick their potato chips in it.
- Serve with a smile on paper plates. The kind with the rippled edges, whenever possible.

Everybody brings her specialty when we all get together, which is a rare occasion these days. Weddings and funerals. We saw Dad's side of the family at Grandpa's service in Hinton. Now everyone on Mom's side has gathered in Tulsa to gab and eat, exclaim over how big the kids are, eat some more, gab some more. It's like that song from *The Music Man*, "Pick a Little, Talk a Little."

I set my Butterfinger pie well away from the potato chips on Aunt Ginger's long dining room table, which is heaped with a whole lot of everything. You can tell a lot about each of the fabulous Smith sisters by what she brings to potluck. Aunt Ginger's warm and nonjudgmental biscuits and gravy are the ultimate comfort food because she's always been the caretaker of the whole family and everyone else in town. Energetic Aunt Gaye serves up green beans and tabouli, which go well with her innate element of surprise. You never know when Aunt Gaye is going in for the love pat, but you know you're gonna feel it when she does. My mom always supplies the dressing for the Thanksgiving turkey because she is a healer, a problem solver, able to transform stale bread and soup stock into something delicious. Aunt Roselan is an earth mother who goes for the organic. She's a breast cancer survivor and in better shape than me, but I always feel a little heartier after a bowl of her special oatmeal with apples, nuts, and honey. Aunt Violet is the most liberal of the sisters, world-traveled and savvy, having lived in London and California. I nestle my Butterfinger concoction next to Aunt Vi's stellar apple and pecan pies because she and I are on the same wavelength: "Life is short. Eat dessert first." Sweet Aunt Tommie Jo is openhearted, a good listener who adopted two children after Mom and Dad adopted me, so it's not surprising that Aunt Tommie Jo's special dishes—banana pudding with Nilla Wafers and broccoli chicken casserole—combine elements that weren't born together but belong together.

Home from Iraq for a brief visit, Aunt Tommie Jo's son Robert is the celebrity in this gathering. A few years ago, he did a tour in Afghanistan and came back filled with pride and enthusiasm about the help being offered, schools being built, progress being made. Now he's in Iraq, guarding prisoners, and when I ask him about it, a deep shadow passes through his eyes.

"You don't want to know," he tells me, and that makes me hug him even tighter.

"Thank you for doing what you do," I whisper in his ear. "You're a good man, and I'm proud of you."

All we cousins are like siblings: Cheri, Shane, Clint, Richard, Pam, Mark, Kristi, Jason, Darin, Cindy, Allen, Katherine, Robert. I love being lost in that bunch. When I was little, Aunt Ginger would ask me to sing and dance at family gatherings, but now I get to be one of the grown-ups who sit on the sidelines in a bank of lawn chairs, getting up to chase a dog away from the table, wipe up a spill with a paper towel, wait my turn to hold the newest baby, or indulge in one of Cousin Cheri's Hello Dollies, these seven-layer bars with chocolate chips, coconut, and I don't know what all.

Hello Dollies were always on the potluck table when I was a kid, but I summoned my willpower and opted for fruits and vegetables. I was a picky eater because of my unswerving dedication to ballet in general and Miss Jane in particular. I wasn't on the Gelsey Kirkland eating-disorder bus, but I was conscientious about the tone and strength of my body. As the years went by, it became apparent that I was never going to have the long, willowy limbs of a prima ballerina. But it's funny . . . as my adult body emerged, I started looking like a tall person—only shorter. Mark says I only look short when I'm standing next to someone. I have long legs, proportionate to my torso, a good pair of "getaway sticks," as we call them in the theatre. I also developed a pretty good pair of Mermans, for such a skinny girl. My interests expanded beyond ballet to tap, jazz, and modern. I was a cheerleader in junior high, but in high school I went out for drill team, which felt more like a dance performance. Of course, I was all about choir, and I went out for every play.

In ninth and tenth grade, I was in Larry Thompson's madrigal group, and he told me about a phenomenal voice teacher at Oklahoma City University. Some of her students had gone on to excellent careers. Lara Teeter received a Tony nomination for *On Your Toes* and was a going concern on Broadway. Susan Powell won the Miss America pageant in 1981, and I remember sitting on the living room floor, a bowl of ice cream clasped between my hands, watching her sing. Mr. Thompson was adamant that this was the voice teacher I needed to study with, and though I loved Mr. Thompson to bits (he's one of those teachers you hope and pray your kid will get), I promptly blew that off. OCU was a pricey private college. My parents couldn't afford that, and even if they could, all my friends were going to state schools. The fun factor had to be considered. But as it got close to decision time, Mr. Thompson went an extra mile, contacted my parents, and told them that studying with this OCU voice teacher could change my life.

"They're having a high school weekend," my dad told me. "We should check it out. You'd get to audition for a scholarship, stay in the dorm, see a show. It'll be fun."

The campus was a grassy, rolling, two-hour drive from home. On the way, I flipped through the catalog and brochures they'd sent. The OCU Mission Statement reads, "Oklahoma City University embraces the United Methodist tradition of scholarship and service and welcomes all faiths in a culturally rich community that is dedicated to student welfare and success. Men and women pursue academic excellence through a rigorous curriculum that focuses on students' intellectual, moral, and spiritual development to prepare them to become effective leaders in service to their communities."

In other words: fun factor zero. But I was intrigued by this voice teacher Mr. Thompson was so big about.

"Florence Gillam Birdwell," the brochure said, "is a master teacher, performer, and force of nature."

∞

Whenever I'm in Oklahoma to visit family, I try to fit in a side trip to see Florence Birdwell. How to describe her here . . . hmm. She's my *person*. Think Dianne Wiest in *Bullets Over Broadway*. That same "I never play frumps or virgins!" sense of self. Flowing fabrics. Orbiting, kinetic earrings. Babe Didrikson hair. Fun, zany, and charismatic, but serious as a jackhammer about her art. I brought her to New York for the Tonys when I was nominated for *You're a Good Man, Charlie Brown,* and I loved watching her cruise the after-parties. The moment she walked in, the room expanded, and half an hour later, everyone in the place either knew who she was or knew they should.

When Dad took me up for the high school weekend, I got to see *Carnival* and fell in love with the part of Lili (which I never have gotten to do). The girl playing it was awesome. (Seriously. Lili girl? Whoever you are? You were *awesome*.) As the big fish in my little high school pond, I'd gotten pretty confident about being cast in leading roles; I could not believe the caliber of the talent on this stage. It was going to be mule-hard work to even get in the game here, but I knew this was the school I needed to be at. As it happened, Florence Birdwell was also performing in concert that weekend, and by the time she left the stage, I was her disciple.

"This is where I want to be," I told Dad on the way home. "I want to study with that bird lady."

He brought me back several weeks later to audition for a scholarship. I followed Ms. Birdwell to the Oriole Room, where master classes were held, and she politely listened as I sang Edvard Grieg's "My Johann," a playful song for a good soprano, and "New York, New York," complete with choreography.

"Okay," she said. "Okay."

The quiet space that followed seemed like plenty of time for her to think of something nice to say. Cue the clock ticking . . . crickets . . . tumbleweeds . . . she just sat there nodding as if she hadn't gotten the memo about how amazingly talented I was.

She finally said, "I want to show you my studio."

Entering Florence Birdwell's studio for the first time was like looking through the wardrobe into Narnia. Glossy black grand piano. A high, upholstered stool, which I always called the perch. Tons of music in heavy file cabinets. A metronome I can't believe she still has. Lots of decor—rich colors, wood, brocade, a table with a plant—the most perfect, unplanned form of shabby chic. The walls were adorned with pictures of her most accomplished students and of herself performing in concert. In the corner, there was a wicker chair where you sat if she wanted to talk to you.

"I'll tell you what," she said. "If you come here, I will take you as my student. And I don't take everyone. You will have the highest of highs and the lowest of lows. You'll have them both. But"—she laughed a little—"you'll figure all that out when you come."

And she was right.

∽

Any separation anxiety I may have been experiencing the day my parents dropped me off at OCU evaporated when the fraternity guys stepped up to help me carry my things to my dorm. These enterprising youths offered Sherpa service to all the girls as they arrived on campus each year, and if there isn't already a statue of the frat brother who came up with that brilliant idea, there ought to be. Mom was crying. Dad was emotional. I was like *See ya!*—and college life began. I wasn't Galinda Upland rolling in on a luggage cart, but I was thrilled to be there and ready to hit the ground running.

"I'm going to have one of our upperclassmen sing for you in a moment," Ms. Birdwell said, indicating a girl we knew to be one of her prize students. "I want everyone to know where they're headed. But before we do that, I'm going to ask Kristi Chenoweth to sing."

Her eyes swept the room like a lighthouse beam sweeps a coastline, her unruffled gaze settling on my face, which felt frozen in one of those classic *Hummana-hummana-wha?* expressions. She directed me to meet quickly with the accompanist, and I went to the piano and exchanged a flurry of questions and answers with him. I chose to sing "New York, New York" because I knew I could deliver that puppy like a wrecking ball. It was my ace in the hole. I belted it out. Everyone applauded madly, but before I could take the *she came, she saw, she conquered* victory walk back to my seat, Florence Birdwell pressed her hand to her heart and said, "Oh. I can't wait to teach you how to sing."

The prize student sang then and blew everybody away. I can't tell you what she did—some aria in some language. I sat there agog. Humiliated. Ms. Birdwell had quite obviously meant to display the *before* and *after*. For the first of many times I left after class struggling unsuccessfully to swallow my tears. But during that first year, I started to get what she was talking about. She took an extremely technical approach. The apparatus of the voice. The nomenclature and physical science of singing, what it is and how it works, control and relaxation of the larynx—a lot of things I was doing naturally, but she wanted me to understand why it works when it works and what to do when it doesn't.

"This is the instrument," she said with a gesture that encompassed my entire body. "The jaw, the mouth, the teeth, tongue, lungs, stomach. You must sing from the vagina! That's how low the breath is."

(While trying to explain this to Ellen DeGeneres on her show a few years ago, I was suddenly unsure about the okayness of saying *vagina* on daytime television, so I ended up blurting, "You have to sing from your—you know—your *hoo hoo*." She never let me forget it. She even produced a big Broadway spoof episode—*Ellen: The Musical*—and had me float in as her musical fairy godmother. The big finish had everyone onstage belting, *"You gotta siiiiiiiiiing from your hoo hoooooooooo!"*)

But beyond the physical, there was an emotional, almost spiritual approach to the music. We learned a selection of art songs we called "The Italians' Greatest Hits," and one day Ms. Birdwell stopped me in the middle of Stradella's "Pietà, Signore," made me start over not once but twice, then stopped me a third time and told me to sit down because I looked out the window. Another day, she stopped me in the middle of Pergolesi's "Se tu m'ami" and asked for the English translation.

"Not the book's translation," she said when I started searching for it. "Your translation. If you have it memorized in Italian, you should have it memorized in English. You may sit down. Please, don't sing to me in another language without knowing what you're singing about."

So I'd go to the library, labor through every syllable and vowel, then show up to my lesson, eager to please her. Some days she simply brushed me imperiously aside with the nebulous criticism "This is not a singing day for you." Other days, she offered a crumb of encouragement. Effusive praise such as "Well, do you feel you made a tiny stride?" or "I think you're getting the gist." Her relentlessly high standards made Miss Jane look like a regular Miss Noodle, but I loved that. Some kids had knock-down-drag-outs with her, and at times I wanted to, but I was so hungry to learn what she was teaching, while other people angled to get out of their lessons, I was badgering to get in and take their time slots.

My freshman year, I'd have to admit, I was a little party puppy. I'd never been much for that sort of thing in high school, but once I pledged Gamma Phi Beta, there was plenty of weekend activity. I got to drinking a little, and for someone my size, a little is all it takes. (Thank you, Heavenly Father, for delaying the invention of the cellphone cam until after I outgrew that phase where the date has to hold the girl's hair back as she leans over a bush.) I was one of the few freshmen getting cast in shows. No leads, of course, but I was grateful just to get onstage in *Annie Get Your Gun*. Of course my family traveled all the way to Oklahoma City to see me dash forward in my little townsgirl costume and deliver the sum total of my lines:

"General Grant?"

I was also in *The Roar of the Greasepaint—The Smell of the Crowd* and even had a small part in *La Traviata*.

"You were wonderful," my brother warmly told me after his first opera. "Please, never invite me to one of those again."

My sophomore year, I struggled with repeated bouts of strep and mono, and Ms. Birdwell cut me not one iota of slack. Going to a juried competition in Norman, I was feeling horrible, so she was driving. (And I need to say here that Florence Birdwell should never be behind the wheel of a car. She's a menace.)

"I don't think I can do this," I told her. "My throat is—I don't know. I can't swallow."

"You won't be able to make excuses in the real world," she said. "People will have more respect for you if you just sing through it. Do what you have to do. I don't care if you have to drink a shot of vodka. You can't go to New York to audition for an opera company or a show and say. 'Oh, hello, I'm not at my best today, but I'm taking up your time anyway.' No! You just sing. If it's not your best, it's not your best. Now, we're in the car, we're going, just *sing*."

I sang. I got third, so I guess it wasn't a complete cat strangler. (I've gotten onstage many, many times since then when I was sick or hurt. I do my best. If I don't sound terrific, I hope my acting will carry it.) Not long after that, I was in her studio, charging through some hideous aria. She asked something of me, took me to task when I couldn't do it, and it was finally more than I could take. I started crying and, for the first and only time, walked out on my lesson.

My mom always knows when I'm not okay. I don't know how she does it—spiritual bond, finely tuned Mom-o-Meter, pheromones, covert operations. Whatever it is, I'm grateful. She was on the phone moments after I walked in the door.

"Kristi, are you all right? You've been so close to my heart all day."

"Mom," I sobbed in pure frustration, "I need to quit. I'm not cut out for this."

"Kristi, are you sick? You don't sound right. Dad and I are coming to get you."

She gave me the nursing-school once-over as soon as she arrived and took me to the doctor when we got home. The following week, I returned to school and told Ms. Birdwell I needed to have my tonsils taken out. She sat me down in the wicker chair. Serious. I didn't know what she was going to say about my scholarship or if she still wanted to teach me.

"Listen to me. *Child*. Do you have any—you can't—" She waved aside whatever she was trying to tell me, demanded the name of the surgeon, and had him on the phone a minute later. "This is Dr. Florence Birdwell of Oklahoma City University. You need to know that you have the voice of the decade—the voice of her *generation*—in your hands."

The voice of *hummana-hummana-wha?*

This was news to me, and I won't lie: my heart soared to hear that from her mouth. For the first time, here was someone who truly believed in me. Someone beside my parents, I mean, and, yes, this meant more than that because she actually *knew* what she was talking about.

"You cannot cram things down her throat. You can not *snip* anything or *nick* anything or make the slightest error." After she finally dismissed the surgeon, she demanded to be connected to the anesthesiologist and raked him over the same coals. Then she hung up and came to sit beside me. "You have to remind them, Kristi. Write it on your forehead: *SINGER*."

"They told me my voice might change. Even if the surgery goes perfectly."

"Don't be afraid. We'll do what we have to do. I don't care if you become an alto. It won't matter. You're a singer *here*—and *here*." She indicated my brain with one hand, my whole self with the other. "I lost my voice when I was getting my undergraduate degree. Studying under the great Inez Silberg. Woke up one morning and . . . nothing. Couldn't sing a note. Couldn't speak a word. She taught me how to talk again, as if I was an infant, and then we applied all that to singing.

Because that's what it is, really. Speaking on pitch. You're so in love with your voice—you've got to stop all that *singing*. Stop listening to yourself and *speak* to us."

My voice did change. It actually went up a step and a half. The first month or two, it felt like a knife-swallowing act. Sitting at the table like the little match girl, watching the rest of the family eat pizza, I downed my nine hundredth meal of green Jell-O. My uvula felt odd and truncated, and I realized that two years earlier, I wouldn't have been able to identify it as anything other than "that punching-bag thingy." My throat felt strange for a long time, but my health was vastly improved. I was stronger, which pleased Ms. Birdwell, and pleasing her lit a whole new fire under me. My voice began to open up to a place I never knew I had.

Healthy food and rest became priorities. Wine coolers and late nights lost their appeal. I wasn't willing to waste my energy anymore. Just like my old ballet days, I optimized my body for the task at hand. I stopped partying and focused on training and studies. Junior year, I got a lead: Adele in *Die Fledermaus*—second cast, so I only got to do one out of the three performances, but still—it was a leading role in a challenging opera. (Sorry, Mark.)

While I worked toward my degree in musical theatre, semesters were spent cramming for classes and performing in plays, and summers were spent doing summer stock, naturally. With the help of an excellent hair and makeup crew, I made a surprisingly believable Tuptim in *The King and I*. I played a Kit Kat girl in *Cabaret*, and years later, when I was doing *Wicked*, I couldn't look at Joel Grey without singing a bit of *tweedly-deet-dee-dee two ladies* in my head. (*Und der is just one man, jah!* See how it gets stuck in your head?) Another summer job early on was singing and dancing in one of those high-kicking review-type shows at Opryland.

I loved Opryland. I wanted to *live* at Opryland. My parents had to come and drag me back to school. Opryland was, however, the scene of an unfortunate incident I call the Cooter Smash. And now, as the Old Lady says in *Candide,* "I shall chill your ears with the tale of my many calamities!" (Feel free to cross your legs as needed.)

How I Acquired the Semimagical Power to Predict Weather with My Cooter
or
Rebel Without a Coccyx

Our story begins when I was at cheerleading camp back in high school. As one of the smaller girls, I was strategically positioned at the top of a pyramid in what they call a monkey grab, which means one girl was holding me up straight while two other girls each supported a foot, and I was basically doing splits about eight feet above the floor. A girl on the bottom of the pyramid apparently decided she had to see a man about a Russian racehorse, got up without warning the rest of us, and I fell.

That. Really. Hurt.

Flash forward a few years. Opryland. Warm-ups. I was doing the paddle-wheeling, high-kicking, Pepsodent-smile routine—specifically the heel-above-the-head-kick-whoosh-down-into-splits combination. I kicked. So far so good. I went forward for the splits, but the worn heel of my character shoe didn't catch quite enough traction, and I ended up doing the pubic-bone-gravity-wooden-floor combination instead. (Okay, now I need to cross my legs just thinking about it.)

The official diagnosis was a fractured coccyx. I also pulled a hammy, but that was hardly noticeable, due to the profound agony radiating from the center of my poor little Georgia O'Keeffe. I missed a few shows, then returned to grin and bear it for the rest of the season with altered choreography and an unswerving devotion to Opryland.

I no longer do the splits. And I can't tell you how happy I am that it's no longer required of me. The lasting legacy of the Cooter Smash is that I'm the first to know when it's going to rain. That's right. I both sing and predict the weather with my hoo hoo. Mozart, meteorology, plus all the usual stuff.

And yet I remain single.

'Splain it to me, Lucy.

❦

As my priorities changed, so did my circle of friends. I drifted away from the party girls in my sorority and started hanging out with the music people, who became my dearest, lifelong comrades. Regina Dowling, who now does a lot of on-camera hosting gigs. Bill Shiflett, who leads a powerhouse music ministry. Destin Owens, who's made his own mark on Broadway. Then there's gorgeous Kandi Johnston, and fabulous Mary Milsap, and of course, then and always, there's Denny Downs. We connected the very first day in choir. Just one of those fleeting "Hey, I know people who know people you know" things, but enough for us to say hello in the hallway and hope we'd have a chance to work together sometime. What eventually bonded us was our mutual lust for the cello player.

Carmen. Bizet's great opera. Originally denounced as "superficial and immoral" and declared a resounding flop. Not unlike My Huge Hit Sitcom *Kristin* on NBC. (Huge hit. Yak-dropping huge. Terribly misunderstood.) Denny was in the chorus; I'd landed a respectable secondary role. We had plenty of time for backstage kibitzing—my breakup with my boyfriend, his breakup with his boyfriend, what we had for lunch, who thought what about this or that current event. At a tech rehearsal, we were standing together downstage and realized we were both gazing into the orchestra pit, making eyes at the same cello player.

"What is it about cello players?" I mused. "Is it the way they embrace the instrument like a lover?"

"It's the biceps," Denny said pragmatically.

He nailed it. Cello players have great biceps. Who needs Bowflex when you have the actual bow? This particular cello player also had a Tyrone Power jawline and tousled Clark Gable hair. He looked up and flashed a smile that hit us like a heat-seeking missile.

"Oh, my gosh. Did you see that?" said Denny. "He is so flirting with me."

"What?" I elbowed Denny in the ribs. "He's flirting with *me*."

"Dream on, girlie."

"You dream on, *Den-whah*." Because that's how we are sometimes. All classy and Frenchified. (Or is that *french fried*?)

After rehearsal, we found ourselves in the crowded hallway behind the dreamboat in question, and Denny kept grabbing my hand and trying to put it on the guy's backside. We both flirted shamelessly with him for the entire run of the show and were inseparable from that time forward. I had a part-time job in graduate admissions and got Denny a job there, too, but he was much better at it than I was. Campus tours were my forte, probably because I loved OCU so much that with little provocation I was willing and able to wax poetic about it.

As an upperclassman, I was getting cast in leads. Guest directors came in from New York, and I soaked that up like a sponge, learning by doing, by bumps and bruises. Everything Florence Birdwell told me and my father that day about the highest highs and the lowest lows—it was all there, and I grew to deeply love this woman who'd lost her voice and had given me mine. I learned the most watching her in concert. I'd never seen a concert like that, but I imagined this must be what Barbra Streisand was doing in the huge venues, what Bette Midler did in the bathhouses of New York. She'd box your ears with "Where Is Flair?" then turn around and break your heart with "If He Walked into My Life"—a song she did for her son, who died the night he graduated high school. "Where's that boy with the bugle?" She was never really able to get through it, but seeing her try was like watching a tall sailing ship leave a harbor.

Ah, I kept thinking every time I watched her perform, *that's how it's done*.

The music didn't come from notes and lyrics; it came from life and mileage. From love. When I was doing that Oklahoma Kids competition, I won with a blow-the-doors-off rendition of Debby Boone's "You Light Up My Life." Yeah, I know the song became an icon for schmaltz, but it's a sweet melody, and then the key modulates, the chorus swells for a big, big finish. I knew every word of that and many other love songs, but I may as well have been singing in Italian for all I understood them.

Then one day I sang the national anthem for a baseball game. The game started, and out onto that pitcher's mound walked a great big, gorgeous uniform full of blond, blue-eyed Oklahoma. I caught the name Shawn Bryant over the loudspeaker just before they started blaring "Wild Thing," which was his theme song because they never knew if his pitching arm was going to be laser scalpel or spaghetti. That day he was a laser scalpel. Amazing. Baseball is my game, and he personified everything I love about it: skill, strength, an unshakable commitment to a craft, blended with an unflappable spirit of fun . . . and really tight pants.

A few days later, I came out to a parking lot to discover I'd locked my keys in my car, and you'll never guess who strolled over to help me. He did the make-a-hook-out-of-a-hanger thing, popped the lock, and handed me my keys.

"You were really good at the game the other day," he said.

"Thanks. So were you."

"I'm serious. We were all talking about it. It's hard to be inspired by a song you hear every day, and . . . you, um . . . I don't suppose . . . would you want to go out on a date sometime?"

"I would."

"Okay. Awesome. How about—"

"Actually," I said, scribbling my phone number on a piece of paper, "before I commit to the logistics, there's one quick thing I need to take care of."

I jammed my keys in the ignition, ripped over to my boyfriend's house, broke up with him, and zipped home to wait for the Wild Thing to call.

Oh, *what.*

"All's fair in love and war," right? I didn't make that up. That's Shakespeare. Or maybe it was Ben Franklin. Or Barry Manilow. In any case, who am I to argue?

So that was Wednesday. Shawn and I had dinner at Chili's on Friday. I had a burger, fries, and a Coke. He smiled his gorgeous smile across the table.

"Wow. You eat a lot for a little girl."

"Yup." I smiled back at him, thinking, *Oh my gosh, he thinks I'm a pig and I am a pig and he's never going to ask me out again. Don't be a pig, don't be a pig, don't—*

"I like a girl who eats."

We went to a party later. Nothing rowdy. Talking and dancing.

"You want to go to my house and watch a movie?" he asked around ten o'clock.

"Yup."

Shawn lived with his parents in Oklahoma City. They'd remodeled the garage into an apartment for him. We sat on the couch, and he plugged in a videotape of *E.T.*

"It's my favorite movie," he said.

I was in love.

My dad's job took him and Mom to Puerto Rico for a while right around the time I graduated OCU with a degree in musical theatre. Exhausted after five years of constant study and performing and not exactly sure what I wanted to do next, I went with them and spent a month lying in the sun, reading books, listening to music, daydreaming about this wonderful guy I'd found, imagining myself in New York. I spoke frequently with Ms. Birdwell, who wanted me to come back and get my master's degree in opera.

"Kristi," she kept nudging, "I need you to come back. You're not ready."

"I don't know. It's a lot of money and—"

"We'll get you a scholarship. Whatever you need. Come back to me."

My father agreed with her. "Get the master's, Kristi. It can only help you. Can't hurt. And you'd be the first person in our family to do it."

Denny and I went to Tulsa and auditioned for jobs on a European cruise line. Small World Syndrome: the auditions were held at none other than the Runyon School of Ballet, and Denny was hugely amused by the old recital photos that showed me moving through my most knobby-kneed "I want to be Carol Burnett when I grow up" phase. We were both cast by the cruise line, but I decided to stay in the United States and pursue my master's degree.

My first year in grad school, Shawn asked me to be promised, and the president of my old sorority invited me to do the traditional promise-ring ceremony. It's such a lovely tradition. Southern as sassafras and sweet as a Moon Pie. All the girls stand in a circle and pass around a pillow with the ring on it. No one knows whose ring it is until it gets to the girl who's promised, and she takes the ring and puts it on, then there's lots of cooing and hugs and tearful congratulations followed by tiny sandwiches and punch. It's a darling custom. Quaint as crinolines.

Shawn was the quintessential knight-in-shining-armor sort, an excellent First Great Love. We adored each other, loved each other's family, and made an unbearably cute couple. The promise turned into an engagement, and though I was in no hurry to get married, I did enjoy the nebulous idea of being his wife . . . someday. I was thrilled for him when he was drafted by the Cleveland Indians, but I missed him horribly when he went off to spring training. I was up to my neck, working through a two-year master's degree program in three hefty semesters and wouldn't have had the money to fly over and visit him even if I'd had the time.

One spring morning in 1993, I was getting ready for school and something on the TV caught my ear: "... Cleveland Indians ... pitching staff killed ..." I ran to the next room. A headline at the bottom of the screen said *Spring Training Tragedy.*

"Oh ... oh, God ..." Every bit of oxygen went out of my blood. "Please, God ..."

My hands were white and shaking as I dialed Shawn's mother.

"He wasn't with them. He's okay," she said the moment she answered, but I couldn't breathe again until I heard his voice on the phone. He told me he'd had a migraine headache and was home sleeping when the boat carrying Steve Olin, Tim Crews, and Bob Ojeda slammed into a pier. Ojeda was badly injured; Olin and Crews were killed. Shawn was understandably devastated, and I didn't know what to say to him other than "I love you" because selfishly, in my heart, all I could think was *Praise God for migraine headaches.* We talked for a while, and it was heart-wrenching to hear him so shattered. More than anything, I wanted to be close to him right then, but he was where he was, and I was where I was, and all either of us could do was our best.

Every song I sang that day—in fact, all the songs I sang for a lot of days that followed—were filled with a different level of love and longing. One day during master class, Ms. Birdwell asked me to sing "My Funny Valentine," and when I finished, she was visibly moved.

"You see that, everyone? That's *it*. She has *it*. You can't teach that."

I'd come into the song, I realized. Six years earlier, I'd walked in this door a precocious belter; now I was a classically trained coloratura soprano. But beyond that, I was growing up, understanding more about love and life, and it showed in the music. Ms. Birdwell kept nudging me to change my major from musical theatre to opera. And she suggested I change my name.

"Not your last name," she hastened to clarify. "But you already look like a *Kristi Dawn*. You already have that to fight against. You need to be a *Kristin*. Insist on being taken seriously when you open your mouth to sing."

I resisted the idea at first. Some names don't fit the person. Such as my dad's middle name: Morris. "Morris the cat," I used to tease him when I was little. He is so very not a Morris. Mom and Mark and I called him "Jeremiah Johnson" sometimes. And Mom was "June Bug." We called Mark "Marcus Welby," and he called me "Christopher Robin," but Kristi . . .

"That's *me*," I said. "That's who I am . . . isn't it?"

I didn't make the connection at the time, but rolling down the highway in my rental car, traveling the familiar road to OCU, I'm thinking of a sermon my friend gave in church a while back. She talked about Jacob, who was sort of a mama's boy until he went on a grand journey, fell in love, and wrestled with an angel.

"They struggled until morning," she said, "and the angel hurt him. But Jacob held on, saying 'I won't let go until you bless me.' So the angel blessed him with two things: the vision of a future and a new name. The angel called him Israel. Not because he was stronger than an angel. Because he was stronger than Jacob."

Everything Rodgers and Hammerstein said about Oklahoma is absolutely true. The fragrant wheat fields. The wind behind the rain. There's enough winter for a healthy snowman or two, plenty of summer for homegrown tomatoes, and in between, during spectacular spring storms, the sky turns green, tar-paper sheds and tin roofs go flying, and you might even get to see a funnel cloud. You half expect to see the cranky, old neighbor lady sail by on a bicycle. The drive from Broken Arrow to the shady campus at OCU has changed very little since my father took me there that first time. Hard-tamped red-dirt hollows, trees hung with kudzu and mistletoe, yards hung with tire swings. On the outskirts of town, old sofas and rocking chairs furnish the front porches. Mom-and-pop businesses mix with modern fast-food chains. It no longer feels like home, but that's probably because I've changed more than the old neighborhoods have.

Florence Birdwell's studio is as warm and eclectic as ever, and now there are a few photos of me on that wall of favorite moments along with Susan Powell, Lara Teeter, and Kelli O'Hara, who's just gotten a Tony nomination for *South Pacific*. I have no idea how old Ms. Birdwell is; it's a closely guarded secret. But I notice she has a hearing aid now, and this is a good thing. Better to hear her students with, those lucky children.

"Florence Gillam." I call her by her maiden name because she looks so girlish today.

"Kristin." She calls me by the name she blessed me with. "Your grandfather. Sweetie, I'm so sorry."

She puts her arms around me, enveloping me in all that flowing fabric. Those *sleeves*. No one carries off a kimono sleeve like Florence Gillam Birdwell. We sit in the corner with the wicker chairs, sipping tea, talking about my family, her family, work, school, and a recent concert I performed at the Met. Bette Midler was there. I was so nervous, my knees were knocking. She's one of those performers I've looked up to since I was a kid.

"I wasn't happy with the first song," I tell Ms. Birdwell.

"I know, dear. Neither was I."

I sigh a deep but not unhappy sigh.

"But once you got there," she offers, "you were there."

"Yup."

"I knew I'd never have to teach you how to sing a song. You were a diva," she says with an grand gesture. "But I had to make you ready. I had to toughen you up."

∽

chapter four

LOVE YOUR HAIR, HOPE YA WIN!
(DON'T TRIP . . .)

We should have dinner at Mudfuckers," says Mom. "They have every kind of burger you could possibly want."

"I think you mean Fuddruckers, Mom."

"Yes, that's what I said."

"You said *Mudfuckers*."

"What? I would never say *Mudfuckers*. Jerry, I didn't say *Mudfuckers*, did I?"

Now, let me say here, my mom is an intelligent woman, so perhaps this is some kind of verbal dyslexia or just a matter of not sweating the small stuff, but in her personal lexicon, I play "Olive Shnook" on *Pushing Up Daisies*. Other credits include *Dames of the Sea* and *Steel Peers*. Suzuki piano method is remembered as "Yamaha lessons." "Achy Breaky" becomes "Yucky Ducky," and Puerto Vallarta turns into "Porta Kolache." Thank goodness, she doesn't even try to say "Cunégonde."

I must have been having a Junie moment during the Miss Oklahoma pageant. I'd rigorously prepared for the interview segment,
cramming my head with current events and state history, but at the
moment of truth, the judge asked, "What do you think of *60 Minutes*
as a television program?"

"I think . . . that's about the right amount of time," I said in all
sincerity.

Now, I know that sounds like the punch line of a blonde joke,
but—well, it *is* about right, isn't it? Just enough time for character
development and a healthy story arc, allowing adequate commercial
interruption to accommodate both capitalism and bladder concerns.
I'm every bit as smart as Mom (shut up, Mark), but I take things literally. When asked if my glass is half-empty or half-full, I want to know
what's in the glass. Kool-Aid? If so, my glass is empty with a quickness
because I love Kool-Aid. Depending on the color. And if it's summer.
And if I just brushed my teeth, because if it's not Kool-Aid—say it's
orange juice—well, you don't want to drink orange juice right after
you brush your teeth, in which case the glass remains full. Pageant
questions are way too ambiguous for my inner Stanislavsky.

Aunt Ginger ran a charm school in Noble outside Oklahoma City,
so she knew her way around the pageant circuit.

"Don't try to be a spelling bee," she coached me. "It's a pageant.
They're looking for poise. Speak from your heart and don't get caught
up in facts and figures."

The toughest question for me was "Why do you want to be Miss
[insert shopping-mall opening title here]?" Because the truthful answer was "So I can sing on TV and get an agent." Obviously, I had to
come up with some altruistic, 501(c)3, banner-sanitized answer, and
because that didn't feel completely honest to me, I always stumbled on
it a bit. A professionally trained actress should be a better liar, wouldn't
you think? But no. I am pathetically underachieved in that area. I can
think of a great lie. I'm plenty imaginative. But before the words are

even out of my mouth, there's a weird tickle of unease in my armpits, a horsefly of guilt lands on the back of my neck, and before I can stop myself, that gassy little bubble of truth belches out.

The interview segment trips up many a contestant (probably by design) because she's standing up there, holding her stomach in, horribly nervous, completely exhausted, desperately trying to convince this guy who's been ogling her chest all week that feeding the hungry children of Botswana is a far larger issue in her life than visible panty lines, despite that if she does indeed have visible panty lines—or if she answers this question wrong—she'll be held up to public ridicule, when all she really wants is enough scholarship money to get her international studies degree so she can actually *do* something to help feed the hungry children of Botswana.

My dad is a self-made man who came up from nothing and did well for our family, but as with any family, our fortunes rose and fell, and the only way for me to attend an expensive private university instead of a state school was on scholarships. I auditioned for and got that first singing scholarship, and Aunt Ginger suggested the pageant circuit as a way for me to make up the difference.

My aunt Ginger, you gotta know, is a lioness. Beautiful. Courageous. Not to be messed with. She's tall and slender—still gorgeous at seventy—a former model who could have gone even further than she did if she'd had the opportunity. She's ambitious and hopeful and has three wonderful kids who are like surrogate siblings to Mark and me. Aunt Ginger has class and God on her side, and she'll tell you so. My grandpa Smith, the father of those six fabulous girls, was everyone's favorite guy. His little daughters thought he hung the moon, so when he was killed in a motorcycle accident, it rewrote the landscape of their lives. Mom was seven or eight, so I guess Aunt Ginger would have been in her early teens. Their mom ran a restaurant to make ends meet, so Ginger became the mama bear, bringing up the rest of the girls, working farm jobs and town jobs, bird-dogging their homework and boyfriends, making sure everyone was happy and fed. She was married for a while to a man named Jimmy, who was a great guy, but she was a good Christian lady, and he was—well, he was a bit of a rascal. We were all around the dinner table one time, and Uncle Jimmy said to Mark, "If you don't stop smacking, I'm gonna tear your leg off and beat you with it."

All us kids were horribly impressed by that. Apparently, Aunt Ginger was not. Divorce was a big drama in this Christian family, but she came through it with her head held high and is now married to my uncle Ben, who is a pharmacist and so good to her. Not the type to tear your leg off one bit. And my uncle Jimmy is still my uncle Jimmy; I stop by to see him whenever I'm in town. Anyway, Aunt Ginger's given me a lot of great advice about my life, and I knew she could help me win that pageant money. I'd been watching her and my cousin Cheri Lynn do the pageant thing all those years, and secretly I'd always wanted to do it because I always wanted to do anything that involved performing onstage.

Aunt Ginger felt I'd do best on the Miss America track, as opposed to the Miss USA track, due to the fact that Miss USA has no talent. The pageant, I mean. Miss USA as an individual has talent oozing out of her immaculately refined pores, I'm sure, but you'd never know it by the Miss USA pageant, in which there is no talent competition. Both Miss America and Miss USA pageants at the local, state, and national levels offer young women an opportunity to score big scholarship bucks if they're willing and able to negotiate an obstacle course of push-up bras and backstage jitters, but Miss USA is a straight-up beauty pageant, and as of this writing, the shortest woman ever to win it is Tara Conner, who stands a not-so-diminutive five foot five. If we ever see a Miss USA under five feet tall, I will hickory-smoke my Louis Vuitton trolley bag and eat it with hot sauce. You have to decide right out of the gate which track you're on by vying for Miss Hooterville or Miss Hooterville USA. Clearly, I had a more realistic shot at the Miss America pageants where I could score points singing.

The first thing Aunt Ginger did to prepare me for the Miss Broken

Arrow pageant was take me to the mall and make me walk up and down the stairs in high heels with a book on my head. Horror. Humiliation. All those people I didn't know. And worse yet, all those people I *did* know.

"If you can't do this," said Aunt Ginger, "you can't be Miss America. Be glad I'm not making you do it in a swimsuit."

Mom had a dress made for me, and I had a swimsuit that would do. For my talent, I sang "Matchmaker" from *Fiddler on the Roof.* Yes, I know I don't exactly look like I just fell out of the kibbutz-mobile, but that number is a charmer, and Aunt Ginger figured I could knock it out of the ballpark. And I did. I won talent . . . and got second runner-up.

(Sound cue: a big fat tuba fart. *Fwaugh fwaaaaugh.*)

Second runner-up is actually third place. Even if Miss Broken Arrow were to meet with a terrible accident—say someone tried to whip a stick out of her mouth or something—the second runner-up still ain't doing any ribbon cuttings.

"This stinks," I wept on the way home, but after some thought, I decided to be undaunted.

There's more than one way to skin a cat, honey. Miss Oklahoma City University gets to compete for Miss Oklahoma, too. So I entered Miss OCU, and *kerbingo!*—I won that sucker, which paid for a major chunk of my undergraduate degree and got me onstage at the Miss Oklahoma pageant. Miss Oklahoma always kicks butt in the Miss America pageant. The Miss Oklahoma pageant show-horses seventy-one perfectly toned, teased, and Galinda-fied contenders, and these are Southern girls, daughters of debutantes and oilmen; if you can sashay to the front of that pack, you're a force to be reckoned with. If I won Miss Oklahoma, not only would I have enough scholarship money to get my master's—I'd get to sing on television in the Miss America pageant and be seen by agents and producers on both coasts. My plan to conquer the world was coming together nicely. I arrived at the pageant buffed, waxed, and ready for action.

I won talent. I won swimsuit. I won . . . second runner-up.

Fwaugh fwaugh.

What can I say? It makes a good story on the talk shows now. Meshed well with all of Letterman's double-entendre breast humor. ("Paul, we should have Kristin play 'Will It Float?' next time." Hilarious stuff like that.) The *60 Minutes* anecdote always gets a good laugh. Sometimes I demonstrate the pageant waves: Screwing in the Lightbulb, Washing the Window, Wrist-Wrist-*Pearls*-Wrist-Wrist-*Pearls*.

"And this is when you see somebody you know," I throw in with a comical good ol' girl howdy-do. "I don't know how you win talent *and* swimsuit and not win, but—hey. I'm not bitter." That always gets a good laugh, too.

They said I lost it in the interview, but when I told Aaron this years later, he said, "What do you have to do to lose it in the interview after winning swimsuit and talent? Seriously. Did you set the interviewer on fire?"

Funny stuff. I'll have to use that.

At the time, however, I was not laughing. I made my way to a quiet corner, where I hoped no one would see me, and—not gonna lie—I was crying. My wonderful acting teacher at OCU, Erick Divine, found me and gave me a hug.

"I don't know what else I could have done," I said. "I thought I did everything right."

"You nailed it, Kristi. But sometimes you nail it—sometimes you're the best—and you still don't get it. Whatever you do as a performer, you have to do it for the performance. You can't do anything with the expectation of winning an award. It's best if you learn that now."

And I did. The pageant experience was good for me in a lot of ways. I got used to getting up in front of people, getting judged, getting rejected. And I discovered an untouchable kernel of confidence instilled in me by my mom when I was too little to know or care about any other point of view. You do your best out of respect for yourself, not to make someone else feel less, and when you know you've done well, no one can take that away from you. At an audition now, I never compare myself to the other girls. It's me and the character. Do we fit? Another girl's performance doesn't change the answer to that question.

The fact is, I knew I wasn't going to win as soon as I heard my name called for Miss friggin' Congeniality. I didn't mean to be nice; I couldn't help myself. The girls were all so terrific, I loved every single one of them. But Miss Congeniality never wins. (Why, God, *why* did you have to make me so dang *congenial*?) I won't say the winner wasn't good, but she was a repeater.

"Sometimes they make you go for it more than once," Aunt Ginger explained. "They want you to *want* it."

"Come back next year," the pageant director told me. "It'll be your year."

I'm sure I nodded and smiled, but I'd walked that dog and picked up the crap; I had no intention of covering the same territory again. Little did they know, these poor fools who thought they could stand in the way of my ultimate world dominance, that my parents had recently moved to Pennsylvania, which made me eligible to compete there. I entered the Miss State Capitol pageant in Harrisburg and (please join me in a full-arm overhead *snap!*) I won it.

Only seventeen girls were vying for the title of Miss Pennsylvania, and I was stoked for the competition. I'd sculpted my body with diet and exercise, crammed for the interview as if it were the bar exam, perfected my talent with every extra hour I could grab in Florence Birdwell's studio. I was doing a rambunctiously great song by Victor Herbert, "Art Is Calling for Me."

To sing on the stage, that's the one life for me. My figure's just like tetrazzini. I know I'd have fame if I sang La Bohème, *that opera by Signor Puccini!*

Funny but operatic. The vocal equivalent of a high-diving horse act. Ms. Birdwell came up with extra trills and frills that made it even harder. So I was feeling pretty confident the week of the pageant. I kept hearing about a certain girl being the one to beat. I'll call her Tessa Von Plotz. I scoped Tessa out, and sure enough, she was cherry-bomb beautiful. But her talent . . . not s'much. I wish someone had told her to do anything other than sing. Twirl a baton. Pull fire out of your butt. *Anything.* She sang "You're My World," which a former Miss America had sung and won with, and, Lord, we'll never get those two minutes back. I'd never heard someone sing sharp *and* flat at the same time. And her platform was "America's Veterans," about which she didn't strike me as super articulate. (I mean, if you want to pick a cream-puff platform that no one disagrees with—"Blankets for Poor Babies," "Crutches for One-Legged Nuns," "No Puppies in the Microwave"—okay, fine, but you should at least be able to talk about it intelligently.)

As the week went by and we worked our way through all the preliminary stuff, I got more and more excited. One of the events toward the end of the week was a photo-op sort of deal with contestants playing minigolf with organizers and sponsors and I don't know whom else. I was teeing up to hit the ball into a clown's mouth when a gentleman came over and asked me if I was excited about the pageant.

"Oh, totally," I said. "But I'm really nervous."

"Don't be. The crown's yours."

"Really? You think?"

"It's already been decided." He shrugged.

"Oh . . ." Something about the way he said it made me uncomfortable. "Really?"

"Wait. Are you—you're the Von Plotz girl, right?"

Fwaugh. Ffffffwaaaaaaaaaaaaaaugh.

Now, let me be clear: I am not saying the pageant was rigged. I don't know who that guy was. I don't know what he meant by that or if he in fact had anything to do with the pageant. I'm just saying. That's what he said.

The next day brought a flurry of controversy when the "story broke" that I was an interloper from Oklahoma, that I had in fact vied for the coveted Miss Oklahoma crown and been defeated. I was clearly the pageant equivalent of anthrax. I'd never tried to hide that I was originally from Oklahoma, never toned down my Southern accent or pretended to be anything I wasn't. Pageant officials rushed to clarify to the press that I was by-the-book eligible. Nonetheless, some folks didn't like it.

"So, Kristi," one of the other girls said, "did you have running water back home in Oklahoma?"

We got to greet our parents after each phase of the pageant, and I was never so glad to feel my dad's big arms around me.

"Don't worry about it, Kristi." He pressed a kiss to the top of my head. "Just go on into that interview and be yourself. They've gotta love you."

When it came time for the interviews, I was called first. The death number. But I was okay with that because in this part each contestant had the opportunity to discuss her platform, which I was excited to do. In this and the Miss Oklahoma pageant, my platform was "AIDS Awareness," something few people wanted to talk about at the time. Thank God, things are different now, but this was back in the day when residents of Kokomo, Indiana, actually started an alternative school so their kids wouldn't have to be in the same building as a boy with AIDS. A family's home was torched when it was disclosed that their three hemophiliac sons were HIV-positive. Those stories hurt my heart, and I felt strongly that people needed to know the facts about AIDS, but it wasn't a popular platform for pageants. There was something unseemly about it, something sexual, or—worse yet— something *homo*sexual. Why would a nice Christian girl concern herself with a thing like that?

I walked into the interview feeling a little shaken by the whole Oklahoma controversy but rock solid about the homework I'd put into my platform.

The first judge gave me the once-over and asked, "Kristi, what's the state flower of Pennsylvania?"

"The Pennsylvania state flower is the Mountain laurel," I said. "*Kalmia latifolia*, a distinctive pink cluster of woodland blossoms that reaches full bloom in mid-June."

"How about the state tree?"

"That would be the eastern hemlock, *Tsuga canadensis*."

"State bird?"

"Ruffed grouse."

"Highest elevation?"

"Mount Davis; 3,213 feet."

"Lowest elevation?"

"Delaware River, right smack-dab on sea level."

"Major agricultural exports?"

"Dairy, poultry, cattle, hogs, hay, and gourmet mushrooms served in many fine restaurants throughout the United States and Canada. Our state is a wealth of natural treasures."

Yeah, baby. Stick that in your *Tsuga canadensis* and smoke it. You better believe I knew my Keystone State minutiae. I'd done my homework on that, too, because (a) I wanted to win, and (b), as corntacular as this may sound, I felt that if I did win, I had an obligation to properly represent the state at the national pageant and at all the Miss Pennsylvania events. The pepper of *Jeopardy!* questions continued until my time was almost expired. Surely, I thought, they'll take the last few minutes to ask at least one question about my platform.

"Kristi, what are your views on the present situation in Yugoslavia?"

"I would have to say . . . about the, um . . . the Yugoslavia situation . . ." *Crap,* I thought, clicking through the fragmented news reports and dinner-table conversations. *Kosovo? Serbia? Shlomo Milosivosovitch?* I cleared my throat and said, "I'm not as knowledgeable about that as I could be, and I don't think it's right to spout an opinion out of ignorance."

They asked a few more questions that dealt with moral issues, which was aces for me; I was still pure as the driven snow. I left feeling pretty good about it. They never did ask me about my platform, but at least there were no *60 Minutes* moments. When they called the ten finalists during the actual pageant that night, I was dead last. Number ten. Which is actually an advantage because you get the last word in the onstage Q&A. It's traditional for the finalists to be asked about their platform, and each of the other girls was asked about hers, but when I stepped up, the emcee said, "Kristi, out of your interview, what's the one answer you'd most like to change?"

"I wouldn't change anything," I said. "I liked all my answers. Life is about each moment, and you don't get to go back and do it over. You can only learn from your mistakes and go on."

After a polite spatter of applause, they did a really lovely thing; they had the finalists dance with their fathers while the scores were being tallied. (Kudos on that, Miss PA pageant event planner. A very special moment.) My father joined me onstage, handsome and confident in his tux.

"I don't think it's going to happen, Dad."

"Don't worry, Kristi. God is in control."

It gave me a little of his strength, the way he said it. Utterly assured. *God is in control.* I tried to hold on to that as they announced the fourth runner-up.

Hang in there. God's in control. Be patient.

Third runner-up.

It's yours. In the bag. Wait for it . . .

"The second runner-up: Kristi Dawn Chenoweth!"

Noooooooo . . . this can't be right! You called my name too soon!

Third again. Out of seventeen contestants. I got my fanny whupped by Von Plotz, who sang like a chain saw and didn't even get to first base at the national pageant a few months later. But it was like a megaphone from God's lips to my stubborn little eardrum: *You ain't goin' to no Miss*

America to get no agent, so get over it. I reminded myself that I'd gotten enough scholarship money to pay for my master's degree, which is what I'd set out to achieve, and I could get an agent the same way everyone else did. (Whatever that was.) If I believed God was in control when I won, I had to believe that his hand was on me at this moment.

Denny, great pal that he is, couldn't wait to get his hands on the videotape, and he still to this day enjoys rewinding it to watch me lose over and over. No matter how many times we roll it back, they consistently get it wrong and declare me second runner-up. The camera zooms in on me, my eyes turn up toward Heaven, and you can see me say, "Okay!" My foot kicks out a little, and I walk on over to collect my roadkill roses. Okay, God, I hear ya, loud and clear.

Backstage after the pageant, one of the organizers asked me if I was going to try again next year, and I smiled and shrugged, thinking, *I'd rather get a Pap smear.*

The next day I was required to go to a luncheon, and I went in a cute skirt and ballet flats, not a spec of makeup on my face, my hair in a casual twist. On the pocket of my jean jacket, I wore a little pin that said NOT! Somewhere in the night, I'd decided that if you can't win it by being yourself, it was never yours to begin with.

One more item was on the pageant agenda. A representative from the Academy of Vocal Arts in Philadelphia was introduced to award the final prize: an opportunity to audition for AVA, which accepted only seven students per year. Auditions were hard to get, and in the unlikely event a girl's audition actually resulted in acceptance, a full scholarship came with it. They felt safe offering this generous prize because—c'mon. What are the odds?

The guy said, "Artists from all over the world apply to audition for AVA's four-year program, and only those with tremendous potential are accepted to the Academy. Very few times have I been truly impressed, and I am now."

Then he said my name.

❦

"I'm glad you lost," Florence Birdwell told me the following week. "I've seen too many girls lose their vision. And there's a certain stigma. Winning pageants can actually work against you in the real world, but the opportunity to audition for AVA—Kristin, this is huge, and if you actually get in? *Well!*" She opened her arms as if that meant everything. "That AVA scholarship is like being handed $280,000. And a career in opera. We'd better start preparing."

Ms. Birdwell outfitted me for vocal competitions the same way Aunt Ginger prepped me for pageant mode. Each year Ms. Birdwell took me to the National Association of Teachers of Singing competition—a six-state thing. Very big deal. At the end of the day, they ask five singers to perform, and my senior year I was thrilled to be chosen to sing "Caro Nome" ("Dearest Name") from Verdi's *Rigoletto*. During the dinner break, I dashed home, put on the gown I'd worn in the Miss Oklahoma pageant, and dashed back to the concert hall, feeling beautiful and effusively soprano. When Ms. Birdwell saw me, her face fell.

"Well," she huffed. "You've lost."

"What?"

"Where's that dear little blue suit you wore today? Kristi, what's so great about you is that you're not one of the women who *goes home to change.*"

Screw her, I thought, as I walked out onto the stage. *I feel pretty.* But as soon as I started to sing . . . oh, I wished I were wearing my little blue suit. I don't know what I was thinking. If I'd been doing "Glitter and Be Gay," yes, of course, the gown, but this was Gilda, the innocent young daughter of the hunchback jester, singing about the name that made her heart beat fast for the very first time.

"Caro nome che il mio cor . . . festi primo palpitar . . ."

I looked down at Ms. Birdwell, and she was looking up at me like . . . meh.

I got fourth. Out of five. Frankly, I had a better voice than some of those women, but I didn't deserve better than fourth.

"All of these are lessons," Ms. Birdwell soothed, putting her arms around me. "All lessons for you to learn, my dear. Go home. We'll start Monday."

I blew my nose and gathered the hem of my gown to trudge across the parking lot.

"Put that dress away," she called after me. "Put it away!"

I finished my master's program with the thesis concert: all legit music, including a difficult song cycle of Emily Dickinson poems set to music by Aaron Copland.

Why did they shut me out of heaven, did I sing too loud?

Emily Dickinson is such a wonderfully obstinate little cuss. I've always wondered what it was in her life that so turned her against comfort, company, and faith. An atheist who wrote hymns, a hermit who wrote love poems—maybe she simply didn't want to be figured out. It took a few years for some of the cycle to sink in, but parts still haunt me.

Heart, we will forget him! You and I tonight!
You may forget the warmth he gave, I will forget the light.

I sang from Carlisle Floyd's great American opera, *Susannah;* Schubert and Schumann art songs; Mozart's "Der Hölle Rache kocht in meinem Herzen"—the queen of the night aria. This was a big, long, hard program. For the written part of my thesis, I decided to present a paper on Leonard Bernstein, specifically three pieces—*Trouble in Tahiti, West Side Story,* and *Candide*—a discourse on whether they were considered operetta or musical theatre. But I let that slide, since I had two years to turn it in, and at the moment I needed to focus on my audition for the coveted fellowship at AVA.

I got it.

Florence Birdwell practically levitated right out of her shoes. Beginning with this prestigious program, a promising career in opera opened up like a magnolia right in front of me. I was thrilled, too . . . pretty much. I'd been focused on New York—on Broadway—since I was a kid. It felt like part of my biology. I was grateful for this tremendous gift being offered to me, but my commitment to the idea kept flickering, like a brownout, when the lights keep dimming and coming back on, teasing shadows at the corner of your eye.

No.

I took myself in hand. It would be insane to turn down this opportunity. And more important, given the serendipitous way it came to me, it seemed to be the direction God wanted me to go.

Looking back on it now, I see that it was.

chapter five

HELLO, I MUST BE GOING

The music at Best Buy in Denver is booming loud and rhythmy. I have to dance.

"Aunt Kristi," Zach groans. "Must you?"

I explain to him that, yes, I must, and he puts up with the humiliation because I've offered to pimp his ride with a new sound system. It's a more extravagant birthday gift than I usually give, but this is a big birthday. Sixteen. Zach has evolved into a big, ungainly puppy version of Mark, a long way from the tiny little biscuit he was the first time I held him, fresh from Heaven, scrunchy-faced and happy, warm and fragrant as a baked potato in my arms. *Now I get it,* I thought. Up until that moment, I hadn't had that gene kick in. Looking at him, I felt this enormous swell of love, pride, and protectiveness, and I knew that was only a shadow of what it must be to have your own baby. I kissed his tiny seashell of an ear and whispered, "You're going to love me."

Thus began my driving ambition to be the Cool Aunt. And so far so good. Thirteen-year-old Emily is easy; Betsye and I have already begun to train her in the ways of the shopping ninjas. Boys are a bit more mysterious to me, hence the clever blend of loud music, electronics, and cold, hard cash. But he is mine. Oh, yes. He is mine.

"Aunt Kristi, if you don't stop dancing, I'm going over there." He points to the video-games aisle.

"Can't stop the beat, Zach. Da funk—it's in the blood!"

He edges slowly away, and I swear, his face is scrunched exactly like that first time. I had just finished grad school. Denny was fresh back from his European cruise-ship gig, and that summer he and I did *A Chorus Line* together at a professional theater in Oklahoma City.

Okay, I'm sorry, but I have to interrupt here for one sec.

Denny! Get in here, honey. You have to meet everybody. Everybody? This is Denny Downs. Denny, everybody. Everybody, Denny.

Hi, everybody. I just have to tell you one quick thing. During that show—

It was the last night of the show.

I'll get to that, but first, you have to know that during the entire run of the show, Kris was complaining about how uncomfortable her costume was. Every night, we'd be standing backstage, and she'd be whining, "This old school leotard is the most uncomfortable thing I've ever worn."

You know the dance clothes we're talking about? Low on the hips, scooped front and back. And the front scoop was way too low. My cleavage was falling out all over the place.

So the last night of the show—

This is the very last night. Last. Show.

We were waiting to make our entrance, and she was tugging at her crotch and fussing with her bust and whining about it like she did every night, and I turn to her, and I go, "Hey—"

He just casually said, "Hey, do you think maybe you have it on backwards?"

And she got this little look on her face like . . . "Shwah?" . . . and then she dashed down the stairs. Went sprinting down to the little bathroom or whatever down there, and came back a minute later. "Yeah, this is a lot more comfortable."

A place for everything and everything in its place, as they say.

Better late than never.

Yeah. Thanks for letting me suffer for six weeks so we'd have this incredibly hilarious story to tell.

Anyway. You were saying?

The very next morning, we loaded up my car—a little Honda CRX—and headed North with all our earthly belongings. Denny had one wrecking-ball-size bag, I had a few little cardboard dressers filled with my clothes, we each had a box of sheet music, and that was about it. Denny was moving to New York to take on the New York theatre world. Apartment hooked up, first audition scheduled—he was really doing it. I went with him to hang out for a few days before I went on to Philly to start my fellowship at AVA. We sang the whole way. Having just finished *A Chorus Line*, we had those songs very much on the brain, but we tweaked them with our own lyrics.

"Everything is beautiful at the buffet . . . at the buffet . . . at the buffAAAAAAAAAAY!"

It went downhill from there. May Marvin Hamlisch have mercy on our blackened souls; we had to pull over to the side of the road several times, we were laughing so hard. Denny and I always laugh a lot on our road trips. We sing, we bicker, we kibitz for miles. If Mark's kids are along, they beg Denny to do the tour-train speech he used to give when he was working at Six Flags.

"All aboard! Good afternoon, ladies and gentlemen, welcome aboard the Little General. Your tour today is sponsored by Friendly's, the friendliest stores in town. If you take a look around the left side of the train, you'll see the sight of the first ice cream cone." Hand gestures are paramount at this point in the speech, so if I'm not driving,

I have to reach across and take the wheel temporarily. "During the World's Fair, an ice cream vendor ran out of bowls and turned to a nearby waffle iron for help. Thus the first cone was born!"

We stopped off to spend the night with Zach (with a baby in the house, Betsye and Mark became a pale side attraction), then dropped off the car at my parents' house in Pennsylvania and took the train to Denny's place in New York. I won't be trite and say that I lay there that first night intoxicated with the sounds of the city, but . . . oh, what the heck—the first night I lay there intoxicated with the sounds of the city. Cue Sinatra and hope to kiss a Rockette; I was in *New York*— mere inches from the Great White Way.

The next day I went to Denny's audition with him. Interesting people everywhere. The colors, the conversations, artists, musicians, tattered posters, worn dance shoes. It was very *All That Jazz* and all that jazz. The audition was for a national tour of *Annie Get Your Gun*, and since I was there, they let me audition, too. Neither of us got cast, but the choreographer came over to me after and said, "Come back tomorrow if you want to. I'm doing this show called *Animal Crackers*. Like the Marx Brothers' movie, you know?"

I smiled and nodded as if I did know, and the next day I went back to audition.

"I don't know if we'll get to you," the Equity union rep told me. "If you're still around after they've seen all the union people, we'll try to find time."

A few other nonunion actors waited for a few hours, then drifted off, but what was a daily grind to them was like a Fellini film to me. I couldn't get enough. I was so intrigued by the people who came and went, I hardly noticed the time. After five hours, the union rep came out and didn't seem thrilled to see me.

"Oh, geez. You're still here."

"Don't worry about it," I said. "I'm just here for fun, anyway, so I understand if—"

He rolled his eyes, went into the next room for a moment, then came back and gestured me to go into the rehearsal space. The choreographer from the day before sat with a few others at a long fold-up table like one you'd see at a church supper. Another guy sat at a battered upright piano that looked like it just rolled off the set of *Lady Sings the Blues.*

"And you are?" said the guy in the middle.

"Kristi Chenoweth?" My voice went up at the end as if it were in question, but I felt Florence Birdwell over my shoulder and said more firmly, "Kristin Chenoweth."

I went to the table and handed the man in the middle my headshot and résumé. (Yes, I did eventually learn what a headshot is. And it does not mean the same thing it does in Texas.) I went to the piano and gave the accompanist the piece I'd pulled from my box of sheet music.

"I'll be singing 'Somebody, Somewhere' from *Most Happy Fella.*"

The director shrugged and sat back in sort of a lay-it-on-us-if-you-must posture.

I laid it on them.

After I finished, he stared at the table for a moment. "Do you have an up-tempo?"

"Of course."

I gave the accompanist the sheet music for "On the Other Side of the Tracks" from *Little Me,* and when I finished singing it, the director asked, "Who are you?"

I wasn't quite sure what he was asking, since he had an eight-by-ten glossy with my name in big letters right there in his hand.

"I'm just . . . this girl. I'm on my way to be an opera singer."

"No, I mean—who—who represents you?"

"Well, I guess you could call my dad. If there's a problem."

"Your dad," he echoed. "This would be the person I negotiate with?"

"Do you dance?" asked the choreographer. "Do you tap?"

"Oh, yes."

He came over and quickly taught me a little routine, and I did it for them. They asked me to read a little scene, and I read it.

"Who *are* you?" the director asked me again. "What are you doing here?"

I gave him the short version: Oklahoma, Birdwell, AVA, Fellini.

"Look," he said, "you need to seriously consider what you're doing here. I'll tell you, we've been looking for three months to cast this role. And I will be calling your father to offer you this part, but you look like one thing, and you're actually a lot of things that—well, are you sure you want to be an opera singer?"

"Well, of course, I am . . . not." Admitting it felt like a deep draw of oxygen.

"You'll hear from us," he said in a tone of voice that even I knew meant *you're supposed to go now.* I thanked them and thanked them and scrambled down the steps to the street. I went back to Denny's, and Denny was as astonished as I was. The next day we took the train to my parents' home in Pennsylvania, and Charlie Repole, who was directing *Animal Crackers,* called while I was there.

"There's apparently some union you have to join," my dad said after he hung up the phone.

"Yes. Equity. It costs—I don't know, but I think it's a lot."

Dad waved that off. "I got him to agree to pay the fee as part of your deal."

"Oh, Dad! You're brilliant. How much does it pay?"

"Five hundred."

"Hmm." I bit my lip and did the math in my head. "It would be tough, but I'm good on a budget. I could get by on five hundred a month."

"No, it's five hundred a week."

"Oh, my gosh!" I shrilled. "Five hundred a *week?"*

I thought I had it made in the shade. And, honey, I did! We get so jaded, don't we? But that was a fortune for a struggling actor. Still is.

"He's faxing the contract over for me to look at," said Dad. "But if you're going to do this, you need to get a real agent. He said you'd probably be getting some phone calls from people wanting to represent you."

"Agents. Calling me." Even through the cloud of elation, I got the irony.

The Lord works in mysterious ways, Grandma would have said.

"Kristi," Dad said gently, "you know that no matter what you decide, we support you. But you need to think hard about what you're giving up here."

"I know. It probably seems kind of . . . not the greatest idea."

It actually sounded like a terrible idea. In Philly, I had a place to live and work for the next four years, stellar training, a wealth of onstage experience. And Florence Birdwell's approval. If I took the part in *Animal Crackers,* I'd be crashing at Denny's, earning a few thousand dollars over the next three months, and then . . . what? I'd basically be out in the cold with the eight kazillion other people who were trying to get the same work I was. Terrible idea. Terribly . . . thrilling . . . and exciting . . . and incredibly, ridiculously blessed.

"What do you want to do?" asked Dad.

Without a flicker of doubt I said, "I want to be on Broadway."

It was a totally "Thus the first cone was born!" moment.

∞

Animal Crackers was a riot. Zany Marx Brothers comedy, physical, broad, and lots of fun to work on. I played a singer/dancer Betty Boop sort of character who sang "I Wanna Be Loved by You" and even got to be the sweet half of the secondary love interest in the script. I was having so much fun, it didn't really sink in until much later what a gift it was to come to New York with that job in place. I need to take a moment here and thank Charlie Repole for sticking out his foot and tripping me on my way to Pennsylvania; he's really the one responsible for bringing me to New York.

The Gilbert and Sullivan style of "Hello, I Must Be Going" and Groucho's signature tune, "Hooray for Captain Spaulding," needled my conscience about that master's thesis. So did my father. He kept asking me if I was making any progress on it, and I kept telling him I was busy taking meetings with agents, who did indeed come to me with offers of representation. (A delicious footnote to my foiled plan to flag their attention by being all pageantastic on television; as Dad said, God was in control. It all happened so much better than what I was praying for.)

We rehearsed at 890 Broadway—a famous rehearsal space, though I didn't know it at the time. I was scared of the subway, so I walked miles by daylight and took cabs at night. Other members of the ensemble quickly spotted my out-of-towner quirks and took me under their wings. They walked me down to the subway and rode home with me the next several nights, taught me to read the maps and figure out which line I needed to be on, and helped me get over my general Big Apple intimidation. This was a wonderful, warm introduction to the amazing community of New York theatre. It's like the song says, *there's no people like show people,* and there's nothing like the Broadway family anywhere else on earth. Since I work on the West Coast so much these days, I have to make an effort to meet the new kids. I try to remember their names, to stay connected, and I go out of my way to help, remembering how my big brothers and sisters in the *Animal Crackers* company brought me in and brought me along without hesitation.

My parents weren't all that surprised by my decision, but I put off telling Ms. Birdwell for as long as was humanly possible. After a few weeks, there was no getting around it. I blurted the big news and waited through a stony silence for her to respond.

Finally, she sighed and said, "Well. You have to do what makes you happy."

"Thank you for understanding."

She remained supportive, but I could hear the deep disappointment in her voice.

She'll come around, I figured. I was on my way, doing a show in New York, auditioning, taking meetings with agents. I made a few false starts in that area, had to kiss a few frogs before I met the handsome princes of Bauman-Hiller, which later became BRS—Bauman, Redanty & Shaul. I loved wise Dick Bauman, and I'm so glad I had the chance to make him proud of me before he died. David Shaul was a brick house of support during my early L.A. days. But Mark Redanty—he was the first one to *get* me. And not very many people did. All the other agents I met with wanted to slap some kind of label on me: singer who dances. Dancer who sings. Comedienne. Character actress. The short girl.

"I see you as everything," Mark said. "That's how we're going to submit you."

He busted out the hustle and moved my career rapidly forward over the next several years, holding my hand and being an unfailing stud muffin through it all. My size and my voice worked against me at a lot of auditions. When I was plugged into a dance line, I couldn't see the chorus for the trees. *(Ba-dum-bum-CHHH!)* But ultimately, being different is a plus, and Mark made sure to send me to auditions where those liabilities became my greatest strength.

The audition fairy sprinkled some magic dust on Denny as well. He nailed a great gig at a professional theater in Houston and headed down there after just four weeks in the tiny one-bedroom sublet on Eighty-first near West End—the first of many apartments he and I have shared over the years—just a hop and a skip from Café Lalo, where we could get dessert on Friday nights for less than $10. (It's still one of my favorite places, with its tall, open windows, creaky wood floor, and boisterous breakfast crowd.) Before we got to be pros at subway surfing, we'd walk dozens of blocks, going to auditions, ferreting out the best bargain shopping, and hitting the off-, the off-off-, and sometimes-even-offer-Broadway plays our friends were in.

When Denny split for Houston, Ashley Mortimer, one of our music friends from school, moved in, and she and I shared the bed Denny and I had been sleeping in. (It took up the entire bedroom, leaving only a few inches between the mattress and wall on any side, so sleeping on the floor was not an option.) After the sublet ran out, Ashley and I moved to a place all the way down on Forty-fifth. Denny came back and squeezed into the little apartment with us. We slept on futons laid on the floor "tic-tac-toe, three in a row," as Ashley used to say. That sublet ran out, and we got a minuscule studio in Midtown.

Denny left to do a tour of *My Fair Lady*. Then I went to Birmingham to do *Little Me,* leaving Ashley to fend for herself, and when I came back, she and Denny were off to somewhere else. I know I'm not keeping all this straight. Denny's the one with the time-line savvy. Knows every show I was ever in. Knows what I wore to lunch on June 6, 1989. He's my touchstone. For me, it all blends into one big, noisy production number. What I do clearly recall is the three of us schlepping Ashley's and my little cardboard dressers through Times Square like a troupe of vagabond players. Which we were.

Completely new to me was the concept of readings and workshops. When a show is in development, the first step is to get a group of actors together with the writer and the director, give the script a voice, and see what pops and what flops. Sometimes it's just the creative team; sometimes potential investors are checking it out. A workshop probably involves getting on your feet a little, possibly putting in some rehearsal time. There might even be minimal set and props, plus a few more people in the audience. You might memorize some of the script and dive into it a bit more as an actor, but you're still on book— you have the script in your hand.

When I got back from Birmingham, I auditioned for a workshop of *Zombie Prom*, a crazy cool pop-rock opera about a heartbroken guy who hurls himself into a nuclear power plant and comes back as a zombie to win the heart of the girl who gave him the air. (The movie featured RuPaul, which pretty much says it all.) Everyone in town wanted to be in it. I looked around the audition, saw all the usual suspects, and figured I was out of luck, but I got cast, and it was a month of pure fun.

After *Zombie Prom*, I was off to Germany, touring with *Phantom*—and I don't mean *Phantom of the Opera*. I'm talking about *Phantom*, the American musical by Maury Yeston and Arthur Kopit. (Yeston calls it "the greatest hit never on Broadway.") Yeston and Kopit actually started their version first and held the American rights to do a musical version of Gaston Leroux's 1910 novel, *The Phantom of the Opera*. Unfortunately, the novel was already in public domain in Great Britain, and when Andrew Lloyd Webber announced his plan to do a musical version, it squashed the Yeston/Kopit version like a bug until four years later, when they revamped the script and produced it as a miniseries on NBC. Same network as My Huge Hit Sitcom *Kristin*. (Huge hit. Beverly Hills breast-implant huge. Until it got squashed like a bug.) The only music in it was opera, and for my taste, if I may be so bold, it's better than the blockbuster. Incredible, beautiful, beautiful play. So much better to sing. (But I love you, Andrew Lloyd Webber! Call me?) Literary and musical purists love the thing, and it's been done all over the world. Just not on Broadway.

The show that toured Germany was—not surprisingly—in German, a language I know my way around, but don't really love. It seems to use a lot of this sound that Maddie makes when she's been licking herself too much. I also didn't love the producer. As the all-powerful elfin queen of my book, I'm going to call him . . . Herr Upderkeister. Herr Upderkeister is brilliant; just ask him. An artist's artiste with Beethoven hair and piano keyboard teeth, he constantly scolded me for riding in the back of the bus with the French and Polish chorus people. He didn't want fraternizing across the caste-system boundaries, I guess, but I wanted to practice my French, and they were a fun crowd back there. None of them acted bored or thought they were slumming; they were grateful to be making the money. (If you think it's tough to make a living as a dancer in New York, try it in Sarajevo.) A particularly lovely dancer named Katja struck up an exuberant cross-cultural connection with me, and we rode along laughing and mangling each other's language for hours. She was in love with this little Hello Kitty jean jacket I had, and when I took it off and put it around her shoulders, not quite sure how to say "Keep it," she was so touched, she had tears in her eyes.

"I tell you und tell you," Herr Upderkeister shouted at me during a rest stop at some *Gott*-forsaken schnitzel-pit, *"der leads needs to ride in der vvvvront of der bus!"*

"Yeah, well, you need to get a haircut," I said, "but I don't think that's gonna happen either."

Nothing at the front was worth giving up the camaraderie back in the cheap seats, but even with the Katja fun factor, I was truly beginning to loathe that bus. I swear, from the first day I could feel my butt expanding to twice its normal size. The German countryside is stunning, and the people are good—I don't blame them for not knowing that corn doesn't belong in salad—but when Herr Upderkeister asked me to continue on with the tour at the end of my contract, that was a big no, *danke*. Crabbiness, bus butt, the phlegmy language and lardy cuisine—throw the Holocaust in there, and like the song says, *Goodbye to you, Mein Herr*.

A few years later, I heard through the grapevine that Katja had been in a train accident in Poland. Her leg was irredeemably crushed and had to be amputated. My first thought was *Oh, no! She can't dance anymore!* Because I knew that for her, the reality that she couldn't *walk* anymore was secondary to that. She and I had kept in touch for only a short time after the tour, so I had no idea how to reach her. It might seem silly, but I was so glad I'd given her that Hello Kitty jacket. I hope she still has it. I hope she can feel my arms hugging her close when she pulls it around her shoulders.

Connections like that are precious to me. People stay with me, even when their phone numbers and addresses don't. And screw anybody Upderkeister if he thinks that some people are not worth knowing or that snobbery is a hallmark of success. I can't bear to imagine the many dear friends I would have missed out on if everyone thought that way. There is, indisputably, a hierarchy in theatre, but it's up to each of us if we want to participate in it. It's good to learn early that every show is a family—complete with dysfunctional relationships, tough love, and plenty of occasion for forgiveness—and my goal is to be the cool aunt.

During a recent revival of *The Apple Tree*, I took the cast out to the Palm for dinner. It was the first Broadway show for a lot of these people, and I just wanted to help them enjoy this moment to the hilt. I like to love people up the way my cool aunts loved me up when I needed it, and just to make sure there's plenty of sugar, I always bake my famous White Trash cookies to pass around backstage or on the set.

In an effort to promote world peace, I will now share with you the recipe for . . .

Chenolicious White Trash Cookies

- Take a cudgel of that frozen chocolate chip cookie dough you buy at the grocery store and resist the temptation to eat most of it raw.
- Bake as directed on plastic wrapper.
- Lick plastic wrapper.
- Crack open a can of Betty Crocker ready-to-spread vanilla frosting and slather that on the bottom of each cookie with a butter

knife—liberally if you're a Democrat, prudently if you're Republican.
- Lick butter knife.
- Clap two cookies together forming one big, fat good-time sandwich. Done!

It also works with Oreo cookies if someone's recently broken up with you and you don't feel like baking. Or if you're interested in finding your insulin-shock threshold.

Full disclosure: A few years ago, I made these cookies during the Broadway run of *Epic Proportions*, and one of my castmates, the dear and brilliant character actor Richard Shull, ate several before we left the theater after the show. I had to do a reading for *Thoroughly Modern Millie* the next day, and afterward I saw the director talking to Jerry Zaks, the director of *Epic Proportions*. They asked me to step into the dressing room. Never a good thing. I thought I was being fired.

"Kristin," Jerry said in the one-stroke, get-it-over-with-way your mother rips a Band-Aid off your knee, "I'm sorry to have to tell you this, but Richard died."

"*What?* Oh, my gosh, but—what—*when?*"

"He went peacefully in his sleep last night after the show."

This was at 4:30 p.m., and we were supposed to go on at eight. The cast gathered at the theater, heartsick and crying. He'd been so special to all of us. Richard was one of those old pro, the-show-must-go-on types, and he had a great understudy who was ready to step in, so we knew we had to go ahead and do the show, but it was hard to imagine getting out there and giving the audience a big laugh riot.

"How did it happen?" I asked. "Did he have a heart attack or . . ."

"He was getting up there in years," said the director. "He had a great run."

Ross Lehman piped up and said, "I think it was those cookies."

We all fell out laughing. Truvy's life-giving laughter through tears. It was a great show that night. We sucked it up and got out there and did it for Richard. The audience never knew a thing was off until the very end, when I stepped forward and gave a brief curtain speech, explaining Richard's absence and saying a few words to honor him.

Flash forward to the set of *The West Wing* in 2006.

I made the cookies. John Spencer ate several. He died two days later. I'm not accepting any liability here, but I will never again make those cookies for anyone over the age of fifty. Denny calls them the "death cookies" and swears he'll never let another one touch his lips.

Apparently, they're just that good.

꩜

chapter six

BOX OFFICE OF THE DAMNED

Madeline Kahn Chenoweth is a Manhattan dog and could not be happier to be back on her home turf. As we breeze through the lobby of our apartment building, I snap a retractable leash onto her bedazzled collar.

"Say good morning, Maddie." I help her wave her little paw at the doorman. *"Good morning, Georgio!"*

"Good morning, Maddie," Georgio deadpans. He's a man of great self-control. "Good morning, Ms. Chenoweth."

Outside in the sunshine, I breathe in a deep whiff of Upper West Side and scruffle Maddie behind the ears before I set her down on the sidewalk. Cesar the Dog Whisperer would say she's the one walking me on a leash. She's a spunky thing who dodges and weaves and refuses to commit to one side or the other. (She and I have a lot in common.) A perfectly nice little schnauzer walks by and wants to play, but

Maddie will have none of it. A block up the street, we meet an English bullmastiff walking in the opposite direction, and Maddie gets all feisty, threatening to beat him up. It's like seeing a side of beef challenged by a kernel of popcorn. He humors her with a brief, condescending sniff and walks away, shaking his head.

"Didja tell him, Mads? Mommy's little baby told that big doggie, yes, she did."

I admit it. I'm one of those freaky dog people I used to hate, promenading my pooch around New York City, talking baby talk to her. I can't help it. She *is* my baby, and she probably doesn't remember any mommy other than me; she was the size of a shortbread cookie when I got her from Little Annie's Pet Salon on Staten Island. My best gal pal, Erin Dilly, has two Pomeranians—Ozzie and Harriet—and she decided I needed a baby of my own. I'd been thinking about getting a Maltese, so we hopped the ferry and went on over to look at a litter of puppies. Two Maltese puppies were still for sale. One was perfectly marked, quiet, and loving, a regular little Marilyn Monroe. The other was more of a Fanny Brice type, the scrawny runt of the litter, cockeyed and hyper. When I picked up the Marilyn puppy, the Fanny puppy raised a big stink, crying and caterwauling. That was Maddie, and she was not about to let me walk out that door with the wrong dog. I picked her up, and the connection was Jello-O instant pudding love.

She wasn't quite old enough to leave the litter, so the day I was allowed to bring her home was the day after the opening night of *Wicked*. Mom and Dad had flown in for the show, so we made an event of it, traveling by stretch limo, dragging Denny and my manager, Dannielle Thomas, along for the ride, to collect Maddie from Little Annie's.

"My grandbaby," Mom cooed as Maddie nuzzled her chin (and the rest of looked on, thinking, *How sad is that*). Then we took Maddie out to the limo, where she settled into the Corinthian leather seat with a distinct air of *I could get used to this*.

Now that I think of it, my connection with Erin Dilly happened just that quickly. I'd been hired to do a pre-Broadway production of *Babes in Arms* at the Guthrie Theater in Minneapolis. I was starting the show in a walking cast because I'd stepped in a hole and broken my ankle during previews for *Strike up the Band* at the Goodspeed Opera House. (I've done that show twice, and I have the scars to prove it; I doubt I'll ever feel the need to do it again.) When I arrived at the airport, gimpy and short on sleep, I saw a girl slumped in a plastic chair near the gate. I figured there would be other people from the show on this flight and instantly recognized that particular brand of physical and mental exhaustion that hallmarks a working actress, so I went over and said, "Hi. Are you by chance Erin Dilly?"

She looked up at me wearily. "You're Kristin."

"Uh-huh."

"I know we're going to be best friends," she said, "but right now, I'm so tired, I just can't make the effort."

"Me, too."

I slumped into the chair next to her, we gave each other an interpersonal hall pass—sort of a get-out-of-small-talk-free card—and have been best girlfriends ever since.

The Guthrie was great. The score had been updated with permission from the estates of Richard Rodgers and Lorenz Hart, and they'd spared no expense on the costumes and set. The story line is pure Depression-era rhubarb pie—a boy puts on a show to keep from being sent to a work camp—and the music is legendary: "My Funny Valentine," "The Lady Is a Tramp," and several other great old standards.

That job led to another job somewhere else, which led to a workshop in New York, which led to an off-Broadway play, which led to something else. That's the way it went, but I couldn't seem to make my father understand that this made it impossible to write that thesis paper I still owed. "I'll get to it," I kept promising, and he kept asking, "When?" Finally he and Mom came to New York to visit, and while we were eating lunch at Subway, they pressed the issue to the wall.

"Kris, it's been over a year," said Mom. "You can't come this close and not get your master's degree for the lack of that paper. Just get it done."

"I will. I promise."

"You promise what?" Dad flipped over his paper place mat on the table, clicking a pen from his pocket. "I want it in writing."

"I promise to write the paper, okay? Soon."

"Within six months." He wrote out the parameters of the agreement and pushed the Subway place mat across the table. "Sign. Right there at the bottom."

"But it doesn't say what you'll give me if I do it."

"Why should I give you anything?"

"Well . . . I mean . . . you know. What do I get?"

"The degree!" he roared. "You get the *degree.*"

"Fine."

I signed the place-mat contract, applied myself to the paper for several weeks, and turned it in. It was accepted without too much rigmarole, thank goodness. When the degree arrived in the mail, I had it framed and presented it to Dad for Christmas. It hangs in his office still today. He is some kind of proud of that master's degree. And I have to sheepishly concede that he did me a huge favor taking me to task about it. At the time, I figured, *Hey, I'm getting the work; what difference does it make?* But of course if makes a lot of difference. I have a master's degree in a classical discipline. That's a little bit of *boo yah!* in the ol' curriculum vitae, if I do say so myself. (Thanks, Mom and Dad. I couldn't have done it without you.)

It's not that I was being lazy. Quite the opposite. I was running myself into the ground. We all were. Before Mark Redanty signed me up, I didn't fully understand that it's de rigueur for New York actors to spend half their time elsewhere. I knew that to make it on Broadway, I needed to be based here, but I embraced the stage experience and growth offered by all the out-of-town jobs. There's no place like New York, but excellent theatre is happening all over the country with top directors either visiting or in residence. Once you get that Equity card, you're in like Flynn. I see God's handprint on each of those stepping-stones that took me exactly where I needed to be to learn what I needed to learn.

After I returned from Germany, I landed a role in *The Fantasticks* at the Sullivan Street Playhouse. I'd studied the show in college, of course, so I knew when I got cast that this was an opportunity to be a small part of New York theatre history. The show was written by Tom Jones and Harvey Schmidt, who's first collaboration was a musical review called *Hipsy-Boo!* (I know, right?) which opened in Texas in 1950 and did well enough to eventually get them to New York, where they began working on a musical version of a little-known Edmond Rostand play called *Les Romanesques,* in which two fathers—knowing that children always do what their parents forbid—build a wall be-tween their houses in hopes that it will make a boy and a girl fall in love. Jones and Schmidt struggled with the script; three weeks before the show debuted at Barnard College, they threw out everything ex-cept the song "Try to Remember" and started from scratch. *The Fan-tasticks* opened to mixed reviews on May 3, 1960, and played 17,162 performances before closing in January of 2002. I joined the cast in 1995, the forty-first actress to play Luisa, the role originated by Rita Gardner. The pay was lousy, but the experience was priceless. The very essence of off-Broadway. And the job kept me in New York, which I loved.

Housing was a perpetual challenge, but we did what we needed to do to make it work, living out of suitcases, sleeping in whatever space was available, and vying for closet space. While Denny was out of town, Ashley and I got a lead on a place near Seventy-second and Broadway for just $800 a month. It seemed too good to be true, so naturally it was. The day after we handed over the lion's share of our meager resources, we saw the landlady's mug shot on television. Denny came home to find us in a panic. He called a friend he'd worked with at Six Flags back in the day—a flight attendant named Brad, a lovely Southern gentleman, who had the biggest heart in the world and a one-bedroom apartment outfitted with four bunk beds, which he generously offered to his fellow airline workers, theatre people, and other wanderers.

Brad loved the *Jenny Jones* talk show, pageants, and *The People's Court,* so he had a huge bank of VCRs, all set to record various programs while he was flying around. The guy seemed as gay as a morning glory, but staunchly remained closeted, and that was fine by the three of us. Whatever floats your boat. We were just incredibly grateful to have a place to live. It was a little odd, however, to share those bunk beds with a revolving cast of strangers, and since everyone came and went on different schedules, you couldn't even count on getting into the same bed every night. I've been told they call this hot-racking in the navy, and that really doesn't help, but you have to understand how deeply, truly exhausted we were. By the time we dragged ourselves home after a show, we just wanted to lie down, and we didn't much care where. Everyone was in the same boat with never enough money or space or privacy to go around. Those were luxuries we were willing to compromise on in order to be New Yorkers.

Denny was temping for Clinique between shows (foreshadowing his later rise to cosmetics world dominance—he's now their executive director of North American marketing), and he was growing disenchanted with me for several reasons. Brad's place was outfitted with the Clapper (you know—"Clap on! Clap off! The Clapper!"), which turned the lights off every time I sang a high note and turned them on in the middle of the night if I sneezed. Cell phones were just beginning to come into vogue, but none of us could afford that or an answering service, so all our casting calls came to the apartment. For whatever reason, Brad had several phones strategically placed throughout the apartment, so every time a call came in, it rang everywhere, including the inside of your head in twelve different ringtones. I was dating three different guys at the time, so an unbalanced number of the calls were for me, and this began to be a source of stress. Denny was irritated at having his business calls interrupted with my social life, and I was irritated at having my social life interrupted by *Den-whah* not-so-cagily asking my dates, "Which one are you?" Between all that and the platinum-precious bar space in the narrow closet, tempers simmered one *clap on!* from boiling over.

The summer was hot and muggy as a dog's mouth, and I wasn't feeling well at all. One night after the show, Denny and I were in the grocery store, and the next thing I knew I was flat on the floor, blinking up at his startled face.

"Kris? Are you okay?" he asked, patting my cheek, pushing my hair back from my forehead.

"What happened?"

"I don't know. Your eyes rolled back in your head, and you were *out*."

He supported me back to the apartment, where I crawled into an available bed. Sharing the bunk below me was an older couple who were visiting New York on their honeymoon, and the bride happened to be a nurse.

"Your temp is up to 103," she said, pressing a cool cloth against my neck. "It's not appendicitis. Based on what you're telling me, I'd say it's some kind of parasite. You're getting seriously dehydrated. Sweetie, you need to be in the hospital."

I lay in a ball in the top bunk, and Ashley was kind enough to take care of me while my dad sped from Pennsylvania to pick me up. I was delirious with pain by the time I got to the emergency room. They dosed me with morphine, ran tests, and confirmed the newlywed nurse's diagnosis.

"You need to come home so I can take care of you," said Mom, and I didn't argue. Dad took me back to the apartment and waited with the car down in the street while Ashley helped me get my things.

It took most of my strength to gather a few clothes and stuff them into a bag. What energy I had left, I devoted to an all-out hissy fit.

"This is great. This is terrific. I'm livin' the dream now, aren't I?"

Suddenly the beaten-down feet, the inadequate sleep, and the too-many-gerbils-in-the-shoe-box dynamic of the past several months started venting out of me much the same way everything else had been venting from my twisted stomach. Desolate and dizzy, I launched into a tirade against the travesty of life in general and underfunded New York apartment life in particular. Because he was standing there, I railed at Denny about cramming his stuff too close to mine in the closet and how I was sick of showing up to auditions looking like I'd just crawled out of the trunk of a car, and he railed back at me about hogging a diva's share of the space. That spiraled into a diatribe about the Grand Central Station sleeping arrangements that had me snoozing sixteen inches from a different stranger every night, which brought out a bunch of hostility from Denny about the phone situation. Next I went off on Brad and his Clapper and his pageants and the idiotic Flintstones sheets on his bed and the ridiculous "Yeah, sure, Brad's as straight as a hitching post" pretense we were all supposed to uphold.

"I just want to shake him by the neck and say, '*Bradley! Baby!* Clap on, pal. You're *gay.* Everybody knows it. You're blipping the gaydar, dude. You're Anne of Green Gaybles. If you were any gayer—' "

"*Kristin, shush!*" Ashley poked my arm and pointed to the top bunk. Protruding from the rumpled Flintstones sheet was Brad's foot.

Luckily, it was not possible for me to feel any sicker than I already did.

Shamefaced and wilted, I gathered the rest of my things, and Ashley carried my bag down to the street where Dad was waiting with the car. I spent the next four weeks at my parents' house, and I'll spare you the details other than to say that the Health Department called and said something about a greasy midtown barbecue joint. After a month in my mom's tender loving care, I was ready to return to New York, weak and emaciated, but desperate to get back to work in the show. I'd heard nothing from Denny. Ashley said he'd moved uptown. I called Brad and left a message, apologizing profusely, blaming the morphine, the heat, the three hundred coiled yards of Dante's *Inferno* in my lower intestine. I got a message back saying that Brad wanted the four of us to sit down and talk.

"Why do I have to be part of this?" Denny groused. "I don't even live there anymore."

"Nice work, Kristin," said Ashley. "You got us kicked out of the apartment."

But when we all gathered at Café Lalo, Brad said it was okay. No hard feelings.

I guess he figured there really wasn't enough room in that narrow closet; he'd decided to come out. Wanted me and Ashley and Denny to be the first to know. And apparently he forgave me for dissing the Flintstones. I still get a Christmas card from him every year.

❧

I cringe when I hear that stupid crack about how you can never be too thin or too rich. That's crap. I've seen people get eaten alive by the wrong kind of riches, and when I looked in the mirror in my dressing room backstage at the Sullivan Playhouse, the specter looking back at me was way, *way* too thin. Despite everything my mother tried to do to help me, my weight had wasted to a skeletal eight-six pounds. Try to put clothes on that. I'm sure everyone who saw me thought I was anorexic, which didn't inspire a lot of confidence at auditions. My contract with *The Fantasticks* ended, and they invited me to extend it, bless their hearts, but I'd been doing readings and workshops for a revival of *A Funny Thing Happened on the Way to the Forum* with Nathan Lane for over a year. It had been indicated to me that I was the director's first choice for the Broadway cast. But when I showed up for the final callback, the powers that be took one look at my Auschwitz fabu-look and . . . *ixnay*. They went with another girl. They told me I could understudy if I wanted, but screw that. Not that I thought I was above being standby. I had no problem with that. But after working on the role for a year—a role I really wanted, working with Nathan friggin' Lane, whom I was crazy about—I was too hurt and disappointed to sit there with my ravaged stomach, watching someone else do it. Fair is fair. She got the part, and that's how it bounces, but when I eventually saw the show, she was doing all my shtick from the workshops, and what made all this even more unbearable was not being able to tell Denny.

After the big summit with the freshly outed Brad, Denny went off on another tour, and I didn't hear from him for two months. We'd hardly gone two *days* without talking since we'd met. I felt like half my ribs were missing. Since he'd become part of the family over the years, Denny was included in our Thanksgiving dinner plans. Dad was taking us all to a semi-swanky place called the Landmark Tavern. Stony silence laid heavily on the table, while Denny and I sulked and Mom and Dad wondered why anyone would be serving pheasant instead of turkey on Thanksgiving.

"To heck with this," Dad finally said, and we trudged up the bitter-cold street to a decidedly unswanky little diner in Milford Plaza, where we ordered turkey with traditional fixings.

"This is more like it," said Mom. "But you all know the tradition. Before we eat, we have to go around the table and say what we're thankful for."

I don't remember what the first few people said, but when it came around to me, I felt overwhelmed with emotion.

"I'm—I'm thankful for my friend—the b-best f-friend anybody could ever have . . ."

I was bawling too hard to say any more, but the next moment Denny was on his feet hugging me, and I kept saying I was sorry, and he kept saying, no, *I'm* sorry. We made up in the sloppiest scene this side of a ninth-grade girls' slumber party and pledged to never fight again. It was all very movie-of-the-week, but we were both completely sincere. It's one thing to face misfortune with your friends, quite another to face it alone.

The food was not great, so the dinner aspect of the day was a dud, but it was our best Thanksgiving ever. In fact, that would be the title of the movie-of-the-week: *Hallmark Presents the Best Thanksgiving Ever,* with Brenda Blethyn and Albert Finney playing my parents. If it was a horror movie, it would be called *Thanksgiving of the Living Dead.* If it was a musical, *A Funny Thing Happened on the Way to the Virulent Intestinal Parasite.* (Since *Hipsy-Boo!* is already taken.)

As much as I loved being Luisa #41, I didn't understand the message of *The Fantasticks* until years later. It's no more or less profound than the simple idea that the ebb and flow of life eventually makes all things even. We move apart, we come together again. We're wounded, we heal. That show is such a gem. Toward the end, the two young people come stumbling back to each other. Luisa takes one look at the battered and bedraggled Matt and says, "What happened to you?" And he replies, "The world happened to me."

We made it through that winter and through another year of auditions, tours, and trials, and as the world happened to us, we started happening back. In 1996, less than four years after that first New York audition, Denny was working his way up the corporate ladder, and I was cast in my first Broadway show. And it wasn't a musical.

Scapin, Bill Irwin's brilliantly physical modern adaptation of Molière's *Les Fourberies de Scapin* ("The Rascalities of Scapin") was a high-traffic farce filled with errors and redemptions, much like real life. Always a heart being broken, a feather getting ruffled, a hole begging to be stepped in. As a musical-theatre and then opera-performance major in college, I'd spent not much time on the classics and no time at all on the neoclassics. The commedia dell'arte school of clowning around was a total news flash for me. I wanted to know everything about it and dove into my own private study, reading everything I could get my hands on—Molière, Voltaire, Shakespeare, Goldoni. People tried to tell me I wouldn't understand it, but that stuff just clicks for me. Maybe because of my opera background. Or maybe I was just born in the wrong century—or at least the wrong decade. I'm a Ziegfeld girl, not a *Rent* chick, and I'm enchanted with the idea that artists such as Mozart and Molière, who in their own time were considered utterly vulgar, are now considered highbrow. It's that ebb and flow El Gallo talked about.

Everything about this play appealed to me, including Scapin's optimistic spin on things. In the face of all life's nose-tweaking "rascalities," he gamely declares, "Ah! Sir, life is full of troubles, and we should always be prepared for them . . . scoldings, insults, kicks, blows, and horse whipping. I always thank my destiny for whatever I do not receive."

Clearly, Scapin never had a lower-intestinal parasite.

∽

chapter seven

QUICK CHANGES

It's a Rodgers and Hammerstein moment in the hypercolorful *Pushing Daisies* universe. The orchestra swells, the camera swoops in from the towering alps to my Julie Andrews twirl. *The hills are alive* . . . and then a pigeon craps on my face. This is how life works for hapless—but never hopeless!—Olive Snook, whose unrequited love and general enthusiasm sometimes compel her to burst into song. I knew from the moment Dannielle handed me the *Pushing Daisies* pilot script that Olive and I were made for each other.

"You must read this carefully," Dannielle told me. "And then you have a huge decision to make."

One of life's little jawbreakers.

I'd been workshopping a Broadway musical redux of Mel Brooks's *Young Frankenstein*. I loved the pilot script, but who turns down an opportunity to work with Mel Brooks? Bryan Fuller's first show, *Won-*

derfalls was—well, it was a wonder, and the script in my hand was even more captivating. They're calling it a "dramedy," which is a word I hate, but there's really no word existing that adequately describes the strawberry-rhubarb combination of whimsy, mayhem, and emotion. Audiences have literally not seen anything like it because every frame is processed with this new Lustre technology, which through some sort of tweaky-freaky magic makes red into *love* and blue into *longing* and yellow into *hilarious*. Everything from Ned the Pie Maker's lips to the matching pattern on Olive's pj's and wallpaper is saturated with the color *wow*. The eyes of the two eccentric aunts (though there are only three eyes between them) are luminous and expressive. Skin looks more sensitive. Digby the celluloid dog is warmer and furrier than the real-life puppy curled up at your feet. Visually, the show is a modern marvel, and Bryan Fuller has created quirky characters, giving us amazing mouthfuls of dialogue.

When I saw the finished first episode, I said, "Oh, it's so *good*! It's so innovative! It's so different! It's—it's—it's never going to last."

But so far so good.

It's a joy to go to work each day as part of this terrific ensemble. Ned is played by Lee Pace, a Southern gentleman from Spring, Texas. This says it all about Lee and me: he bought his dad a meat grinder for Christmas and couldn't wait to tell me all about it. Who else was he going to share that with but a fellow down-homer? Nobody. Anna Friel came over from London, bringing with her a fabulous sense of style and her adorable daughter Gracie, who is crazy for Maddie, my little Maltese. They're together so much, I swear, she's got this dog barking with a British accent. Chi McBride has been around the block and doesn't put up with any crap. I learn just watching him work. He loves his job, basketball, and his new baby.

The two aunts are played by drop-dead-gorgeous Ellen Greene and Swoosie Kurtz. My mom and I both loved Swoosie when she was on *Sisters*, and it meant a lot to me that she was the one who handed me my Tony. When they told me she might be on this show, I told Dannielle, "If they get Swoosie, I'm in." I wasn't going to miss the opportunity to work with her. Ellen Greene is a complete whack-a-noodle and an amazing actress—a huge Broadway icon with the sweetest, most generous spirit. And she can make a German chocolate cake that looks as if it came from a bakery. I know this because the writers and cast often get together during hiatus to eat, gab, and watch *America's Next Top Model.* (I swear, we're not catty. Much.) We're a happy troupe.

One of the most deliciously different elements of *Pushing Daisies* has been the opportunity for Ellen Greene and me to sing on the show. It's something audiences aren't used to seeing, so it was a risk, but the buzz seems to indicate that people want more, so Bryan asked me to make a list of songs that Olive might sing. I went him one better and asked my music director to sit down with me at the piano for an hour to record a few tracks that might spark Bryan's imagination. (It doesn't take much.) The piano we sat down at is at John Kilgore Sound, an intimate recording studio in the Film Center Building. The place is as New York as it gets, an art deco icon designed by the architect Ely Jacques Kahn, who's secretary, Ayn Rand, spent her lunch hours working on her novel *The Fountainhead.* You can feel the history of the place in the wood grain.

I adjust the microphone in front of me. "Hi, Bryan Fuller. Say hi, Andrew."

"Hi, Bryan. It's Andrew Lippa."

"The Genius."

And I'm not teasing. He truly is. Lippa is the man who produces my concerts, conducts the orchestra, plays piano, and chimes in as needed, much to the delight of the crowd. If this were a French neo-classic, he'd be Cyrano, crafting these wonderful songs that come out of my mouth. If this were *Phantom of the Opera,* he'd be my Angel of Music, only not with the Halloween costume face.

"We are in the recording studio and this is the first option for Olive. And, Bryan, these are just options. Songs I feel Olive could do."

Lippa and I are offering Bryan about a dozen pieces to choose from. A few old standards like "Someone to Watch over Me" and "Till There Was You," plus a few contemporary pieces.

"Okay, Bryan, just go with me here," I tell him. "Just think about it."

Lippa lays down the familiar piano ramp into Lionel Richie's "Hello" and I give it an Olive Snook spin. Anything goes. Last season Bryan had Ellen Greene and I do a little bit of a They Might Be Giants ditty called "Birdhouse in Your Soul." If the suits could handle that, they can handle anything. (And it was a major thrill for me to sing with Ellen.)

"Okay. Here's another one, Bryan. We're just throwing 'em down."

We dig into Lippa's beautiful arrangement of "Boy," a song that kisses unrequited love on the forehead and puts it to bed. Lippa volunteers that the piano solo at the opening could be cut, but I tell him to lay it down here just because, hey—nobody lays it down like Lippa.

∽

I first heard of Andrew Lippa when Denny, Ashley, and I were cohabiting in one of our many Midtown sublets. Denny came home from a tour feeling pretty flush and said, "Anywhere you want to go. On me." Dangerous thing to say to starving artists.

"There's this little show playing across the street," I said. "I don't know anything about it, but I'm dying of curiosity."

For several weeks, I'd been watching people come and go from *john & jen,* and on the way out, they definitely seemed . . . changed. Denny and I went and sat through this astonishing little show. Two actors, piano, cello, and percussion. The staging could not have been simpler. Nothing distracted from the music, which ends up telling the richly complex story of a woman, her brother who dies in Vietnam, and the brother's namesake, her son. After the final curtain, I floated out the door thinking, *I have to know Andrew Lippa.*

A year later (or maybe two years, I don't know—ask Denny) I was doing *Scapin* by night, rehearsing and workshopping *Steel Pier* by day. I have to digress here and tell you that this was the first time I woke up with the room spinning. I'd never heard of Ménière's disease. Had no idea what was wrong with me. This wonderful man I was dating at the time, Marc Kudisch, came in and found me on the bathroom floor.

"Don't touch me," I whimpered. "If I try to move . . . I have to hurl."

Marc Kudisch and I were working together in *Steel Pier,* and I can't begin to tell you how important this show was to me. From the moment I first heard about this show about a dance marathon by Kander and Ebb—Kander and Ebb, for crying out loud, Kander and Ebb!— well, everybody was buzz buzz buzz about it. Susan Stroman, the choreographer, brought me in to audition with the chorus, and all I saw was miles and miles of nothin' but legs. The top of my head barely cleared the nipple region in that lineup. But there's a rottenly yummy little character in the show who—*tra-LA!*—sings opera. Kander and Ebb called me in to sing and read for them, scrapped the song they'd originally written for the character, and created a number for me. (Kiss my grits, tall girls.) And then Marc Kudisch, my second First Great Love, also got cast. In what universe does *that* ever happen? Heaven! We were back in the rehearsal space at good old 890 Broadway, and everything was going swimmingly. The show was bound for Broadway, and this performance was for potential backers.

"Perfect," I moaned into my hands, shivering on the bathroom floor.

Marc paced the hallway outside the door, talking on the phone to the director, Scott Ellis, whom I loved and respected. I was so grateful (and still am) to this man who cast me in my first Broadway musical; the last thing I wanted to do was disappoint him.

"I don't know what's wrong, but she's really sick," Marc told him. "She *is* trying, but she can't even—I'm telling you, she can't even stand up without barfing."

I'm going to be okay now, I told myself sternly. *Suck it up, Roller Girl. Just open your eyes and be okay.*

Marc came in and knelt beside me. "Kristin. You've got to pull it together."

"I know. I am. I'm . . . I'm . . . yeah."

On the way to the theater, the cab had to pull over so I could throw up in the street. Huddled on the floor in the dressing room, I begged God to help me. Susan Stroman came in and asked if I was okay.

"No."

"Well. You need to get okay. Real quick."

She wasn't being mean. Dancers are tough, that's all. My partner, Jim Newman, basically held me up through the show.

"We won't spin," he whispered in my ear. "We'll just take it step by step."

After the show, there were notes, but I told the director he had a choice: I could do notes today or a show tomorrow. He told me to go home, and Marc walked me out to help me get a cab, but I told him, "No, you have to go back in for notes."

"Are you sure?"

"Yes. Go. I'll see you at home."

He left me leaning against the wall, and as soon as he disappeared through the stage door, I knew it was a mistake. Some time went by in a blurry mess of nausea, whirling cobblestones, more begging God, *Please, please help me.*

"Miss? Do you need help?" A man in a tweed coat touched my elbow.

"Please," I said, sounding very Blanche DuBois depending on the kindness of strangers. "I need a cab."

He hailed a taxi, poured me into it, paid the driver, and wished me well. Because that's how New Yorkers are. People answer each other's prayers a million times a day in this city. The next morning, feeling significantly better, I said to Marc Kudisch, "Wow. That was weird. Thank goodness that's over." Famous last words.

Anyway. Life goes on.

So—*Steel Pier*. Broadway. It was a great show. Screw what the *New York Times* had to say about it. The lousy review ("Party's Over, Chum. Just Keep Dancing") plotzed all over the great Kander and Ebb and the leading players and didn't even mention me.

"Kristin, you're the only person I know who bitches about being left out of a bad review," Marc chided. "You should be thanking your lucky stars."

The show didn't run long, but talk on the street about it was good, and I think this is how my name came up in conversations about a workshop opportunity at the Eugene O'Neill Theater Center, an extraordinary facility in Waterford, Connecticut, where they gather an ensemble, get a show on its feet, and at the end of the week bring people up from New York to see it.

"The show's called *Wild Party*," my agent told me. "Written by a guy named Lippa."

"What else has he done?"

He mentioned a few things, including a little show called *john & jen*.

"I don't know who he is," I said, "but I gotta do it."

Arriving at the Eugene O'Neill Theater Center, I had a bit of a *Private Benjamin* moment. This place is not like a theater, it's like summer camp, and I've never been a big camper. It's not that I have a problem with nature; it's just that so much of it is outside. I like my nature with a little Plexiglas. The kitchen served nothing but carbs.

There was nothing but a narrow bed and small desk in the room. Bathrooms were shared. The first night, I spent a few hours slapping at bugs, then went and slept in my car. I woke up cold and cranky, thinking, *What am I doing here? Forty-eight hours ago, I was on Broadway.*

And then I met Lippa. Huge blue eyes. The blunt brown haircut, precious heart, and skinny legs of a schoolboy. He spoke with utter clarity—I loved his speech and admired his faith. Because Marc Kudisch had become important in my life, I was eager to learn about Judaism, and Lippa and I had many thought-provoking conversations about it. He'd written a terrific song for my character, a comedic role that goes deep at the end. Hearing his music the first day of rehearsal, I felt as if I were in church.

Early one morning toward the end of the week, I sat by the water and said, "Thank you, God, for bringing me to this place, to this person."

A bright green bug landed on my shin, and I didn't even bother to slap at it.

∞

Over the next year, the opportunities got better, which made the choices harder. (Not that I'm complaining!) In the spring of 1998, I played mean Nurse Nancy in *A New Brain* at Lincoln Center, and the director invited me to join a revival of *Annie Get Your Gun*, headed for Broadway later that year. The sassy supporting role of Winnie offered opportunities to sing, dance, and participate in a knife-throwing act, and if that's not enough to whip the stick out of your mouth, Bernadette Peters (cue the angel chorus) had signed on to star. The show was a guaranteed Broadway smash.

Meanwhile, I'd been hearing rumblings of another revival show: *You're a Good Man, Charlie Brown.* In its original incarnation in 1967, the musical, based on the *Peanuts* comic strip by Charles Schulz, was a big off-Broadway hit. But in 1971, they took it to Broadway, and it went over like a burp in church. That version became a favorite high school musical with its low-budget set and the big "Suppertime" number for the talented kid. Michael Mayer was planning to workshop and revamp the show completely with the addition of new music by (cue that angel chorus again) Andrew Lippa. Of course, the objective was Broadway, but there was no guarantee this thing was going to make it past Toledo.

Denny and I were sharing another little studio apartment, and I kept him up late debating the issue, weighing my options.

"Bernadette Peters . . . Andrew Lippa. Guaranteed smash . . . potential burp in church. More money . . . more Lippa. More money plus *knife-throwing* . . . Lippa. Obviously, I have to do *Annie Get Your Gun* . . . right?"

"Obviously," Denny agreed. "If you want to."

"Of course, I do! I mean—who wouldn't? It's a great role."

"It's a terrific role."

"But with *Charlie Brown,* I'd be creating something totally new."

"That does sound like fun."

"Dang it, Denny, do you have to be so neutral? It's like sharing a closet with Switzerland."

Marc Kudisch and I were still going strong, and I drove him crazy agonizing over it while the fun factor kept nudging, and Michael Mayer kept telling me, "Trust me. You want to do this show."

"Marc, please," I begged, "give me one sane, practical, all-about-the-business reason to do *Charlie Brown.*"

"You'll get more stage time in the small ensemble show."

Marc Kudisch, ladies and gentlemen. Handsome hunk of helpfulness.

I hadn't really thought of it that way—small ensemble versus the cast of thousands. It wasn't easy to let go of the knife-throwing. And Bernadette. But in my heart, it felt like the right call.

Though I'd originally auditioned for the role of Patty (not Peppermint Patty; she was created in the comic strip after the original show was written), I arrived at the first rehearsal and found my chair marked SALLY. Part of Michael's redux of the script was to eliminate Patty altogether and expand the role of Charlie Brown's little sister. He was still noodling out how he wanted to do it and gave me reams of *Peanuts* comics to read in hopes of ferreting out a few inspired bits and pieces. While we workshopped the show, I experimented and played with the character, eventually coming up with a composite of fidgety tics and ball-bustery. Michael didn't say much, so I figured it was okay. The creative process was such a toboggan ride, I couldn't wait to get home and tell Denny about it every day.

The show has traditionally been owned by Snoopy, and it was clear from the beginning that Roger Bart was going to be brilliant. Ilana Levine was a fiery Lucy, B. D. Wong our lovable Linus, and Stanley Wayne Mathis the thoughtful Schroeder, with Anthony Rapp fearlessly leading the cast as Charlie Brown. A terrific ensemble of smart, seasoned, hilarious actors, and a wonderful group of friends to work with. The lone piano and building-block set from the original production had been supersized to include special effects and a full orchestra, and Lippa had written a song called "My New Philosophy" with a wealth of comic opportunities, Zen wisdom, and vocal range for Sally and Schroeder. It's a little piece of genius. Sally is able to marshal all meaning necessary for living her life into a series of concise axioms:

Oh, yeah? That's what YOU think.

Why are you telling ME?

No!

And *I can't stand it!*

Give it some thought. I defy you to come up with a life circumstance in which one of these doesn't come in handy.

I have to give credit where credit is due: my inspiration for many of Sally's little mannerisms was my brother's bodacious blue-eyed baby girl, Emily. She was a toddler right around this time, just beginning to discover her long, lean, and naturally athletic limbs. She'd tapped into the power of *"No!"* and wielded it without hesitation, her little arm straight out, index finger pointing slightly off to the side, as if to tell you how out of line you were in trying to boss her around. She's a lovely fourteen-year-old now, and Betsye and I are doing our darndest to coax forth her inner girlie girl, but every once in a while I see a flash of the old Sally Brown determination that will undoubtedly serve Emily well in later life.

We opened the show in Skokee, Illinois, and the audience went ape wild for it. After the curtain call, Michael gave me a big hug and said, "See? See? What did I tell you?"

Nothing! I wanted to yell at him. *You told me nothing! I thought I was part of the wallpaper.* The next night, I figured I should rein it in a bit, but after the show Michael came charging back again.

"What happened? Where was the character I saw last night?"

"I thought maybe the balance was off a little. I don't want it to look like I'm trying to upstage people."

"Those guys can take care of themselves. You play your role and respect them enough to let them play theirs."

He told me to let it rip. Run with the big dogs or stay on the porch with the puppies.

In February 1999, we opened on Broadway. Mom, Dad, and Florence Birdwell all came up to see the show. We went out after and laughed and talked, but I couldn't stay up late because my castmates and I were scheduled to perform Stanley's big number, "Beethoven Day," on *The Rosie O'Donnell Show* the next morning. (And can I just say here that I love Rosie O'Donnell? They didn't used to call her the Queen of Nice for nothing, and even when they stopped calling her that, it didn't stop being true. She's one of the coolest, most generous people I've ever known, and she did for New York theater what J. K. Rowling did for magic hats, bringing Broadway to millions of folks who had previously never given it much thought.)

I was sound asleep when the phone rang at two in the morning, and I rattled it off the cradle, thinking somebody better be on fire.

"Kristin." It was a friend—actually my doctor, but I got hurt often enough that we were on pretty familiar terms. "Go get the paper. Now."

"What? Why?"

"Ben Brantley says you're a star."

My dad went out and returned with the *Times,* and he and Mom sat at the table reading, their heads close together, tears running down Mom's face.

"What does it say?" I asked.

She held up the paper to show me the headline: "Your Sister's Gutsy, Charlie Brown."

"It says . . . it says 'one of those breakout performances that send careers skyward.' "

"Oh." I would have laughed had I been able to breathe. "What does it say about the rest of the show?"

Mom bit her bottom lip and shook her head. Basically the review started with some positive stuff about Sally, then trashed the show, tearing down the production values and either slamming the rest of the cast or damning them with faint praise. With a weird sort of survivor's guilt, I allowed the blessing to wash over me. This didn't bode well for the show, but something huge was happening for me, and I was way too grateful to pretend otherwise. I've ridden at the back of the hay wagon plenty of times and been genuinely glad for the person enjoying his or her moment in the sun. This show was going to be my moment.

It was a quiet gathering backstage at *Rosie* later that morning, but the moment B. D. Wong walked in the door, he wrapped his arms around me and said, "I'm so happy for you." Out on the set, Rosie talked up the show like crazy, said great things about everybody, and flatly stated that the role was going to win me a Tony. Stanley blew the walls back with "Beethoven Day," and the audience ate it up.

Just before the end credits rolled, Rosie looped her arm around me, pulled me toward the camera, and said, "I love this girl! I love her!"

It was a perfect nutshell of the entire day from my perspective.

And it was great, okay? What—am I Mother Teresa? Am I a wooden peg? Of course, I *loved loved loved* every second. It was thrilling. My agent's phone was ringing all day. After the show that night, I sat in my studio apartment with Denny, trying to encompass how my life had changed in the hours since the sun had come up.

❧

When the Tony nominations were announced, *You're a Good Man, Charlie Brown* was nominated for Best Revival (Musical). Michael was nominated for Best Director, Roger Bart for Featured Actor, and me for Featured Actress. Producers hoped this would overcome the bad buzz from the *Times* and other reviews to keep the show afloat, but as awards night approached, we all knew we were circling the drain. The Tony producers came to the show and asked us to do "My New Philosophy" plus a few bars of "Happiness," which had been spiffed up from the original.

The week before the Tonys I was back on Rosie O'Donnell's show, and she asked me what I was going to wear when I accepted the Tony, which she and my mom had already decided would be mine.

"Tommy Hilfiger made me a beautiful dress," I said, "but we're going to perform right before my category is announced, and they told me there wouldn't be time to change."

"What? No, no, no," said Rosie. "You have to change."

"Well, they're telling me it's only about thirty seconds."

"Plenty of time. It's theatre. People do quick changes all the time. Don't you worry. I'm going to have my dresser back there for you. Bobbi's a magician. He'll have you out of the costume and dressed with time to smoke a cigarette and fall in love."

I was a little ambivalent about assembling a team to quick-change me backstage at the Tonys. The potential for humiliation here was not small. I had some stiff competition: Gretha Boston, Mary Testa, and Valarie Pettiford. If I didn't win, it would be the most awkward moment in the history of all-dressed-up-with-no-place-to-go. I'd be in my Tommy Hilfiger dress just in time to wave to the winner as she breezed on by.

The night of the awards, we did our thing and trucked off the stage to huge applause. In the thirty-four seconds it took for Swoosie Kurtz and Ben Stiller to list the nominees and crack the seal on the envelope, two dressers peeled off my costume and poured me into an evening gown while the hair wrangler whipped off my short, mopsy wig and whipped on a long Farrah Fawcett hairdo. (B.D. said it turned me into someone he'd never seen before.) Somebody yanked off my Sally Brown clodhoppers and ankle socks and jammed high heels on my feet at the moment my name was called. A scream went up from my castmates, who surrounded me with a windstorm of congratulations and shoved me back onstage, breathless and elated as if I'd been shot out of a cannon.

Roger had won his Tony earlier that evening, and finally the moment came to announce the Best Revival. And the winner was . . . *Annie Get Your Gun*. Nothing left to do, we figured, but go out and party like rock stars.

We received our closing notice the following day.

⌒∞⌒

My Tony sat on the piano at Mom's house for several years.

"I don't want it to get lost in the shuffle," I told her, but the truth is, I found it intimidating. The Oscar seems to be styled so that recipients are not tempted to sit on it. The Antoinette Perry Award for Excellence in Theatre—*Tony* for short, after the actress, producer, and World War II–era leader of the American Theatre Wing—features a nickel-plated brass and bronze medallion, suspended over a black acrylic base on a pewter swivel. It looks a bit like the suspended garbage-can lid that Chuck Barris used to whack in *The Gong Show* when the contestant had worn out his or her welcome on the stage. Seeing it hovering there on the shelf impregnated the air with the possibility that all this could be over in the space of a single cymbal crash.

When I bought my apartment in New York, Mom brought it to me and insisted I put it on the bookshelf. After all those years of anywhere-I-hang-my-hat, I was settled in one place now, and she figured I should keep track of my own things. And it's fine. Between then and now, I've won and lost enough awards to blow off *The Gong Show* pastiche.

In 2004, I was nominated alongside my castmate Idina Menzel for *Wicked.* I wasn't at all surprised when she won, and I couldn't have been happier. She'd been nominated for *Rent* and lost in 1996. This was her moment, and she earned it. I think everyone was a little surprised when *Avenue Q* kicked *Wicked*'s butt in every other category, but—there you go. It was their moment.

In 2006, I cared more than I like to admit about the Tony nominations. I'd invested blood, sweat, and tears in a revival of *The Apple Tree.* I played four roles, worked harder, sang stronger, and had more fun than I'd ever had in any show *ever* and received the best reviews of my life. After the nominations were announced, a fabulous photo of me in a spanglicious golden gown appeared in *New York* magazine online—right under the headline "Tony Nominations: Who Got Snubbed?" Below my fabulous photo, it said, "Kristin Chenoweth. The once-beloved pixie of Broadway fails to get nominated."

Once. Beloved. Pixie.

In other words, *GONG-ng-ng-ng-ng.*

The item asked, "Does Broadway resent her alternating stage projects with TV and film?" As if "Broadway" sat down at their Friday-night poker game and came to a collective decision about the earth-shattering question of whether I'm on TV? Ironically, the day of my nomin-*not!*-tion, I was scheduled to do up-fronts for *Pushing Daisies*. Up-fronts are yearly press events at which each network has a day to trot out the shows for the next season. The actors and directors are seated at long tables in front of a firing squad of cameras and microphones. Entertainment journalists lob questions at us, and we lob answers back.

The very first question put to me was "How'd you feel about getting snubbed by the Tonys?"

A few answers unbecoming to Miss Congeniality sprang to mind. *How'd you feel about waking up with a fork in your eye?* Then I thought about Uncle Jimmy. *How'd you feel if I tear your leg off and beat you with it?*

But I smiled and said, "A wise teacher once told me never to do anything with the expectation of an award." Then I spent the rest of the day in a funk.

The next morning, my mom called:

"Kristi, I have some bad news. I had this lump biopsied, and, honey, I have breast cancer."

In one paradigm-shifting, perspective-galvanizing, attitude-adjusting moment, the difference between drama and melodrama was starkly outlined. I put my life and career on hold and went to Houston, because once I got past the initial cancer-bomb stuff—all the information that has to be assimilated, decisions, logistics, private tears, and public transportation—I realized that *this* was my moment. All my life, I'd been on the receiving end of my mother's endless tenderness and vigilant care. I'd never had the opportunity to be the one who's *needed*—for her or anyone else—and until it was my turn, I never had an inkling of what a privilege it is.

Before Mom's double mastectomy, we went shopping for gowns that would be easy to get in and out of and spent the day talking, reminiscing, just being together. The first month or so after the hospital, it was basically the two of us most of the time, and I'll always cherish the closeness we had during those weeks. The nurses taught me how to empty and measure Mom's four surgical drains, tend the suture sites, monitor temperature and pain meds (which I was tempted to sample some days). Sterile fields had to be maintained with latex gloves and proper protocol, and everything was carefully logged in a binder. I bathed her as best I could and helped her in personal ways you wouldn't want a stranger to help you. Believe it or not, we laughed a lot. We talked about things we'd never talked about before. We held hands. We prayed.

"How do you feel, Mom?" I asked her the first day she was more awake than sleeping, and she wrecked me by answering, "Grateful."

A friend of mine had cancer when her daughter was in kindergarten, and she tells me that her five-year-old used to sit beside her on the bathroom floor, singing songs for her sick mom, and that seemed to make the little girl feel less afraid. Being allowed to care for my mom was a gift, the single greatest lesson, the best blessing—the most *rewarding* experience in my life.

∽

chapter eight

I'M NOT THAT GIRL

I want to run through the trees on a sweet summer day licking peach juice from a cardboard plate . . ."

Now there's a first line for ya. That's a Lippa line.

"I want to curl in a ball and feel free for a moment and not get caught up in some kind of net I always make . . ."

After I did this song at the Met, I got a lot of requests for it. I love that audiences are open to a quiet, contemplative moment in the middle of a high-energy, ninety-minute concert set.

"I want to drink coffee with half and half and sugar and skip the damn skim and Sweet'n Low . . ."

It so succinctly states where I am in my life at this moment. It says everything I want to say to (and about) Mr. Right and Mr. Writer.

"I want to dig down in my soul and lose my self-control and find out what I'm not doing right . . . I want to love somebody now . . . I want to love somebody now . . ."

Hours after I sang it in the recording studio, it's still drifting through my head, wrapped around me like a pashmina as I stand in line at Starbucks. People who hear it in concert tell me it lingers with them the same way.

"Tall soy chai latte, please," I tell the girl when it's my turn.

Skip the damn Sweet'n Low. Lippa is a genius.

I nip someone's discarded newspaper from a wire basket and take it to a corner table. In the arts section, an item catches my eye. There's a picture of me and a blurb about the benefit concert I'll be doing later this month for the 3 Angels Memorial Fund. I'm pleased to see the benefit getting some press because it's such a worthy cause, but it hurts my head a little when the reporter describes me as "Broadway performer Kristin Chenoweth, who has been romantically linked with virtuoso violinist Josh Bell." As if dating a virtuoso violinist is a much better classical-music credential than . . . oh, I dunno . . . a master's degree in opera? Singing at the Met? Selling out Carnegie Hall? A publicist once told me they do that to counteract rumors that I'm gay. Or that Josh is gay. Or that classical music is gay. I don't know. I can only say that it's vaguely disturbing to see a fractured love affair listed in the arts section as if it were a performance credit.

I'm not unlucky in love. I consider myself extremely lucky when I think of the good, good men I've loved. I've had four First Great Loves, and the fact that I'm so willing to love again could be seen as a performance credit for them, I suppose. The problem is meeting men whose love won't be overwhelmed by the logistics of dating me. If I did register on eHarmony, what would I say? "Bicoastal, type A Tony winner seeks same. Must love dog." I used to sing every night in *Wicked,* "He could be that boy, but I'm not that girl." Is it possible that any or all of these men were Mr. Right, and I am simply destined to be Ms. Not? I never saw myself as the runaway-bride type, but somehow it's worked out that way.

The first boy I loved was Brett Breedlove back in Broken Arrow. This was high school, so I don't really count it as a Great Love. More of a Warm-up Love, if you will. He was in a core group of guys who were friends with my core group of friends, so we all went out together, which is so much healthier for kids that age, I think. Perhaps the root of my runaway-bride/serial-fiancé issue is that Brett Breedlove simply ruined me for other men, spoiling me like crazy with flowers, listening skills, and love notes. Brett was the sweetest, most thoughtful boy in the world. Never pressured me to do anything I wasn't ready for. He had model good looks, actually did some modeling, and didn't like it if I messed up his hair when I kissed him. School wasn't his thing. Neither was football. He loved to go shopping with me and even helped me coordinate my prom dress—a Madonna-inspired number complete with fingerless lace gloves.

"Oh, my gosh, Kristi!" Brett enthused when I came down the stairs. "You look exactly like Belinda Carlisle!" And then I knew I loved him, because that deconstructed Go-Go's vibe is *exactly* the look I was going for. What guy *gets* that? Brett was a finely manscaped, Sharper Image metrosexual before the word was even invented.

Brett Breedlove and I amicably broke up after graduation, both knowing our lives weren't headed in the same direction, and I had a summer fling with a soccer player. It's good to have a summer fling between Serious Great Loves. Some relationships aren't meant to be Great Love; they're meant to be like a hot fudge sundae—enjoyable but not something you can actually live on. He's got talent or intelligence or some other great little cherry-on-top quality that makes him a treat, but if you keep him around too long, things get soupy. I got a little too involved with a stage-crew guy I was fling-dating once. (Crew guys are invariably hot. It's in the Equity contract: "Theaters have a fiduciary duty to uphold crew hotness.") Anyway, this particular fellow was actually making some headway with me until I got a call from his pregnant girlfriend, which instantly moved him from "hottie" to "fudgie." (Helpful Love Hint for all my young Galindas out there: if you have to call another girl to find out where your boyfriend is, he's not worth the ninety seconds off the life of your cell phone battery, much less whatever time he's taking up in your existence.)

In college, of course, there was my first First Great Love, Shawn the "Wild Thing" baseball pitcher. If you're wondering whatever happened to him, well, so am I. We never did the flying-dishes, bitter-words breaking-up thing. He struggled to deal with that terrible incident that happened during spring training, and as much as I loved him, I was wrapped up in my own thing, so I wasn't a good helpmate. After I moved to New York with Denny, Shawn visited me in this strange new world, and it was obvious to both of us that he was not part of it. I still think of him fondly now and then (whenever I see a pair of adorably tight britches taking the pitcher's mound, for example), and I wonder how things are going with his beautifully boisterous extended family, whom I loved. I heard through the OCU grapevine that he got married and became a daddy. He called and left a message wanting to catch up a few years ago, but after giving it some thought, I decided not to call him back. (I'm not that girl either.)

About nine months after I moved to New York, while I was doing *Box Office of the Damned*, a friend fixed me up on a date with Marc Kudisch. There were social faux pas on both sides. He asked me to meet him at his place, then answered the door dripping wet, talking on the phone, a towel around his hips. (I couldn't help but notice that he had an incredible body, but, c'mon. That was rude.) He talked a lot and didn't listen. When I did manage to get a word in, I blurted like a hick that he was the first Jew I'd ever gone out with, and he fell out laughing at me and made me feel like a yokel. We went to see the movie *The Mask*—his choice, not mine—and he paid for his own ticket, then looked at me expectantly. I paid for my ticket and sat in the dark, wishing the whole thing could be over. Talk about *Box Office of the Damned*. As we left the theater, he invited me back to his place for a drink.

Yeah. Right.

"Why not?" he asked, genuinely surprised when I said no.

"Because I'm tired," I said, "and frankly, this has not been a success."

But he called me the next day, apologetic and on his best behavior: "Look, I'm used to going out with women who want to pay their own way, level the playing field, whatever that is. I'm sorry, and I would like to see you again."

He didn't grovel or backpedal, offered no explanation or excuse; he simply suggested that we try again with a clean slate. And I liked that about him. That says a lot about a man, don't you think? We went out the next day, had a wonderful time together, and started seeing each other pretty steadily. There was so much to love about Marc and so much that drove me crazy, often at the same time. When Marc walks into the room, it's just a whole lotta Marc. He has a presence that makes him electric onstage but can be a little exhausting in real life. (The woman he's with now is formidable. I salute her. And I like her a lot.) I kept going back and forth, telling Denny one day, "I'm madly in love with Marc" and the next day, "I've had it. I'm breaking up with Marc."

Then he and I were cast together in *Phantom* in Boston. Marc blew me away with his raw talent and gung ho work ethic, and I loved that he loved the same things about me. We had a lot of respect for each other, and that's key in any relationship. By the time the show closed, he was officially my second First Great Love. During the five years we dated, he grew exponentially as a performer. He wins the golden uvula for Most Improved Singer, that's for sure, and I'd like to think I was a good helpmate to him in that area, not because I taught him anything, but because I challenged him, and not many people do.

I leased a rent-controlled apartment in a crummy old building and lived with Marc for three months while it was being fixed up, and that was absolutely not okay with my parents. Mom grudgingly got on my side when she realized that living in sin at Marc's place was safer than living by myself over in the work-in-progress place while all those strangers were coming and going with keys to my front door. Dad, on the other hand—well, there was some friction there. Marc and I talked about getting married, but I wasn't ready for that, so I was stunned on New Year's Eve when he proposed in the middle of a big party. At midnight. With a diamond ring in a glass of champagne. And everyone looking at me expectantly.

"Five! Four! Three! Two! One!"

"Wow . . . oh . . . Marc . . . oh my gosh . . . this is . . . really . . ."

He reached into my bubbly, fished out the ring, and put it on my finger. What was I supposed to do? I loved the man. I wasn't going to humiliate him in front of all these people by hemming and hawing about it. *Anyway,* I thought, *why shouldn't I be that girl? I* am *that girl, dang it, and he's that guy.* I called my parents, and they came up to visit shortly after. Marc came over in paint-stained jeans and a torn shirt and argued bitterly with my dad about their could-not-be-farther-apart political views. Another song in *Wicked* is about "Loathing! Unadulterated loathing!" and this was kinda like that. A big blowup ensued. Drama, drama, drama. The next day, Marc tried to apologize, but Mom and Dad were unmoved.

"Sir, I know I screw up sometimes," Marc told my father, "but your daughter makes me a better person."

"Well," Dad harrumphed, "*you* don't make *her* a better person."

My mom had made a beautiful quilt with our names and engagement date embroidered on the edge, and as she and Dad were getting ready to drive off, she clutched it against her heart and quietly told me, "Kristi. This? This can never happen."

More galvanized than ever, I assured her that it was most certainly going to happen, and they could like it or stay home. It was horrible and jolting to have them drive away with gauntlets thrown down and ultimatums hanging in the air, but I realize now that I needed to grow up and assert myself with my parents a little, and this definitely facilitated that. By the time they got home, they'd decided that if the only way to have me in their life was to have me plus Marc, they would learn to love him.

And they did.

I have to give Mom and Dad a lot of credit here. They did a complete U-turn for Marc and genuinely embraced him as part of the family. They've supported my personal choices with the same acceptance they showed me back in my "What would a bunny do?" days, wanting nothing more than for me to be happy and healthy.

Marc's family was all for us, and I was excited to be part of that wonderful bunch. (Even after Marc and I broke up, I never could bring myself to let go of the Kudisch clan.) Once we became engaged, I felt it was important to learn everything I could about their faith because I fully expected to have a family with Marc, and it wasn't possible in my mind to separate faith and family. Sarah Silverman irreverently suggests that the difference between Judaism and Christianity could be explained to a child as "Mommy is one of God's chosen people, and Daddy thinks Jesus is magic." I don't recall the name of the comic who answered that with "Daddy has the blood of Messiah-killers on his hands, and Mommy is going to leave you in a driverless car when she's taken up to the Rapture." Neither of these meshed well with my anticipated parenting style, but I felt strongly that if we had children, they should know and respect both sides of the fence, so I embraced it the way I'd embraced the state of Pennsylvania. I bought and studied several books, including *What Every Christian Should Know About Judaism,* and was surprised to learn that there is no fence. Marc's faith and mine, in large part, share common ground.

I wanted to give him a gift symbolizing this, so I went down to the diamond district to have a jeweler create a special gold pendant on a chain. I'd read that the Magen David had one triangle that strives up toward God and another that strives down toward the real world, and in my mind, Jesus brings the two together, so I'd carefully drawn the six-pointed Star of David with a cross at the center.

"Can you do this?" I asked, sliding my little sketch across the counter.

The jeweler said he could have it ready for me the following week, just before the High Holidays, which was perfect because Marc was having a hard time. His father was dying of leukemia, and because I was wrapped up in all that *Charlie Brown* hullabaloo, I hadn't been there for him the way I wished I could be. If anything, he was there for me, holding my hand through the Tonys and everything that came after. He understood what was at stake for me in that moment. He knew how hard I was trying to handle it right and was a bastion of tough love anytime I was in danger of being sucked up by an ego tornado. I thought this gift would be a lovely, hopeful gesture about our life together.

When I presented it to Marc with my whole heart, he lifted the lid from the box, inhaled sharply, uttered something that sounded like *guh-fwaugh?* and clapped the lid down.

"No," he said. "No, no. That's—no."

"What? Why not? How is that wrong?"

Marc howled with laughter.

"Well, at least I'm making an effort," I sniffed. "You haven't done a thing to learn about Christianity, and I bet I know more about Judaism than you do. And I don't know why I'm going to all this trouble because you don't even care. You make a big deal out of *being* Jewish—maybe you should try *doing* Jewish like your father. If all that matters is being born Jewish, who's to say? I could be every bit as Jewish as you are!"

Marc did his best to backpedal, but I was hurt and angry. A few weeks later, we went to see his father, and when Marc was out of the room, his dad took my hand.

"I saw your gift," he said, and when I started to stammer an apology, he shook his head. "It's the sweetest, kindest gift I've ever seen."

He smiled and pressed a gold necklace into my palm. A chai—the simple but elegant symbol that is (I knew from my studies) the Hebrew word *living*.

Almost two years later, I sat at Marc's kitchen table, waiting for him to come home, thinking about his father and my father. They reminded me a bit of the two bold gentlemen in *The Fantasticks*, who want so much for their children, but more than anything else hoped they would have a life filled with love. I'd flown in that afternoon from L.A., dreading seeing Marc, not knowing if I had the strength to say to him what I wanted to say. Needed to say. *Had* to say.

Or not.

No, I did. I had to say it.

"Denny, I don't know if I can do this. Tell me I'm doing the right thing."

Denny said the best thing a friend could possibly say in the situation: "I can't tell you what to do, but I'll be here for you when you get home."

I hung up the phone when I heard Marc in the stairwell.

"Oh . . . Jesus . . . I can't do this unless you help me. You have to show me. Make me see clearly that I'm doing the right thing."

Marc walked in the door, seeing me for the first time in a month, and said, "Geez, we had a terrible audience tonight."

A curtain of heartbreak fell over me. There was such an absence of joy in the air between us. I'd been thinking that the distance was time and geography, but now, even in the same room, we weren't *living* together, and I knew we never would.

I said what I had to say and walked forty blocks home, weeping.

Ten years later, I was doing a revival of *The Apple Tree* at Studio 54 (which has been revamped since its disco-balls-and-cocaine-spoon days). When a producer asked me whom I'd like to have cast with me, I said without hesitation, "Marc Kudisch."

"We were hoping you'd say that," he grinned. "I wasn't sure you'd be okay with it."

But why shouldn't I be? I still love the man, admire his work, respect his commitment to his craft. *Could it have worked out between us?* I occasionally wondered during the run of the play, which is all about what works and doesn't work between men and women. *He's so handsome and talented and funny and . . . oh.*

Suddenly, I'd remember. He's that guy. And I'm this girl.

Which is why I love him. And why it didn't work out.

∽

Do you know what a magical kingdom is in your ear? A fairy cave leads to an Ali Baba doorway, beyond which the bony little ossicles— Malleus, Incus, and Stapes—guard the great snail, Cochlea, to whom God has given the power to transform the indiscernible movement of air into music. I don't know if it's coincidence, karma, or mechanics, but those bastard angels Malleus, Incus, and Stapes are my greatest allies and most dreaded enemies. My hearing is finely tuned; I have perfect pitch. But I also have that stupid frigging Ménière's disease.

During one particularly devastating bout with Ménière's, I was told that the only help for me is a surgical procedure called a cochleo-sacculotomy, which has been shown to give a lot of relief but can cause significant hearing loss, which for me is the loss of music, and I can't risk that. Even in my most miserable moments, I am not even tempted to risk that. And I feel the same way about love. To protect yourself from heartache, you have to close down parts of yourself that are also a source of joy, and that's so not worth it.

The happy married life—the "normal" life—I naively envisioned for myself and my baseball player is never going to happen. That ship has sailed. I've known men who can handle the complicated logistics of my life. A few who were willing to work around it, loved me in spite of all that. But I want to marry a man who genuinely loves all the logistical and ideological quirks and cabbages that come with loving me. I want to marry a man who loves *living* with me, even when we're not on the same coast. If I cease to be myself, I'm shut off from that possibility. I won't give up on it. I'd rather put up with the emotional vertigo. Even if that means perpetually being the wedding singer instead of the bride.

In 2002, Ashley got married, and Denny and I sang at her wedding. This was post–Josh Bell and pre–Aaron Sorkin. I was in a particularly unsatisfying hot fudge phase, and not in much of a mood for a wedding. But Malleus, Incus, and Stapes were on my side that day, and as we waited for the beautiful bride to make her grand entrance, I tipped my head and listened to a finely tuned rendition of Pachelbel's "Kanon und Gigue in D."

"Don't forget, Denny. You said you'd be my maid of honor."

"I've given up on that dream, honey."

"Oh, c'mon, it's possible that someday—"

"Kristi." Denny knuckled my back, and I followed his startled gaze to the string quartet in the corner. Sitting there between the viola and a tall spray of hydrangeas was . . .

"No. Way. It can't be . . ."

But it was. The Tyrone Power jawline. Tousled Clark Gable hair.

It's our cello player!

The guy hadn't aged a day in ten years. I swear he looked exactly the same.

Immediately, I started to cry.

"Oh, Denny," I hiccupped, hugging his arm. "That brings back such memories."

After the ceremony, we made a beeline for the poor bloke, introduced ourselves, poured out the whole story—OCU, *Carmen,* tech rehearsal, blather, blather, blather.

"We have to know," I said. "Who were you flirting with, me or him?"

Of course, he said it was me. Would I be including it in my book if it had been Denny? I think not. But to this very day, Denny refuses to believe it. Six years later, as we ascend the steps of Lincoln Center, girding our loins for an evening of Mahler, it's still a bone of contention.

"He was *so* flirting with me," Denny says.

"Dream on, *Denwhah*. He was straight."

"You can put a wire hanger in the closet, sister; that don't make it straight."

"Oh, for crying out loud."

I hear my name across the evening air. It's an old beau. Not so much a hot fudge sundae as a . . . Dilly Bar. He was attractive and intelligent and very dear in many ways, but he'd vociferously condemned the institution of marriage. Said he'd certainly never bring a kid into this world. But as we stand on the steps chatting, I sense the seasoned warmth of fatherhood about him, and I make a wild guess: "You're a daddy."

He gives us all the details with that Babies-R-Us air of every person who just invented parenting. He says, "What are you in the end if you don't have a child?"

As he walks away, I stand there feeling like I've just been bludgeoned with my own biological clock. Then I feel Denny's arm around my shoulders.

"Don't even go to that place," he tells me softly. "Plus—he's fat."

I've said it before, and I'll say it again: on a scale of one to ten, Denny's a tenor.

∞

Chillin' in my crib, 1968. (Like the man says in *Dirty Dancing*: "Nobody puts baby in the corner!")

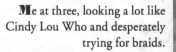

Me at three, looking a lot like Cindy Lou Who and desperately trying for braids.

Finally growing some pigtails, much to my mother's delight.

The hours I spent practicing at that piano . . .

My first time *en pointe* at the Runyon School of Ballet in Tulsa.

Q: What's the sound of an exploding sheep? **A**: "Siss boom bah!" (Cheering on the Broken Arrow Tigers, 1984)

Looking as thrilled as any teenager would at posing with mom and grandparents.

Brett Breedlove, my first First Great Love, offers a gentlemanly smooch as he squires me off to the prom at Broken Arrow High, 1986.

Cinderella and her leading man, Jeff Cordle, Broken Arrow High.

Getting a dip as Ado Annie in *Oklahoma!* at Oklahoma City University.

Crash landing in the greenroom (and probably dreaming of the gorgeous cello player) between Chamber Choir concert performances at OCU.

Kristin get your gun at Opryland. Obviously, the show was a blast!

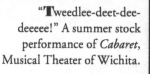

"**T**weedlee-deet-dee-deeeee!" A summer stock performance of *Cabaret*, Musical Theater of Wichita.

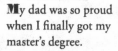

My dad was so proud when I finally got my master's degree.

Cruising the runway at the Miss Oklahoma pageant in 1991 (I was second runner-up, but hey, it's all about world peace, right?)

Meet Miss Oklahoma City University, 1991.
(When God closes a door, He opens a window.)

The glamorous life of a working Broadway actress . . ! After the Tony win, wearing Tommy Hilfiger and a wig cap!

On the set of my Huge Hit Show, *Kristin*. Huge. Iceberg-hitting-the-*Titanic* huge. Maybe you've heard of it? (Courtesy of CBS Paramount Network Television.)

The creative genius behind *Kristin*, John Markus.

The amazing cast of a magical show on the night of my last Broadway performance: Idina Menzel, me, Joel Grey, and Norbert Leo Butz. (Photo by Erin Collins.)

Between takes on the set of *Annie* with Kathy Bates and the ridiculously talented Rob Marshall.

How fabulous is Florence Birdwell? She came to see me the night I won the Tony . . . and I couldn't have gotten there without her.

My manager, Fireball Dannielle Thomas, gorgeous as usual, and me with some kind of animal on my head: backstage at an L.A. Opera performance.

I've said it once, and I'll say it again: on a scale of one to ten, my best friend Denny Downs is a tenor.

On location with *The West Wing* in 2005. A great script, John Spencer, and a pocketful of Jolly Ranchers. Who could ask for anything more?

Looking tough as media consultant Annabeth Schott on *The West Wing*. (THE WEST WING © Warner Bros. Television, a division of Time Warner Entertainment Company, L.P. All Rights Reserved.)

Starstruck and thrilled to be standing next to my idol, Miss Dolly Parton, at a red carpet event in 2006.

The Fast and the Frivolous! Sang the national anthem and hitched a ride at a NASCAR race at Watkins Glen, New York, summer of '06.

"**H**ouston, we have a problem." The new definition
of Bad Hair Day. And it's just hours before
the AFI red carpet. Holy shiz!

Maddie and me.
(I know, right?)

On the set of my beloved *Pushing Daisies* with the great Swoosie Kurtz.
(PUSHING DAISIES © Warner Bros. Entertainment Inc. All Rights Reserved.)

Life's too short. I'm not.

chapter nine

HOLD ON TO WHO YOU ARE

I'm on my way to a meeting about my hair.

Yes, there are meetings. About my hair.

I don't make the rules, people. I just go along to get along, okay? My hair used to be a subject of deep and constant concern because in its natural state, it is frinky, flyaway, three-year-old-boy hair. Mosquito thin with manic cotton-candy ends. When I was a little girl, I wanted that perfect ballet bun, and the skinny hair actually worked pretty well for that. During my pageant days, I had those Southern girls helping me out backstage, and nobody knows big hair like us. We do big, bigger, and *juuuuuust* right. I got used to wearing wigs on Broadway, and for film and television, hairdressers abused, begged, and cajoled my bonny locks into shape, which only left my real-life hair sadder and wispier, pleading into the mirror for a baseball cap to cover the frizzled specter of its fading self-esteem. Poor-little-match-girl hair.

But all that changed while I was shooting the pilot for *My Huge Hit Sitcom Kristin* on NBC. (Huge hit. Wagnerian breastplate huge. Perhaps you've heard of it.)

One day on the set, the hair dominatrix was teasing and poofing, trying to achieve some continuity with the more vigorous hair I'd had earlier in the day. She finally sighed and said, "What you really need is extensions."

I was hesitant, afraid of the damage it would do to what little hair I had.

"They have amazing technology these days," she assured me. "And it's not like you suddenly have this Lady Godiva hair. It's more for volume than length. We can keep teasing it all night if you really want to, but if you get hair extensions, it'll stay."

She sent me to this guy who was *the* big fa-shizzle of the day. Piny from Israel. His family was famous for rugs, so in my mind this was a natural tangent for him to follow. Great thing about L.A.: the best personal fixer-uppers on the planet are all here. If you want a brain, heart, or courage installed, go to Oz. For anything else, it's L.A. all the way.

"The *weft*," Piny said, draping the silky curtain over his arm. "We braid across the scalp. Teeny-tiny little braid. Then with great skill, we sew the weft."

It took several hours for Piny to work his wefty mojo, but when he was finished, I had a thick, gorgeous head of absolutely natural-looking hair. Every two months or so, I went in, spent a few hours in the chair, which was no hardship compared to all the hours I'd spent on the set every day for results that were never half this tresslicious. I was hooked like a rug, honey, and I have never looked back. Piny had me addicted like a crack ho to that weft. But wefts were just the gateway drug. I was soon on to the hard stuff. Copper. Nylon. Glue.

When a revolutionary new extension technique was recommended to me, I was reluctant to try it, but a charming woman named Kimarie sweetly seduced me to the next level. She had a tragic past, which she alluded to during our long hours together, and she didn't shave her underarms, adding to her mystique. With the individual bonds, you could get volume where the weft wouldn't go, closer to the hairline, and not in straight lines, so it looks even more natural. Which is not to say it *feels* completely natural. When I was dating Josh Bell, he went in for that first kiss, teasing his concert-violinist fingers through my hair and—

"Gah!"

He recoiled like he'd encountered a tarantula on the back of my head. Wasn't quite the moment we'd both been hoping for. It was kind of like the first time I met Julie Andrews. She came back to my dressing room to meet me when I was in *Steel Pier*, and I was so thrilled my legs were shaking. She glided into the room—this woman I'd worshipped since the camera had swooped in over the alps and found her twirling on the hill, alive with the sound of music. I managed to squeak some sort of greeting. Julie Andrews extended her lily-soft hand and parted her lips to speak *in the voice of Julie Andrews*—

At that exact moment, the stage manager's voice graveled across the intercom instead: "Anybody order chicken from Pluck You?"

So . . . yeah. I feel your pain, Josh. Sometimes you gotta let go of the dream and love life for the yodeling goatherd that it is.

Once I committed to a long-term relationship with my extensions, I had to find an East Coast person, too. We'll call him Cartoosh. He used nylon instead of copper and was very conscious about the morality of the hair-extension ecosystem.

"Very important to reuse the hair," said Cartoosh. "Someone grew this beautiful hair. Some woman in Russia or Scandinavia. To throw it away—where is the respect? We must be grateful to this woman." (And I am. Thank you, thank you, thank you, Svetlana, Ingaborg, Olga. You girls rock. If there's anything I can do for you, please let me know.)

I had a disastrous affair with glue bonding. When the hairdresser on the set hair sprayed me the next day, it was like a marshmallow in the microwave. Some kind of freaky chemical reaction took place, and it took Kimarie nine hours to pick out the sticky, coagulated mess and place the new extensions. There was also a bad moment involving a lit candle I'd set on the back of the toilet. (Big Hair Safety Tip: Unless you pee standing up, set the candle by the sink.) By the time I started asking myself, *Hey, what's that smell?* the smoke alarm had deployed, and moments later the maintenance men pounded through the door and found me beating my head with a towel. I had to go out and walk Maddie with a big charred spot, and Denny complained for days about the lingering stench, which was like burned tire with a twist of lemon lip balm.

My worst hair mishap unfortunately coincided with a big benefit for the American Film Institute. This was a major televised red-carpet event so I had fresh extensions put in. Slated to rehearse my number ("I Could Have Danced All Night") with the orchestra at ten in the morning the day of the benefit, I got in the shower at ten the night before. So *tra-la-la,* there I was, singing in the shower, washing my hair . . . which started feeling a little weird . . . so I combed a little extra conditioner through it . . . except the comb kind of didn't want to skim through the hair . . . which was getting more and more tangled, so I used *more* and *more* conditioner, which made it even *more tangled,* even though I kept *combing* and *wrenching* and *dumping on more and more conditioner,* and I started to panic because *oh my gosh, oh my gosh, oh my gosh! What is wrong with my HAIR?*

By the time I got out of the shower, it had matted into three dense plugs. Like Princess Leia's bagels plus a large inoperable tumor. At the time, I was dating a man who was younger than me and is now in jail. In fact, you might have seen him; he was on that show *Prison Break.* (Long story. We don't have time for that now. We're in the midst of a serious crisis that requires our full attention.) He was a cool customer (probably what led to his downfall), so I called him, and he came right over.

"Geezes," he said with a low, horrified whistle. "It looks like something you'd pull out of a drainpipe."

"Could you take this comb and—"

"No."

"Denny!" I sobbed. "I need Denny!"

Cool Guy called Denny, and Denny came right over. When I opened the door, he laughed so hard, he practically had to have oxygen. We worked at it for an hour or so, wrenching and pulling, all three of us falling out in fits of nervous laughter. But after a while, I wasn't laughing. Just crying. It was now about two in the morning. I called my manager, Dannielle Thomas.

"You're waking me up to tell me about your hair?" she said.

I told her about the epic battle being pitched in my kitchen.

"Oh, for crying out loud," she groaned. "Come over."

We all piled over to Dannielle's, pounding on the front door. She opened it, stared for a moment, and said, "Houston, we have a problem."

Instantly grasping the gravity of the situation, she sprang into managerial action. She wasn't able to get Kimarie on the horn, but she finally rousted out Jonathan Hanousek, a guy who often does my hair for photo shoots. He came right over.

"I've seen this before," said Jonathan, with a keen eye which thank the Lord, was not wasted on neurosurgery. "The hair was bonded on the wrong end. So when you comb it, it's like backcombing, and now you've basically ratted your own hair into it."

He worked at it for about two hours before he knelt beside my chair.

"Kristin, I need you to start thinking about cutting it off."

"No, Jonathan, no," I whimpered. "It's taken years to grow it this long."

He took pity on me and noodled at it for another hour. The darkest hour just before dawn. He knelt beside me again.

"Baby girl . . . ," he said.

"I know."

I cried as he cut it all off, leaving pinkish bald patches between a scattering of scrubby blond thatching. Looking like a little grass beach cabana in the wake of a tropical storm, I lay down for a sad, fitful nap, then donned a baseball cap and a tragically brave smile and went to rehearse with the orchestra. As I walked in, Catherine Zeta-Jones came over to say hello, and rather than make strained small talk, I lifted my cap. It was actually a lot of fun seeing the look on her face.

"Oh, my Lord!" she gasped. "Honey, what happened?"

"Extension mishap," I said darkly, and she nodded with awe and understanding, as if reacting to the sinking of a commuter ferry. It's not that actresses are fantastically vapid and vain (much), it's that our persona, our appearance—that's a large part of our stock-in-trade, so a major hair issue for us is like a computer crash for a commodities broker. It matters.

Kimarie was beside herself when she saw what had happened.

"I always check to make sure it's bonded on the right end. *Always*. I can't believe this happened." She guided me to the inner sanctum of the salon and set out a tray of long golden hair. "You see this? Eighteen-inch, guaranteed virgin blonde. I got it special from the Ukraine. I was supposed to put it on Nikki Ziering later today. But it's yours if you want it. Seriously. It's yours. No charge."

"Who's Nikki Ziering?"

"Playboy bunny. Wife of Ian Ziering from *Beverly Hills 90210*."

"Do it."

A few hours later, courtesy of Kimarie and one gorgeous Ukrainian virgin, I walk out of the salon with the high-potency mane of a California playmate. Tough break for Nikki, but I figured she had other natural resources with which she could muddle through.

An amusing footnote to this harrowing tale:

A few days after the event, I baked muffins to send my mom and dad, and when my assistant was packing them up to FedEx, one of the hair tumors somehow got tossed into the box. Scared the bejeebers out of poor Mom, who thought it was a dead mouse. For reasons I hope to never understand, Mom sent the hair tumor back to me, and I thought it would be a funny little sight gag if I coughed it up on Jay Leno's desk when I was on the *Tonight* show. You know. Like a kitty coughs up a hair ball. Funny, right? So I did that.

(Love ya, Jay! Call me?)

∞

My Huge Hit Sitcom *Kristin* on NBC was the brainchild of John Markus, a writer and producer who'd worked on lots of great shows, including *Cosby* and the *Cosby* spawn *A Different World,* the unfairly hilarious *Larry Sanders Show,* and lots of other stuff dating all the way back to *Taxi*. John first saw me on an audition tape for a show called *Blind Men*—a sitcom about a couple of guys selling venetian blinds. My TV résumé was pretty slim. I'd played a scrappy 1940s reporter in the miniseries *Paramour,* which got great notices but was discontinued when Ted Turner bought AMC and canceled all original programming. That was the humble but heartfelt beginning of what a theatre friend calls my "bicoastal disorder" and my first inkling that television might be something that I could do.

I was one of three women brought to L.A. to test for *Blind Men,* but one of the other girls got it. Okay by me. I learned a lot about the TV process, so the experience was a plus. John did ask me to do a guest shot on the show; I was a hot tamale in need of window treatment and seduced Patrick Warburton when he came to do the installation. (Seducing Patrick Warburton—another plus right there.) The shoot was loads of fun, and John Markus was one of those people I just immediately wanted to know. His mad skills and my mad skills are an instant eHarmony hookup.

After the Tony Awards show, there was a lot of excitement and he was part of that rush. My agent told me my acceptance speech was a nice little icebreaker that showed I could smile and form cohesive syllables under pressure. Phone calls were generated. Meetings were taken. It was weird, but wonderful. John came to visit me backstage after one of the last performances of *Charlie Brown* and invited me to a meeting at Paramount. I was going to L.A. to shoot *Annie* anyway— a new TV movie version with Kathy Bates as Miss Hannigan—so I thought, *Cool. Two birds, one stone,* and all that. Why not go to the studio for a quick meet'n'greet? I didn't know what I didn't know.

At the meeting, we talked about my life, Broken Arrow, church, Mom and Dad. I thought we were just small-talking so they could get to know me, but then the talk turned to actual deal making. I wasn't sure I wanted to do this. Or that I was even *available* to do this. I'd been involved in workshops for a revival of *Thoroughly Modern Millie*, and the producers wanted me to do it on Broadway. A dream gig, if there ever was one. Turning my back on that to do a sitcom—this would be a major lane change in my career.

"It would have to be something I really care about," I told John Markus. "And it would have to be fun."

John's high concept was basically "a small-town-Oklahoma Christian girl trying to make it as an actress in New York City." (Rings vaguely familiar, doesn't it?) As the talks progressed, I loved the idea, but barfed in my mouth a little when the studio suits suggested using my name for the title. For one thing, this was an ensemble show, not about one person, and for another, if the show was a turkey, *Kristin* would be a turkey, and that scared me. I wasn't interested in being the Southern-born synonym for *Ishtar*. Sadly, the other proposed names were hideous—*Short and Sweet, Sweet and Sour*—I guess they hire companies to make up these titles, and no one was clever enough to come up with something like *That Girl.* So . . . okay. Go along to get along. I decided *Kristin* wasn't so bad.

The show was actually done by Paramount, but Garth Ancier,

who was the current God-of-all-whatever at NBC, liked me and loved our pilot episode, so NBC bought it right up front and ordered thirteen episodes. Jon Tenney signed on to play my boss, Tommy Ballantine, a jaded but basically good-hearted real estate developer. Larry Romano was his faithful sidekick (a contractor or something), Aldo Bonnadonna. The forever leggy Ana Ortiz played Santa, the vampy sales rep. Dale Godboldo lent the cast some cool as Tyrique, a hip bicycle messenger. I was Kristin Yancey, an aspiring singer/dancer working as Tommy's secretary. In addition to the music we'd been workshopping for *Thoroughly Modern Millie,* Jeanine Tesori and Dick Scanlon had written "The Girl in 14G"—a crazy great song, one of my favorites to do in concert—and I asked if they could write a theme song for the show. I loved what they came up with:

No red light can stop me. Hold on to who you are.

That's what I'm about, right there.

The show was fun, fun, fun. John had a great eye for inspired physical-comedy bits that used my petite stature without making me feel like a clown. The first episode opens on a dance audition; first, the camera pans across the line of dancing feet, then it pans up and back across the dancers' hopeful faces, but of course, all you can see of me is a little *Who down in Whoville* ponytail bobbing between shoulders. I had the opportunity to sing—and I mean really sing—in several episodes. (When was the last time you heard Mozart's Queen of the Night aria on a sitcom?) The wardrobe had sort of a 1940s flair, which suited both me and Ana beautifully. There are some fabulous pumps on that show, let me tell you. Ana looked amazing in her pencil skirts, and someone made me the cutest charcoal peplum jacket with red piping.

John Markus did the scripts, which were a step up from the usual set-up-joke, set-up-joke, set-up-joke, commercial. The comedy was more about character than situation. And the dialogue—well, let me give you a little taste from a scene in which Kristin Yancey is at a planning meeting for a church fund-raiser:

CHURCH LADY: Our spring fund-raiser is just around the
corner. We need ideas galore. Kristin?

KRISTIN: You know, every year it's the same old thing.
A pie-eating contest, ring toss, make your
own belt. How about a booth where we can
dye our hair a crazy color for a day? Like
bright orange or purple?

CHURCH LADY: Purple hair? Sounds like someone's been
watching the MTV.

KRISTIN: I don't mean to be a pain, but there are a lot
of people out there who think that church-
goers can't be any fun. C'mon! Let's shake
things up a little.

REVEREND: I'd like to try something new. Maybe it could
replace the Dunk the Reverend booth.

KRISTIN: All right! We're doing a hair-dyeing booth.
Who's with me?

CHURCH LADY: If we do this, I'm stepping down as chair-
woman of the spring fund-raiser.

KRISTIN: Here's an idea. A snoring booth. And we
won't call it the spring fund-raiser. We'll call
it Snooze-a-Palooza.

CHURCH LADY: Maybe you don't need to be there. Or here
either. Maybe you need to be . . . in hell!

KRISTIN: Last year I made my own belt and choked
down three pies. Trust me, sister, I've been to
hell.

Every table reading felt like a birthday party. On Monday, we'd get
the script and gather to go over it. We spent the week putting each
scene on its feet, preparing to shoot on Friday. I was like a greedy little
sparrow snarfing up all these seeds of wisdom and expertise and

knowledge—everyone from my costars to the prop kids knew what he or she was doing and patiently brought me up to speed. When I saw the finished episodes, my character visibly changed as the weeks went by. And it wasn't just the hair extensions. As I became more at home in the process, the lines were less labored, the bits flowed back and forth between the actors, rhythm and melody started coming together. The premise was still intact, but it had grown past a one-note joke. (Kristin Yancey summed it up in one episode when she glared at Santa: "Get used to it, 'cause I'm gonna keep on being good *right in your face*.") The first few episodes were chemistry experiments, as they are with any series, but by the thirteenth episode, we'd found the added dimension in each of the people and were building the dynamics and relationships that become the real lifeblood of a show.

We were to have a March airdate—midseason replacement—and we were excited about that. In the spring, the failed shows go off the air and the wannabes get their shot while plenty of people are watching. But as our opportunity approached, Garth Ancier left the network (or it left him), and the incoming president, Jeff Zucker, saw things differently.

"I don't think they're going to air the show," John told me as gently as possible. He'd gotten to be like my big brother. "He says they have a lot of respect for you as a performer. It's the show they hate."

"But . . . but . . . why?"

"One of the big complaints is that no such girl exists."

We had a good laugh about that because the show had drawn so much material from my real life. The broad strokes—being a Christian in a business that's largely jaded, being small in a world that's largely large—and lots of little details, too. In one episode Tommy and Aldo come to Kristin's place for Hum Dum Ditty. In another, Kristin's high school boyfriend, Brett Breedlove, shows up from Broken Arrow, Oklahoma. John Markus used almost word for word a conversation in which he and I argued about the ethics of making dinner reservations at both Moomba and Balthasar. (He wanted to keep his options open; I thought it wasn't right to hold an extra table, which keeps some nice person from dinner and screws the waiter out of a tip.) People kept telling me not to take it personally, but a thousand small things made this show extremely personal for me, from the Hum Dum Ditty to the name on the door.

Without going into the minutiae of contract law, John explained to me that sometimes it's necessary for the network to "burn a show off" by airing it in such a way that no one notices when it's on or cares when it disappears. *Kristin* was dumped into the midsummer replacement landfill during the months when the fewest viewers are watching television. The advertising campaign consisted of exactly one thirty-second ad. But because the show was aired at eight thirty on a Tuesday night, right before *Frasier,* the numbers didn't actually suck. I felt a surge of foolish hope. The following week, *Kristin* was shown in a different time slot, and the numbers fell. The time slot was changed again the following week. Not even my parents knew when it was going to be on. The angel of sitcom death was swift and unmerciful. After a total of six episodes, *Kristin* was replaced with a new reality show called *Fear Factor,* in which people were going to do stunts and eat bugs or something.

"*Ugh,*" I huffed. "Like *that's* ever going to make it?" More famous last words.

So that's what happened to my show. The boob-tube equivalent of winning talent and being second runner-up. It's a mercy, I suppose, that we didn't anticipate any of this while we were shooting, so we were all high-spirited and hopeful when we said good-bye and broke for hiatus. The last line of the last episode was "Get your hand off my ass."

Epitaph for a flameout.

Obviously, Jeff Zucker is a genius at what he does. This is a tough business in which tough decisions have to be made, and he has the balls to make them. You can't fault the guy for that. Three years later, I joined the cast of *The West Wing*, and at the up-fronts, he came over and introduced himself to me.

"Hey," I said. "Thanks for canceling my show, ya party pooper."

He laughed, gave me a hug, and said, "I'm so glad to have you back on our network."

I hugged him back. No hard feelings. Really. I love that Jeff Zucker.

I'm baking him a nice batch of my special cookies.

⌘

Because I've always been a happy person by nature, I wasn't prepared for the depression that settled on me that summer. Something inside me felt mummified, afraid to feel, and when I did allow myself to care about anything, I had a deep foreboding sense that no matter how hard I tried, it was just going to fall to crap anyway. Thinking about my personal life made me feel worthless. Thinking about my professional life made me want to hit myself in the head with a hammer. *Thoroughly Modern Millie* created a lot of buzz, with people saying it was sure to win the Tony for best musical (which it did) and that Sutton Foster would nail it and walk off with a Tony herself (did and did). It's not like me to look back and question my decisions, but now I was overwhelmed with the feeling I'd made a terrible mistake doing this television show, which made me wonder about every decision, all the could haves and might haves. I'd always seen the opportunity to learn, laugh, and make a great story out of it when circumstances went awry. Now all I could see was the opportunity to fall in a hole.

Maybe it was all too good to be true, I figured. Maybe I hadn't paid my dues enough or clawed my way up enough. Maybe I was going to have to do that now. During pilot season, I auditioned for a show called *Seven Roses* with Brenda Blethyn. I'd always wanted to work with her; she's one of those actresses who is so kind, so smart, and so Mozart-talented, anything she does is going to be a great experience for the people around her. But I have to admit, it tweaked my nose out of joint that I was having to test for it. I'd won a Tony, had my own show, and now I was back on the cattle wagon auditioning? In the midst of my *Bullets Over Broadway* moment, as I was heading in the studio door, I saw Patty Duke heading out. *What on earth?* I wondered. *Why is she here?* I rarely pipe up and introduce myself to people because I don't want to bother them; I've been shy about that since I was a kid. I'd rather admire people like that from afar. But I had to know . . .

I went over and introduced myself and told her I'd been a big fan since I could remember, then without even trying to couch it in casual form, I said, "Ms. Duke, I'm dying to know—what are you doing here?"

"Oh, I had a great opportunity to test for this new show," she said, those famously vivacious eyes bright with excitement. As she was happily telling me all about it, a production assistant called my name. Ms. Duke reached over and squeezed my hand and with her signature girlish giggle said, "Good luck, sweetie!"

I went in, and it went well. They called two hours later to tell me I got it. A few days later I saw that someone else had gotten the role Patty Duke had auditioned for, and it made me feel sick inside.

"You can have an Oscar and it doesn't mean jack," I bitterly told Erin Dilly on the phone. "You can be Patty Duke—a *legend*. They should be offering to cut off a thumb to get her on their show. But no. That's the capricious, soul-consuming business we're in."

"Oh, for pity's sake. What is *wrong* with you? This isn't you, Kristin."

When the summer was over and it was time to go back to New York, Erin decided that I should come straight from the airport to her place on the upper west side of Central Park.

"Spend the night with me," she said. "We'll have girls' night and sleep in till noon."

I was grateful to have a break before facing my empty apartment. We stayed up late talking, but the sound of sirens in the street woke us up long before noon.

"Welcome to New York," I grumbled, pulling a pillow over my head, but the sirens kept wailing, and I couldn't get back to sleep. I got up and turned on the TV. A vast blue sky was boxed in the small screen. Smoke billowed up from the familiar skyline.

The first tower fell, and I said to Erin, "What movie is this?"

"Oh . . . God . . ." Her voice was choked and frightened. "It's really happening."

Still wearing the boxers and T-shirts we'd slept in, we jammed shoes on our feet, grabbed our cell phones, and ran. Down the stairs. Out into the street. Into chaos. Into Armageddon.

⌒∞⌒

I'm not going to tell "My 9/11 Story" because my 9/11 story is a pale inconvenience compared to what so many others went through. I will say that it was wrenching to see Broadway sitting dark and silent.

Over the following months, my little heartbreak about my little television show came into a very different perspective. Instead of dwelling on how it got snuffed, I made the conscious decision to gather all the good things about it and hold those under my nose like a bouquet of marigolds for the rest of my life. Every table reading where we laughed until our sides ached, every zingy line that hit the mark, every good soul in this excellent team of talented people, my peplum jacket with red piping, cherry tomatoes and doughnut holes from craft service, tap dancing on a table, singing Mozart over spaghetti, smiling at pictures of the cameraman's grandbaby. I did what Ellen and I sang about in that They Might Be Giants song; I built a little birdhouse in my soul.

I haven't heard from John Markus in a long time, and that makes me sad.

"Maybe he feels bad," a friend suggested recently. "Because he got you on this bus and it went over a cliff."

But I love that bus. I'm proud of that bus. In my heart, it's not a flop, and I will never talk it down or apologize for what it didn't become. It was a thoroughly enjoyable experience and, in retrospect, an oasis. A completely sweet kiss before the lights went out.

A huge hit. Grandbaby-picture-smile huge. I wish you could have seen it.

∽

chapter ten

DEFYING GRAVITY

Denny's cat is seriously grating on me.

Now, please don't go blogging about what a cat hater I am. I promise I love all God's creatures like a Care Bear loves high-fructose corn syrup, but Sally is a malcontented wheezer, a shoe-chewer, a three-hundred-pound ball of contempt and shedding who hisses and spits like a python every time I walk by.

Denny has moved in, camping out while builders finish his condo on the other side of the river in Jersey, and while Denny and I get along like peas in a pod, Maddie and Sally are—well, they're like cats and dogs. Sally seems to be carrying some hair-borne toxin. The moment she enters the room, my skin starts to itch, and I can't breathe. I'm convinced I've developed an allergy, and so has Maddie, who's been sneezing and having bad dreams.

Sally gets on my bed, staring daggers at me.

"No, kitty!" I scold. "Off the bed."

"Mrrraaaw," the cat says disdainfully.

The cat is not invited on my bed. Only Maddie is invited on my bed. And Mom. And on rare occasions, Mr. Writer (though I sometimes have a little trouble breathing when he's around, too). The cat glares at me. Her eyes glow with loathing. I find myself surreptitiously opening the window six inches or so.

"Here, kitty kitty kitty . . ."

Okay, excuse me, but I have to step in here.

Denny? Nobody asked you. You stay out of this.

Something you need to know about Sally . . .

Shut up, Denny.

That is Kristin's cat.

Okay, technically, that is true. I will admit that. But Denny, the cat doesn't like me. The cat doesn't *want* to belong to me. The cat wants to belong to you.

When Kristi was doing Babes in Arms *at a theater in Minneapolis, her dance partner thought it would be sweet to give her this little kitten. Sally was the name of her character in the show, so they named it Sally. She came home with it, and I was like, "A cat? Does this man know you at all? You can't take care of a cat. You're never here. You're way too busy, and—no. This is ridiculous. No cat." But she loved this little kitten and couldn't give it up, so I ended up taking care of it for her whenever she was out of town. She brought Sally with her when she was living at my place in L.A., and when she went back to New York to do* Wicked, *she got Maddie, and that was it. She wanted nothing further to do with the cat.*

Good-bye, Denny! Thanks for playing. We have some lovely parting gifts for you.

Excuse me while I close the window.

All right. Fine. Sally did start out being my cat, but things change, and if there's one thing you learn in the theatre, it's how to roll with the changes.

Things were different after I returned to New York. New York was different. The world was different. Broadway was hard hit emotionally and financially by 9/11; it took a while to recover our joie de vivre. I shuttled back and forth to L.A. over the next year or so, singing concerts, doing my Miss Noodle thing on *Sesame Street* and *Elmo's World,* and making brief appearances on *Frasier* and a few other shows. Denny and I did major road trippage, driving from Houston to L.A., eating at Sonic, stopping in Vegas for a spa weekend. I spent three months in beautiful Toronto, shooting *The Music Man* with Matthew Broderick for ABC. But I kept my home base in New York because I was workshopping a show that I knew was going to turn the world on its ear.

Gregory Maguire's bestselling novel *Wicked: The Life and Times of the Wicked Witch of the West* was a witty perspective flip on L. Frank Baum's *The Wonderful Wizard of Oz,* and a small aspect of his *just suppose* story was that Elphaba (an homage to the original author—her name is drawn from his initials) and Galinda (who evolves into Glinda) were roommates in college. This makes me wonder about Maguire's college roommate, but it made Stephen Schwartz wonder what would happen if that story was translated to the stage. (He did the music for *Godspell,* so you can see how he and I are soul mates.) He brought in Winnie Holzman, who's written for some great shows, including *My So-Called Life,* which you gotta love (the Emmys did). They took the idea to another dimension, creating the script and transformative music and lyrics. Like a cosmic game of Telephone, the story evolved as it was passed along.

At the heart of Maguire's novel is the idea that layers of good and bad exist in everyone, and those layers are most effectively excavated by love. At the first reading of *Wicked,* the script was mostly about the love affair of Elphaba and Fiyero with Madame Morrible as the antagonist in the mix. When Stephanie J. Block and I brought voices to Elphaba and Galinda, yet another dynamic emerged. The two of us had only one scene together, but it really popped. Six months later, at another reading, another Galinda and Elphaba scene had been added, and it popped, too. I sat there thinking, *Am I crazy, or is this really about the two witches?* Apparently, Winnie's crazy, too.

Now, let me say here, I'd have done the show even if the Galinda role had remained small. I love a mighty little spicy-tuna-hand-roll of a role. (One of my favorites was the eager poet Fern, who becomes Annette Bening's lover in *Running with Scissors*. A total of four minutes on the screen, but what a plum!) Winnie's language is delicious, and Galinda's lines were like tasty little bonbons—enough great moments to make it juicy, plus the song "Popular," which was the one all the little girls were going to be singing. I knew that the first time I heard it. But something more was there. Everybody knew a Galinda in high school. (She's the one who was so happy, it made you want to beat her up in the girls' bathroom, right?) Everything was easy for her. She floated around as if her life were a magic bubble. But when we grow up, we learn that no bubble remains unscuttled in this world. So what happened to that girl? Who did she become?

Stephanie and I reached deeper into the characters, and the story evolved to focus on the relationship between the two witches. This is Elphaba's story, but parts of it we need to see through the eyes of her friend. It's the transformation of Galinda the Giddy to Glinda the Good that makes Elphaba's journey a victory instead of a defeat. Glinda takes the story into the future after Elphaba melts away, and that's how Elphaba truly defies gravity.

During three years of workshops, the great script got even better. The terrific music took flight. This was something very special, and everyone involved knew it.

Nearing the out-of-town tryouts, making our way toward Broadway, I was offered an extremely meaty roll on *The West Wing*, which had premiered the year before to great critical acclaim and was now a huge commercial success. I was thrilled that my name even came up in that conversation. It was an amazing opportunity. A serious acting role. The producers of *Wicked*, Marc Platt and David Stone, have a good-cop/bad-cop thing going. You don't know from day to day which is which, but that's the well-tuned team they are. They'd gotten me into this at the beginning and were not about to let me walk away now, but truthfully, they didn't have to work too hard at it—partly because I loved working with them. There was not one scrap of doubt in my mind; *Wicked* had the legs to get to Broadway and was going to be a hit. And along the way, the Galinda role had evolved into a substantial challenge. She belts, she sings legit, she dances, she girl-fights, she's funny, she's poignant, the character matures emotionally and vocally over the arc of the show—oh, honey. You couldn't have gotten me out of that magic bubble with a crowbar.

Stephen had had me in mind for Galinda from the beginning, but before we started out-of-town performances, auditions were held to cast the role of Elphaba, and I was asked to sit in. Of course, I was pulling for Stephanie; she's a good friend, and I'd loved working on the show with her, but all five women being considered were terrific. Any of them would have brought something different and exciting to the production. Producers and our director, Joe Mantello, decided on Idina Menzel, an amazing performer who'd blown everyone's socks off in *Rent*. I was excited about working with her. (Stephanie played Elphaba in the national tour, in a later Broadway company, and in Chicago's long-running production, and she rocked it.) Norbert Leo Butz was cast as Fiyero and Robert Morse as the wizard.

The out-of-town shows weren't exactly charmed. Some of the reviews weren't stellar. Anxiety was high at times. In one spectacular meltdown, the powers that be all stormed out, and just to break the silence that fell, I grabbed Idina and dipped her for a big kiss. Everybody left on the stage fell out laughing, then Idina cracked us up again by saying, "The scary part is, I enjoyed it." During our final rehearsal in San Francisco, a light tree crashed down on my head and conked me out cold. That evening, while I was in my hotel room nursing my battered noggin, I got a panicked call from the lobby.

"We've got a problem," said Winnie.

My first thought was *Noooo. I need to sleep.* My second thought was *Oh, crap. Am I getting fired?* I went downstairs to find Winnie and Stephen pacing and exchanging notes. Long story short, several of Galinda's lines hadn't originated in Maguire's novel (to which they had rights) or Baum's original book (which had passed into the public domain); they played off the movie, which is so ingrained in the collective conscious, it makes for great laughs. It had begun to sink in that this show was going to get seen by a whole lot of people, including the lawyers for Warner Bros., who owned the rights to every word in that movie. We were going to have to cut, tweak, or improvise around stuff like *lions and tigers and* [you know what] *oh my!* and somehow make the new lines play as well as the movie send-ups.

I did what I always do when I'm trying to think: I went power-shopping. I know what that sounds like, but I find shopping meditative. One minute I'm stroking the seam of a perfect pair of pants in Olive & Bette's, the next moment, I'm having an epiphany about that Judy Garland song from 1942. (Not the one you're thinking; the one nobody does.) In New York, I'm supported in my endeavor by dear friends: Barney, Mrs. Fields, Filene, and Ben and Jerry. Out of town, I have to hit the mall. Being a shopper savant is not about spending money; it's about making choices and finding what fits. That's the process, the circle of life, the story of the glory of shopping.

The next morning, I found Winnie with her feet up.

"I'm exhausted," she groaned, and I said, "Of course you are!"

She'd never written a musical before. That's a man's world statistically, but she'd busted down the door and done something truly inspired. I have tremendous respect for her, and I can't wait to see what she does next. Stephen had decided the night before that changing even one word of any questionable line protected the production from legal snares and actually made the script funnier because it caught the audience off guard. They expect the little dog to be named Toto, so saying "Dodo" tugs the rug out from under their feet a little. Lesson learned: it's dangerous to be SuperGlued to anything in any show. (Or in life.) You have to let go of what's not working no matter how dearly you wish it would work; put that ol' thinking cap on and step up to the next thing. The changes played great. Unfortunately, during the show that night, I was playing the heck out of my hair-flipping bit and herniated two disks in my neck.

The show underwent major changes between San Francisco and New York. Joel Grey was brought in to replace Robert Morse. An entire number—"Which Way Is the Party?"—was scrapped and replaced with "Dancing Through Life." Because of my neck injury, my costume had to be retooled to include a neck brace, which we Galindafied with the Bedazzler. We rolled with the changes.

Wicked officially opened at the George Gershwin Theater on October 30, 2003. It went on to smash box-office records set by *The Producers,* then went on to smash the records set by itself. While 80 percent of Broadway shows never earn back the money that's been invested, and a solidly successful show takes two or three years to break even, *Wicked* was in the black—or in the green, I guess—after only fourteen months.

Richard Zoglin wrote in *Time,* "If every musical had a brain, a heart, and the courage of *Wicked,* Broadway really would be a magical place."

∞

Tweedly-deet-dee-dee, two ladies . . .

Dang, there it is again!

When you first meet Joel Grey, all you can think of is *Cabaret.* Then you get to know him, and you discover this deep-river soul and dear, dear heart. He's one of those old-school pros—part of a dying breed, I'm afraid—show people who are all about the work. There's an unspoken bargain among the players—we're in this together in the hokiest "C'mon, kids, let's put on a show!" kind of way—and it feels wonderful. Standing next to Joel onstage, you can feel how happy he is to be there. Swept along by this completely boyish joy, you're willing to try anything and everything and then try something else, make a fool of yourself, look less than pretty. Heck, I'd have let the man whip a stick out of my mouth!

Carole Shelley was right there with him. She shares that same brand of professionalism that rules out any fear of failure. I loved working with her and learned a lot by watching her. This was not her first rodeo, as they say, but she still cracked herself up and took everyone with her. Onstage, she was a powerball, but in her dressing room she was gracious and quiet, serving tea and scones in her silk robe and wig cap between matinee and evening performances, telling me stories about a different time when theatre was a life and not a job. Once I fell asleep on her sofa and woke up when a little mouse ran across my face.

Eeeek. I know.

That's the Gershwin. It lacks the history of the Richard Rodgers, but it's one of the biggest Broadway houses, which means more people get to see the work. The facility has a few gremlins. One night the Vari-Lite system started grinding and crackling like the eight-track player in a '72 Impala. When a gel in a light starts to burn, the buzz quickly escalates to the sound of a jackhammer, and there's nothing to do but let it run its course, which takes approximately two minutes. There was no point trying to continue, so I started to tap-dance, and Joel and Idina joined in. Willie Nelson and Amy Irving were in the audience that night and said it was their favorite part.

Doing a Broadway show is hard as H-E-double-hockey-sticks, so it makes me guffaw when people refer to a performance as "effortless." When you're singing that intensely every night, you have to conserve your energy and your voice all day. If people saw me working hard, the effect would be ruined. It's like the iron bubble. The audience sees Glinda in her frilly gossamer gown float weightless up into the sky. In reality, the bodice of the dress is reinforced with steel safety gear, and a crew member slips behind her to latch and unlatch her from the ironclad, Teamsters-approved, computer-mechanized flying bubble. Likewise, the frothy character is reinforced with years of training, technique, and plain hard work.

At our final tech rehearsal, crew hotties hitched me into my rigging and sailed me up into the dark rafters for one last test-drive.

"It's great!" I called down to the ladybugs and ants bustling around the stage far below. A busy grasshopper waved up at me and hopped offstage to check some other equipment. Five or ten minutes went by. Then another ten or fifteen minutes went by, and I noticed that they'd all moved on to other projects.

"Hello?" I called, but no one looked up. "Hey, anybody?"

I guess they got sidetracked reblocking some stuff and forgot I was up there. I couldn't yell because that's like taking a cheese grater to your vocal cords, so after about twenty minutes, I busted out a high F and caught someone's attention.

Other than that small hang-up, the rigging and flying went off flawlessly. Flying is all about the crew, and Idina and I never felt insecure about our safety. The equipment was immaculately maintained, and the design was ingenious. It was all about the flying underwear; I had my ironclad corset, and Idina had her computerized petticoat. Just before Elphaba's spectacular rise in "Defying Gravity," the lights distracted the audience eye long enough for her to step onto a small platform. A steel gate in the waist of a thirty-foot black skirt locked around her middle, and a safety sensor sent a message to the lift mechanism. If she wasn't locked in, it wouldn't budge. As soon as she was securely on board, up she went, and the music went with her. Breathtaking every time.

It's a luxury to go to the same workplace day after day for many months. The cast and crew become a family, and their families become our extended family. I loved seeing Marc Platt and his wife, Julie, herding their kids up the wide lobby steps: Samantha, Jonah, Ben, Hannah, and last but not least, Henry, who was for some reason terrified of Glinda. Everyone knows everyone else's business, and there's no such thing as a dull day. Even when everything goes exactly as it's supposed to (and it practically never does), you have moments in the show that are fresh and emotional every time. I looked forward to so many moments every night in *Wicked*. I'd hear a music cue or feel the lights change, and a little thrill would flutter through my stomach.

Oh! Here's where I get to fall in love with Fiyero!

Yay! Here's that part of "For Good" with the perfect harmony!

Throughout the show, you have these moments with each other, and if there's any danger of things falling into muscle memory, someone sticks his finger up his nose or makes a fart noise behind your back. (Yes, Norbert, I'm talking about you.) I did it, too. I'll admit it. Eight shows a week? C'mon. I used to be all Olivier purist about it back in my *Charlie Brown* days. Since that time, I've disintegrated into the mess you see before you. Sometimes great moments are born out of those shenanigans.

That live-in-the-moment vibe is something I love about theatre. The audience knows you're up there on this flying trapeze and anything could happen. It draws them in and actually involves them in the creative process. On film, you craft something, offer it up, and the audience will take or leave it. But live performance is a relationship. The audience lets me know what works and what doesn't, I get a sense of what's important to them, and I do my best to go there.

The hard thing is when the moments begin to lose that potency. Then you know it's time to go, and that realization is hard. After nine months on Broadway, I knew it was time for me to go. I'd been working on this show for over four years, and for all that time it fit. When I felt that change, it broke my heart, but I knew hanging on would be wrong for me and for this show I loved.

Some people thought I left the show because Idina won the Tony, and I can tell you flat out, that is crap. I'd made the decision to leave the show before the Tony nominations were announced. Having worked with Idina side by side for a year, I watched her earn that sucker with love, sweat, and fierceness. It didn't bother me a bit. It does bother me to hear people say that we hate each other. I'm not a hater, for one thing. It takes too much energy. I'm sure there have been moments when I inadvertently stepped on a toe or hurt someone's feelings, but I try to be nice to everyone I work with. An actress who behaves badly—backstage, on set, or worst of all "in the moment" during a show—is really shooting herself in the foot. At times I just want to shake a young actress by the shoulders and tell her, "You have a long road to travel in this career, and things come back in the weird-est ways." Word gets around. And it's not a long trip from "Gosh, she's a pill, but she's so talented!" to "Gosh, she's so talented, but she's not worth the aggravation." No matter how good you are, people in this biz are willing to put up with only a certain amount of doo-doo.

Which is not to say that a girl has to be perfect.

Take a look at the next cab you see passing by, or the billboard, or the Playbill in your hand if you're lucky enough to be at the Gershwin tonight—you'll see a little glint of green in Glinda's eye. What ulti-mately makes this character resonate is the thing that makes us human: we're all just a little bit wicked. Galinda *thinks* she's good until she sees her own mean streak and faces the sad consequences of it. When she steps up to make it right, when she learns from her mistakes and grows stronger through tough experiences—that's when she truly becomes Glinda the Good. (And there's another name change, too, reminding me of Jacob's wrestling match with the angel.)

So, sure, I've got my wicked streak, and so does Idina, but our paths haven't crossed enough for a mediocre rivalry, much less a healthy steam of hatred. Enquiring minds want to know, but the unsensational truth is that we're two hardworking girls, both doing pretty well for ourselves in a tough industry. And for those of you who are fixated on the idea that Idina is my lesbian lover, if you'll direct your attention to the left side of the tour bus, you'll see Denny Downs laughing his fanny off. That's ridiculous. Everyone knows Janeane Garofalo is my lesbian lover.

KIDDING! KIDDING!

I'm just *kidding*, for crying out loud.

(Sorry, Janeane. Please don't beat me up in the girl's bathroom.)

Producers asked me to stay through the Tony's, and that was a blast. I floated in to open the show and introduce Hugh Jackman, who is almost hot enough to be an Equity crewmate. At an after-party, I heard someone grouching that if they'd nominated Idina for Best Actress and me for Best Featured Actress, we both could have won, and I suppose that's possible (though I wouldn't make any assumptions; there were some great performances in the Featured Actress category that year). But winning another Tony would not have made me happy if that meant reducing Glinda from a lead to a sidekick.

I love the idea of two lead actresses in one show. How often do we see that in a major Broadway musical? Before *Wicked*, you basically saw a male and a female lead, two male leads, or *Gypsy*. Winning another Tony would have been nice, but the joy, the challenge, the ridiculous thrill of helping to create this character and grow this soul-beautiful, mind-expanding, box-office-busting show—that was huge.

Makes me feel like I defied some gravity my own bad self.

chapter eleven

YOU LIKE ME
(YOU REEEEEEEEALLY LIKE ME)

O h, baby. Talk nerdy to me.

Maddie and I are deeply involved in an episode of *Dr. G: Medical Examiner*. It's the one where a thirty-six-year-old woman died after experiencing inexplicable itching all over her body. Yes, I am one of those geeky kids who loves that sort of stuff. I wonder if I'd get a different sort of fan mail if people knew how spectacularly Herbert I really am, sitting here chain-chewing Super Bubble, wearing flannel pj's my mother bought for me at Target, and watching science shows on the telly. Not the slick *CSI*-type dramas, the real thing, starring the actual forensic-science nerds and procedure buffs: *American Justice*, *First 48*, *Cold Case*, and anything having to do with a handheld camera in a coroner's lab. It's my latent Nancy Drew tendencies; if I hadn't ended up floating around in magic bubbles, I would have been a detective.

So you'd think I would have had a *clap on* moment when I first met—oh, let's call her Evelyn Draper, after the scary stalker chick in *Play Misty for Me*. Which gives you some idea of where this chapter is headed.

Now let me start by saying that I love and appreciate my fans. Hey, y'all! I love and appreciate you! Seriously. I am enormously grateful for the time you've spent with my work and for the love and kindness you've shown me.

Thank you, from the bottom of my heart.

Nine hundred ninety-nine times out of a thousand, every member of the audience is wonderful. There are days, of course, when some guy is snoring or there's a foot-bouncer on the front row or some stockbroker is hissing into his cell phone, which plays "Apple Bottom Jeans" every time it rings. Once the security officers had to drag a guy out of *You're a Good Man, Charlie Brown* because he was masturbating during "My New Philosophy." I remember a performance of *The Fantasticks* where a mom brought her teenage son with Tourette's syndrome to the show, and it was explained to me that because he liked me a lot, it became especially difficult for him to control his outbursts when I came onstage. Throughout the performance, every time I said or sang anything, he would snort, howl, or bellow some expletive about bodily function or female anatomy. (Apparently, I was really on that day. Five out of five F-bombs on the Blurt-o-Meter.)

One rainy Fourth of July, a total of two—count 'em, *two*—people showed up to see the matinee. They were offered their money back, and we were all backstage begging God to have them take it so we could have the afternoon off, but they wanted to see the show, and we gave them the same performance they would have seen in a packed house on Friday night. If you have a dud audience, you can't get mad at them or let the dead air push you to overcompensate. That's when you deliver the goods based on what you know how to do. You find that energy inside, play for each other, play for the crew, and most important, play for that person who's never seen a Broadway show and was unlucky enough to buy a seat next to the foot-bouncer on Dud Audience Day.

Really, it's the audiences who made *Wicked* what it is. Reviews were mixed, but word of mouth was *You gotta see this show.* "Reviews are reviews," Stephen Schwartz used to say. "I know we divided the critics. But we didn't divide the audience, and that's what counts." Before *Wicked,* I'd never been in a show where the audience actually became its own tour de force. So many people became regulars, seeing the show again and again, spiriting the music and characters out of the theater into pop culture—the anime series *Red Garden, Buffy the Vampire Slayer* comic books, a soap called *Passions,* the delightful comedy *Ugly Betty,* shows as diverse as *Brothers and Sisters* and *Saturday Night Live.* Elphaba and Glinda showed up in far-flung places, parties, and pride parades. The first time I saw a bevy of drag queens dressed as me, I knew I'd seriously arrived.

So when good ol' Evelyn wangled her way into a private part of the lobby, I had no reason to believe she was anything other than a fan who was absolutely gaga over this show that left a whole lot of perfectly nice people absolutely gaga.

"Miss Chenoweth," she said with big, limpid eyes, "I want you to know how much this show means to me. Especially your performance. You've changed my life."

"Well, you're so sweet. Thank you so much," I said, eyeing the door.

"I just found out I have liver cancer. I have about six weeks left. And I'm going to spend every single night of it here. All I want is to see *Wicked* every night. As long as I'm able to . . . to make it . . ."

"Oh, my gosh, you poor baby! Do you need a chair? Do you need a glass of water?"

Go ahead. Say it. Kristin is a big ol' gullible sap.

I invited her to come back to my dressing room after the show the next night. She showed up bearing a boatload of designer-label gifts.

"Oh, honey, I really can't accept these . . . these fabulous . . . Prada and Fendi handbags? Dolce and Gabbana? Gucci shoes that are *just my size*? I really can't . . . can I, Kay?"

"No," said Kay, my dresser.

Well, Evelyn fed me and my dresser some all-out Persian tapestry of crap about how she worked for a famous designer and all these were freebies. She asked Kay her size and offered to get some things for her, too. Blinded by the Gucci glare, we quashed our doubts and took Evelyn entirely at her word. But over the coming months, Evelyn remained remarkably healthy, and I started getting suspicious. I started testing, sleuthing, and baiting.

"You look terrific tonight, Evelyn. How are you feeling?"

She must have gotten a vibe that I was onto her, because the next thing you know, I got a message that she was in the hospital. Then I received e-mail from a nurse named Nancy, updating me on Evelyn's critical condition. (Earth to Kristin: I played Nurse Nancy in *A New Brain*.) I called Evelyn's cell phone to see how she was doing, and when she called me back, I could hear chirping in the background, the beep beep beep you'd expect to hear in conjunction with total hepatic encephalopathy.

"Kristin, all the children in the chemo ward just adore you," Evelyn told me wanly. "They all drew pictures for you. Where should I send them?"

Pink with shame that I had doubted this poor dying woman when she was using the last of her strength to color pictures with the cancer children, I said, "I'll come get them. I'd like to come visit you."

"I'm not allowed visitors," she said with a soft, frangible cough. "The nurse said she'd send them over if you give me your address."

I know this sounds pathetically gullible, guys, and really, I'm not that dumb. But in no part of my heart or brain could I imagine someone lying like that. So now she had my home address. And my cell number. And my e-mail. She made a miraculous recovery and basically dropped the pretense about having cancer, acting like we were just good buddies now. I realized what a dope I'd been. Fortunately, I was about to leave for L.A. to shoot a movie, and I figured the distance would give her time to focus on something—or someone—else.

But just in case, I checked into my hotel under the name Sally Upland. (Sally Brown plus Galinda Upland. Not super sly, I guess.) Evelyn quickly located me and left a bag of gifts for me at the front desk. I sent my dad an e-mail about a car I wanted to buy. Five minutes later, I got a text message from Evelyn, saying that she was in town, and guess what kind of car she'd rented? Yeah. Right down to the color of the upholstery. While I was working, I got a text message from her: "Hi! Guess what! I'm on the lot!" Gotta hand it to her; those gates are not easy to pass, but she'd somehow talked them into believing she had a meeting in one of the buildings. I called security, and they escorted her off the lot, but I was getting really scared.

Cue the lonely saxophone. Enter John Artez, a hunky LAPD sergeant with nineteen years under his gunbelt, fifteen of which he's been moonlighting as a Sam Spade class gumshoe, watching over the hothouse orchids of LaLaLand. (I never actually saw gum on his shoes; I just like saying "gumshoe." And "LaLaLand.") Artez took a few notes as I laid out the tangled tale. When I got to the part about the chemo children, the corner of his mouth twitched a little.

"You gotta be kidding me," he said.

"I know. I was an idiot to believe all that, and now it's like *Help, help, I'm being showered with designer handbags*. But she leaves these things for me, and I have no way to return them, and she won't leave me alone."

He held up his hand. "You're not an idiot, and what she's doing is not okay. I don't get the feeling she'd hurt you, but it needs to stop."

He started digging into the case and sat me down a few days later with a very *just the facts, ma'am* look on his face.

"Understand that I'm not able to use police department resources to look into any individual's background until a crime has been committed, and right now, we can't say that it has. What I can do is access certain information in public record. Having done that and having looked through some of your correspondence with the subject, I'm seeing red flags."

"Like what?"

"For starters, her income doesn't support her lifestyle."

"So maybe she comes from money. Maybe she's an heiress, and maybe she paid high-tech hench-geeks to hack into my BlackBerry, which is how she knows everywhere I go, everything I do."

"Or she's stealing and she's gotten friendly with someone close to you."

"No," I said, because the very though left me hollow. "It's got to be hench-geeks."

"Kristin, you're one of the sweetest people I've met in this business. You want to see the good in everybody. People come up to you wanting a hug, and you *hug them*." He said it like it was unthinkable: the dreaded YaYa Congeniality Gene. But then he smiled a kindly Hector Protector smile. "That's a great way to be, but from a security standpoint, it concerns me. We gotta tighten up on that."

Ultimately, Evelyn's spendy gift shopping was her undoing. Turns out, she was embezzling from the big name designer she worked for, spending her ill-gotten gains on theater tickets, flowers, and pricey presents for Catherine Keener, Cherry Jones, and me. Long story short: she got indicted, I got schooled, some homeless girls in Soho got the Gucci goods, and John Artez got hired to be my West Coast security muscle.

On the East Coast, I have a guy named Carmine. It makes me feel like a mob princess.

≪∞≫

The state flower of Oklahoma is the mistletoe, *Phoradendron serotinum,* which climbs wild on trees, is particularly bountiful in the southern regions of the state, and encourages kissing, which is almost always a good thing to encourage.

The state tree is the blossomy redbud, *Cercis canadensis*.

Oklahoma's state bird: the scissor-tailed flycatcher.

State rock: rose rock, barite crystals formed during the Permian age.

State reptile: collared lizard.

State fish: sand bass.

The Sooner State motto: *Labor omnia vincit!* ("Labor conquers all things!")

The official state meal of Oklahoma (a state in which folks are easygoing enough to devote legislative-session time to determining a menu for an official state meal) is fried okra, squash, corn bread, barbecue pork, biscuits, sausage and gravy, grits, corn, strawberries, chicken-fried steak, pecan pie, and black-eyed peas.

That's generous, industrious, homespun *you're doin' fine* Oklahoma.

In case you haven't heard me say so on eleventy-seven different talk shows, I am proud of being from Oklahoma. I love it when the people of Oklahoma want me to represent them, so I was happy to do several events celebrating our state's centennial, including the Macy's Thanksgiving Day Parade, in which I rode on a float with some other well-known Oklahomas and sang "Oklahoma!" by Rodgers and Hammerstein. The Oklahoma centennial organizers had created a spectacular Clydesdale-drawn float, which featured an oil well, a covered wagon, and a rocket ship (your guess is as good as mine) and was populated by a galaxy of Oklahoma stars including the transcendent soprano Leona Mitchell, football coach Barry Switzer, sparky gymnast Shannon Miller, and baseball legend Johnny Bench.

It was a hoot and a holler. Lots of fun. But when they asked me to be part of the Rose Bowl parade on New Year's Day, I had to say no. I was doing a show on Broadway, and no commercial flight could get me to Pasadena for the parade and back to New York by curtain time. No problem, they told me; some generous Oklahoman donated the use of a corporate jet (again, your guess is as good as mine) to ferry me across the country and back again. This was generous indeed, and I didn't want to be a wimp, but I'm afraid of those little airplanes. Too many late-night viewings of *La Bamba*. So I asked Denny to go with me.

"No," he said flatly. "I refuse to be *and others*."

"What? What do you mean?"

"I mean *Kristin Chenoweth AND OTHERS die in flaming puddle-jumper crash*. Fiery death is not part of my plan for New Year's Eve."

I owe Denny big-time for this one. He was living in L.A. at the time, but after some cajoling, he flew to New York, helped me get myself together for the event, organized my suitcase, sent my gown by messenger to the hotel in L.A., and brought me a sandwich and Coke to snarf in the car on our way from the theater to the airfield. We made a mad dash for the waiting jet, and the pilot took off without saying so much as howdy-do.

As we taxied, I said to Denny, "Dang. I already need to go to the bathroom. I guess I drank that Coke a . . . a little . . . too . . . fast."

We looked at each other, first in dawning realization, then in cold horror. Then we started laughing. Because the fact that there was no bathroom on this airplane was very funny. For about thirty minutes. After that, not so funny. And after another thirty minutes, *so* not funny.

I scootched forward to the cockpit area and said, "Excuse me? Hi, I'm Kristin. Your passenger. Um, I'm sorry to bother you, but I didn't realize there was no restroom—"

"Oh, sure there is." The pilot flipped up the lid of a chemical toilet between the pilot and copilot chairs. "There's a little curtain there you can pull around you."

"*Denny . . .*"

"Actually," said the copilot, "if you can hold it a while longer, we'll be landing to refuel."

"Oh, thank goodness."

"They're having some nasty weather tonight," he added. "You might want to buckle up back there."

As we swooped in over the mountains of Wyoming or Estonia or whatever it was, the little jet rocked, dipped, and shuddered, and I clutched the armrest in one hand and Denny's wrist in the other.

"Oh, no. We're in trouble. *Oooooh*—Denny, did you feel that? That was free fall. We're going in. We're going down."

"Kristi, get hold of yourself. If we die, we're dying with dignity."

"Oh, God, please don't let Denny be *others*. Please let us land so I can pee."

The landing gear galumphed out, and the plane skidded and slid to a stop. Denny yanked that door open, and we hit the tarmac running. As we loped toward the restrooms, he shouted over his shoulder, "Don't drink! Don't drink anything! Not a sip!"

Like he had to tell me.

I peed a reservoir of urine, paced while they refueled, then peed again before we took off in the pitching wind. The rest of the flight was relatively uneventful, so shortly before we landed in Pasadena, Denny said, "We'll be getting in around eleven, and you have that walking rehearsal at three thirty a.m. Not much time to sleep. You should take your Ambien now so it can sink in before you get to the hotel."

As someone who struggles with insomnia, I'm not even going to pretend to be valiant about it: Ambien was my saving grace. Because I'm often double- and triple-tasking—juggling a show, workshops, music, and promotional events—it's not possible for me to function without sleep, and left to my own nature, I lie there with my mind racing, trying to shut down the day, staring up at the ceiling until it cracks. I know Tom Cruise would not approve. "Eat some placenta! You're on the ship or you're not!" Well, he can kiss . . . kiss my . . .

Zzzzzzzzzzzzzzz . . .

I was soundly out with my head on Denny's shoulder when we landed. He dragged me down the steps and oozed me into the limo. I vaguely remember the driver calling, "Where to?"

"The Ritz-Carlton in Pasadena," Denny called back.

"Hmm. Do you know where that is?"

"Well, no. Don't *you* know where it is?"

"Driver don't know wha dis?" I said woozily, and I have no memory of anything after that until Denny hitched me out of the limo and schlepped me into the lobby à la *Weekend at Bernie's*. He got us checked in while I hung on his arm thinking, *Shiny . . . pretty . . . where be room?*

"*Wha me druh?*" I blurted.

"Excuse me?" said the desk clerk. She was being played by Olivia de Havilland. Tiny winged piglets circled her head.

"*Spez ma gwan.*"

"She's asking about her gown," said Denny. (That's how well we know each other.) "It should have arrived by courier earlier."

"Oh, the dress. Yes. It's here," said Olivia, and the piglets clapped their little cloven hands. So happy for shiny, pretty dress. "I'll have the bellman bring it to your room."

Zzzzzzzzzzzzzz . . .

I awoke to a soft pat-pat-patting on my cheek.

"Kristi? Wake up," Denny said. "It's three a.m. Time to go to rehearsal."

"Oh . . . okay . . ."

"Sweetie, we have a problem. The dress is gone. I've searched from one end of this hotel to the other. It's nowhere to be found."

"Crap . . . crap . . ." I jumbled myself upright, pushing my hands against the sides of my head. "Denny, what do we do?"

"I don't know. I'm very upset. All I can think is that some little dip'n'chips is out partying in that red dress."

"Oh, my gosh . . . New Year's Eve . . ."

Now, please understand that this dress—a fabulous red Emanuel Ungaro gown—was worth several thousand dollars and had been precisely tailored for me as a gift. Not only was it supposed to be dancing down the street on television five hours from now, I fully expected my children's children to wear it to their weddings and bat mitzvahs.

This was a job for gumshoe John Artez.

I called him while Denny dug through my suitcase and came up with a pair of jeans and a red leather jacket he'd packed for me just in case, then I stood in the shower, which smelled unpleasantly of someone else's overwarm body.

The winter weather in Pasadena is almost perfect. Not once in its hundred-year history has the Tournament of Roses been called on account of rain. Only one time has there been heavy rain during the parade. This was the time. I stumbled through the rehearsal and did my song-and-dance thing in the parade. Meanwhile, John Artez had made the scene and rattled his saber, and the dress eventually reappeared. After the parade, I went back to get it, looking and feeling like a soggy little rag doll, and determined to tell somebody off.

"Would you let me take care of it, please?" John Artez said, but wearing my *Oh, yeah? That's what YOU think!* hat, I stormed to the desk and demanded to see the manager.

"What's the problem?" asked the manager.

"Oklahoma float dress airplane jet pee driver supposed to be a Ritz Carlton where hotel dress dress gown what kind of service dress six thousand dollars out partying with chips'n'dip parade rain and and if you think three in the morning wearing a red dress rain dress hotel gown words words words yab yab yab. And the shower smelled like BO!"

"I'm terribly sorry, Ms. Chenoweth. What can we do to make your stay better?"

"Well. . . ." I said, disarmed by her accommodating smile. "Perhaps a free weekend?"

"No."

As I swirled into another word hurricane, John Artez reached out his arm and hooked me off the stage like a vaudevillian. In the car on the way to the airport, Denny reached out and nudged my shin with his foot.

"Happy New Year."

"You, too," I said wearily. "Listen, it's silly for you to fly all the way to New York just so you can turn around and fly back home again. You should stay here."

He agreed quicker than you can say "collateral damage."

"You sure you're okay?" he said when he dropped me off.

"I'm a big girl. I'll be fine. Thanks for everything, Den."

I hugged him and sent him on his way. The pilot was suddenly being very friendly. I gathered from our conversation that during the layover, someone had schooled him about me supposedly being someone.

"You didn't tell me you were on TV." He grinned. "Need to use the ladies' room before we take off?"

Hardy har har. "No, thanks. I'm fine."

Before we took off, he called back from the cockpit, "We're going to land in St. Louis to refuel since the weather looks pretty bad in New York."

That scared me a little, so I called my buddy Anne Nathan and asked, "How bad is the weather? Do you think I'll be able to land in time for the show?"

"What are you talking about?" said Anne. "The weather's fine."

Hmm. I figured the pilot must know something I didn't. He must have radar or something that—well, whatever. *I'm* the one who should have had my radar up.

"Let's grab a quick bite to eat," he said when we landed to refuel, and envisioning a drive-through window, I gratefully said yes. Instead, he took me to a nice restaurant. As "quick" turned into an hour, and an hour turned into two hours, I kept asking if we shouldn't really be getting back, and he kept shrugging it off and asking me about movies and TV shows I'd been in and various famous people he thought I might know.

"Do you mind taking a picture?" He waved the waiter over. "I can't wait to tell all my friends that I took a TV star out on a date."

"What? *No*. No picture. I need to get back to the airport. I have a show tonight."

When we got to the airfield, the pilot who flew next to a toilet told me, in all seriousness, "We're not taking off till I get a picture."

For the sake of moving things along, I stood like a wooden Indian long enough for the chagrinned copilot to snap the photo, then I got in the airplane, pulled my jacket over my face, and pretended to sleep the rest of the way back to New York, where the skies were sunny and fine.

Grin and bear it, I told myself. *Your newfound popularity.*

∽∾

chapter twelve

A GRIM FAIRY TALE

*P**lease, God, help me be a good prostitute today.*

It's an odd request, but He knows what I mean.

When Ann Luster called my manager, Fireball Dannielle Thomas (actually, my dad calls her Fireball, Ann calls her Dannielle), and asked if I'd be interested in playing a suicidal hooker in writer/ director Patrick Coyle's *Into Temptation*, Dannielle said, "We've been looking for something exactly like that!"

From the fireball point of view, it's an opportunity for me to show my range.

"It's a risk," she said, "but we need casting directors to see that you can be serious in one breath and seriously funny in the next."

The premise is fertile ground: a hooker confesses to a priest that she has decided to kill herself. Coyle's harrowing script follows the two characters through what might be the last days of this woman's life. Sounds like a laugh riot, huh?

I didn't have to be talked into it. I grabbed hold with both hands. But playing someone like Linda, giving her my skin and bones for a time, allowing her to take me to the dark places—it's been tough. Studying what made her choose to do this, I've had to look to my own dark places, and that's stirring so many ghosts and questions to the surface. This part has put me in a deeply melancholy mood, and I know that when the movie comes out, it might be hard for my family to watch and even harder for them to understand why I chose to play a role like this.

Shooting *Into Temptation* has been like Rolfing—that brutal deep-tissue massage that hurts like hell but gets all the toxins out of your system. There is a misconception about me (and probably about most people you see on Page Six): my life is perfect, I'm always happy, I never have a bad-hair day. But depression is a real thing for a lot of people, and I've battled my way through a couple of tough spells.

I've come to accept that I occasionally fall in holes. Literally, as in the hole outside the door that grabbed me and broke my ankle during *Strike Up the Band*. Or the hole in the set of *The Apple Tree*—one of the openings that symbolized the unfinished quality of the earth at the time of Adam and Eve. I stepped back, found myself unbalanced at the edge, and basically did the Nestea Plunge. Brian d'Arcy James saw me going over the edge and screamed like a soprano. I landed on my back six feet below the stage, groaning like a baritone. I had to do the run of the show with fractured ribs. (It was still the single most enjoyable theatre experience of my life. That's how great that show was.) Then there are these rare but undeniable down-the-rabbit-hole kind of holes. Emotional lows that make me feel swallowed, body and soul. Some people say that depression can be defeated solely on prayer, determination, or just a healthy bucket of "get over yourself" (which is easy to say if you've never been there), and maybe that's possible for some people. It wasn't for me. I got through it with Mom, God, and Zoloft.

While I don't want to go into all that at great length—because some things are sacred, other things private, and others just none of anyone's beeswax—it's important to me that the young women who watch me know that my life isn't perfect; it's filled with challenges and sorrows, highs and lows, just like theirs.

A group of girls from Glitter, my official fan club, waited for me after a concert in Chicago recently, and I was so moved when I saw them. They were so beautiful and vibrant, so fresh on the brink of it all. And let me tell you something, those little Glitter Girls are a force to be respected; they've raised close to $100,000 for charity. I love that they've chosen to come together, centered on something bright and positive and pink, with the goal of doing good. I'm honored to be the host of our cosmic slumber party.

So I want all you girls to gather round while I tell a little bedtime story. Meghan from Toronto? Where are you? Ah! There she is. Get on over here, you. Let's all snuggle into our down comforters, plump our ruffled pillows, and gather a few soft stuffed animals. Meghan, you hold Maddie in your lap.

Now, I won't say where this little story fits on the time line of my life because—you know what? It doesn't. I didn't have time for this episode, and, Glitter Girls, neither do you.

Everyone tucked in? Good. This is the story of . . .

The Princess and the Bogsnart

Once upon a time, a levelheaded type A princess went momentarily barking mad and thought she was in love with a bogsnart. If you're wondering what a bogsnart is and questioning why, oh, *why why why* do princesses routinely fall in love with them, I'm afraid I must tell you that virtually every woman in the world has been bitten by one of these pernicious ticks. At the very least, she's been hit on by one at a party. The bogsnart wanders the streets disguised as a perfectly companionable prince, his facial hair impeccably manscaped, his metrosexual manners as charming as Paddington Bear. But beneath the gym-built shirt-stuffing and pseudo-intellectual patter, an unsalvageable *bogsnart* lurks, and at nightfall he is driven by instinct to skulk like a bedbug toward the nearest warm-blooded host.

The type A princess was fooled by the bogsnart's clever disguise and invited him to tea one day. But as day turned to evening, the bogsnart's witty banter turned mean.

"It's a pity," snorted the bogsnart. "Such a beautiful evening and I'm stuck here with this ugly girl."

"I beg your pardon!" cried the princess. "I looked at myself in the mirror just yesterday, and the result, while not perfect, was overall quite acceptable."

"Please. You're the homeliest thing I've ever seen."

From his dastardly bag of tricks, the bogsnart drew a mirror that was cracked and de-silvered, spidered with flaws, and smeared with bog offal. When he held it up to the princess's face, she saw herself smirched and malformed.

"You're right," she said sadly. "I'm terribly ugly. How could I have thought otherwise?"

"I suppose I could tolerate your shortcomings," hissed the bogsnart, "if you give me your treasures. Your golden voice, your ruby lips, the diamond sparkles in your eyes."

The princess fell into a deep sleep, and in her feverish dreams she danced with a handsome prince. When she awoke, she was alone, and the fever had left her. Looking down from the castle window, she saw the bogsnart scuttling off into the woods. He'd taken her treasures and left the distorting mirror under her bed. Late at night, she would sadly gaze at her smirched and spidered reflection and be reminded how poor and ugly she was.

The princess cried, and she couldn't stop crying.

Fortunately, the levelheaded queen knew immediately what she was dealing with.

"Bogsnart. Up to the usual tricks," she correctly surmised, pushing the broken mirror aside. "Look into my eyes, Daughter. What do you see?"

"I see . . . *me*," said the astonished princess. "All my treasures—they're still here."

"Because the treasure is *you*, my girl, and you are still as *you* as you ever were. The most perfect you there is. The best and only you that God ever made."

Without making the princess feel young or dumb or judged, the wise queen applied love and chocolate and pharmaceuticals and held the princess's hand through dark forests and long cab rides until the princess recovered her natural vivacity. Never again was the princess fooled by a bogsnart, and when she saw that particular bogsnart on the street one afternoon, his warty nose pushed against a shop window, she saw how small and today he was, and she actually felt a bit sorry for him. Not sorry enough to resist flipping him the finger. But a little sorry. She continued down the street and lived happily (which is of course a relative term, but usually applicable) ever after.

So remember, all my glittery princesses, we must never allow a bogsnart (or a prince, in fact) to tell us who we are, no matter how handsome his disguise, no matter how needy our own hearts. Our best and truest reflection is found in the eyes of those who love us.

Now, good night. Sleep tight. Don't let the bogsnarts bite.

chapter thirteen

WALK AND TALK

I never wanted a manager. I wanted to do it all myself. But when I recorded *Let Yourself Go,* Sony Classical made me hire a publicist, and after a year or so the publicist begged me to hire a manager. Here's another of those I-didn't-know-what-I-didn't-know situations. What did a manager actually do? I didn't want to pay someone to boss me around. The PR wizardress assured me that's not how it works. She narrowed the field to five. I met the first four, they all seemed fine, and I was ready to sign one and head home to New York. Frankly, I didn't think I'd be giving this person much to do, so it didn't seem like a critical decision. The publicist asked me to stay one more day and meet the last candidate.

Vibrating with energy and knockout, grape-stomping, raven-haired gorgeous, Dannielle Thomas walked in and said, "I'm Dannielle. And I'm going to change your life."

"Oh. Hi. I'm . . . I'm Kristin. I'm not sure if I want my life changed."

"You need to play Dolly Parton."

Okay. I don't know how she reached into my head and pulled out this secret dream. But I immediately knew with my whole heart that I was supposed to be here. When I called to tell her she was hired, she yelped. Gave a big ol' *"Yeeeooooow!"* as if she were at a football game, and I loved that. She didn't bother to play it cool. She never does.

The following week, working out a game plan over coffee, she told me, "You need to be doing movies and television."

"I never really saw myself in the movies," I said. "I don't think I'd get cast."

"Well, stop thinking that. Just wait. When you get your Oscar—"

I coughed my latte across the sidewalk.

"Don't think it's impossible." Dannielle set her hand on my arm. "I'm serious. Sissy Spacek in *Coal Miner's Daughter.* Reese Witherspoon as June Carter. You as Dolly."

She sent me to read for Steve Martin, who was doing *The Pink Panther.* (Oddly enough, as I was on my way out of that audition, Idina was on her way in.) They told me I was too young for the lead but called me back for a smaller part, and I got it.

"First movie." Dannielle made a check mark in the air over her desk. "Now let's get you on TV." And about five seconds later, she'd hooked me up with *The West Wing.*

Things I love about Fireball Dannielle Thomas:

1. She's unfairly good-looking.
2. She never stops for a moment.
3. She changed my life.

Things that drive me crazy about Fireball Dannielle Thomas:

1. She's unfairly good-looking.
2. She never stops for a moment.
3. She sometimes has to be reminded whose life this is.

Right away she started scolding me for doing too many benefits, but she did encourage me to do one for the American Film Institute. They asked me to sing a song from a movie, and I chose "My White Knight" from *The Music Man.*

"The people and I talked," Dannielle informed me. "We all agree. That song's boring."

"Excuse me?"

"Oh, not that it's boring the way you do it," she backpedaled. "They're just looking for something more fun, you know? More of a movie song. Light, showy . . . do 'Glitter and Be Gay.' People love that one."

Cue Sally Brown: *Oh, yeah? That's what YOU think!*

"I'm going to get in my car and drive away now," I said. "I did 'My White Night' in a movie. I do it in concert. It is not boring. And if the ritzy, glitzy people of Los Angeles don't understand what Meredith Wilson meant when he wrote that song, well, *words words words words words.*"

I went off on her about being tired of doing what other people want me to do, and I guess I know a good song when I sing it, and I'm going to sing that song because I feel like it, and then I went up there and I sang it.

It flatlined. There was not enough juice in the defibrillator to goose a response out of that crowd. I followed up with "Glitter and Be Gay," and they went ape wild.

Oh, well. That's okay. I have no problem with being proven wrong, and I have to be prepared to go down in flames once in a while. But I've learned that going down in flames for something you believe in is a lot less painful than going down in flames for something you got talked into, so I have to make my own decisions, prepared to stand by them. In the years we've been together, Dannielle's learned a lot from me about the theatre world, and I've learned a lot from her about the business end of show business. She knows her stuff. She has a lot of respect for theatre, and not everyone in L.A. does. She's my biggest fan (other than the designer-handbag stalker), and her belief in me feels totally genuine. She does her job so well, it's easy to love all her quirks. When Power Up named Dannielle one of the Ten Amazing Gay Women in Showbiz, I presented her with the award, gave her credit for changing my life, and sang "You'll Never Know (Just How Much I Love You)."

Her particular brand of ball-busting honesty isn't always appreciated. Sadly, she and my agents at Bauman, Redanty, & Shaul didn't click, and after a lot of sleepless nights, I made a change in representation. It was one of the hardest decisions I've ever made. Mark Redanty was my champion from the beginning, and David Shaul held my hand through the whole *Kristin* of it all. They were unfailingly supporting and loving, and they negotiated like gladiators on my behalf. Leaving them felt like leaving home, but leaving home is part of life, and it was time for me to grow up. Since signing with my new agent, Tony Lipp, I've done half a dozen movies. Giggling offscreen with Nicole Kidman, horsing around in the heartland with Robin Williams, reading poetry and making out with Annette Bening, tackling scary, wonderful, so-juicy-you-gotta-eat-it-over-the-sink roles such as Linda in *Into Temptation* and Fern in *Running with Scissors*. And I'm developing projects on my own. I'm wearing the big-girl pants now, and I like it.

When Tony calls me on the phone, he always begins by asking, "How's your life?" When he cuts to the car chase, I never know from his tone what to expect. "Li'l chicken?" he says. "You got the job." Or "Li'l chicken? They went with someone else." "Li'l chicken? You're gonna sing on the Oscars." "Li'l chicken? So-and-so died." Trick or treat, the news is always delivered with the same it-is-what-it-is equanimity. It's like that line in the Rudyard Kipling poem: *If you can meet with Triumph and Disaster / and treat those two impostors just the same* . . . Tony's approach reminds me that first, there's your life, and then there's whatever blossoms or bombs.

❧

Outside a Midtown rehearsal space, I wave good-bye to the backup dancers and head toward home. I opt to walk instead of flagging a taxi. To be in New York is to be in motion. But five or six blocks up the pike, I'm feeling the rehearsal from the back of my neck to my Achilles tendons. To be in concert is to be in motion, too, and preparing for that is a workout.

The ninety-minute set involves backup dancers, full orchestra, a rambunctious onstage homicide, and no rest for the *Wicked,* pardon the pun. Andrew Lippa always has my back. He had to chime in and rescue me in Chicago when I completely went up on the lyrics in "Popular." I'm not sure how I managed to screw that up, as many times as I've sung that song, but it's all good. I think those moments make it more fun. My Glitter Girls have heard the perfectly polished CD version a thousand times. This is *live.* Buckle those seat belts.

By the time I walk offstage, I'm spent, but I can't bring myself to skimp on the afterglow. One of the first concerts I went to as kid was by Amy Grant, and I remember how much it meant to me that she took the time to greet people afterward. She made a moment for each person, as crunched as her time and energy were.

"What's your name, cutie?" she asked.

"Kristi," I said, barely able to exhale the two syllables.

"Let's see. What should I say? How about *God bless you, Kristi . . . Love . . . Amy.*" She jotted it on a piece of paper and handed it to me. "How's that?"

Utterly smitten and fairy-dusted, I managed to peep, "Good."

And it was. It was just plain *good* of her. That's what I aspire to.

World peace, one small, sweet moment at a time. I've come a long way from my Emily Dickinson song cycle, performed for as few as five people, and sold out Carnegie Hall. Low point: the Mohegan Sun casino in Connecticut. I delivered a heartfelt Jerome Kern number, there was a spatter of applause from the dozen or so folks in attendance, and then a drunk loudly said, "Geezes, yer *short*." High point: that night at Carnegie in 2004.

That audience was alive, involved, and entirely willing to go for a ride. My parents, Ms. Birdwell, and many friends were there. The dressing room was crowded with love and flowers. After the show, as a huge crowd thronged the alley outside the stage door, it suddenly occurred to everyone inside that perhaps some security should have been arranged. Dad went out to do recon and came back in to report.

"Here's whatcha got," he said in full gatekeeper mode. "You got a lot of kids, you got some old folks, and a bunch of guys dressed like you."

You gotta love my people. Glitter Girls, grandparents, and fansvestites.

We decided the best way to handle it would be for Denny to shepherd me through the bustle to a waiting limo while Dad did his best to bully the crowd back a bit. I hung on Denny's arm as he plowed through the fray, he chucked me into the back of the car, and I rolled down the window to tell the people gathered outside how grateful I was for their kindness and enthusiasm.

"Thanks for coming," I called. "You all are so sweet. Thank you so—what?—*Mom?*"

"Hi, honey!" She waved to me from the curb, where she stood wedged between two octogenarians and a Glindafied trannie.

"Mom! What are you doing?"

"I just wanted to see you exit." She beamed and waved me off as if I were riding the short bus. Denny and I couldn't stop laughing for thirty minutes.

The 3 Angels benefit concert will be scaled down somewhat from the usual song-and-dance extravaganza (though not an ounce less energy is involved). It's going to be an intimate performance in a small venue, which is perfect for the theme—"This One's Personal: A Concert to Stop ACD"—and the cause is good. A heartbreaker, like all good causes, but particularly close to home because the heart broken belonged to a good friend, my *West Wing* castmate NiCole Robinson, whose seven-week-old son, Lincoln, died a year earlier from alveolar capillary dysplaysia, a genetic disorder often mistaken for SIDS.

NiCole was like my big sis from my first day on the set. Broken Arrow, Oklahoma, meets Burley, Idaho. A recipe for reality-based girl talk if ever there was one. When people ask her what's with the capital *C* in the middle of her name, NiCole replies, "It's what poor people do to look fancy." That's NiCole. Funny, smart, real as rimrock. She took me in immediately and made sure I knew the scoop on everyone.

When she came to visit me on the set of *Pushing Daisies* after Lincoln died, I couldn't hug her hard enough, couldn't find words to tell her how sorry I was. But sorry isn't what she was looking for. She was on a mission, galvanized by grief, needing to transform her terrible reality into a more hopeful possibility for someone else.

"It has to change," she said. "But that takes money. I was thinking you could sing."

"Tell me where to be. I'll be there."

❦

I don't think Aaron Sorkin set out to create a family when he created *The West Wing*, but that's what he did. No one who worked on the show came in unchallenged or went away unchanged. When I was first offered the Ainsley Hayes role during the *Wicked* workshops, Marc Platt told me, "You have to do *Wicked*. It's iconic. There'll never be another show like it." The same could actually be said for *The West Wing*. When Dannielle roped a second chance for me to join the cast,

I jumped in with both feet. I believe in that old saw "Run with the big dogs or stay on the porch with the puppies." And these were some mighty big dogs.

The women of *The West Wing* could be a calendar if they felt like it. Raving beauties. And the brainiest coffee klatch since Gertrude Stein.

Allison Janney had a party where everybody had to wear a wig. Just to shake the snow globe a little. How great is that? Our first scene was a walk and talk, in which she looked down at me from her full five foot twelve and said, "I can't believe we're members of the same species." She and I look like two people on an escalator, even with me in heels and her in flats. We decided it was her job to check me for dandruff, my job to check her for nose debris. I've never seen anyone else master complicated dialogue in such a short time, and she taught me a trick she got from Meryl Streep: "If you've got a string of words you just can't get in your mouth, write the first letter of every word at the top of the page. It sets the words in your brain just a bit differently." Works like gangbusters. (There you go, young actors. From Meryl Streep to you via the great Allison Janney.) She's a great lady. I look up to her. Literally and figuratively.

My first scene with Stockard Channing was about NASCAR racing, and we laughed a lot. She's such a mom, supportive and deeply kind. I'd been a fan of hers since *Grease,* of course, and the way she was able to shift so seamlessly between theatre, movies, and television set an example I hope to follow throughout my career. We go to the same voice coach in L.A., and sometimes she's arriving as I leave.

"Oh, Lord," she always groans. "Do I have to go *now*? After *her*?"

I love listening to her sing. She nails that speak-on-pitch dynamic Florence Birdwell talks about. Stockard is one of those rare women whose voice has—well, it's got *balls*. She can do anything—plays, musicals, movies—I wouldn't be at all surprised to see her NASCAR racing.

Something sweet and wonderful about all the *West Wing* men is how unabashedly they love their families. It's touching and reaffirming to see such good men walking the halls.

Jimmy Smits is living proof that gallantry is not dead. In a van going to location, he'd get in last and out first to help the ladies. One day, I showed up on set late and crying; I'd gotten a car with a navigation system that somehow left me even more lost than my old car and Key Map. Without making me feel like an idiot, Jimmy said, "Let's go figure it out." I don't know where I would have been without him. Literally and figuratively.

Brad Whitford needs a good spanking. He was always horsing around, putting something in someone's muffin, going off on politics. One day, I wore a skirt that laced up the back, and as we cruised down the hall doing a walk and talk, he unlaced it. I was oblivious; everybody else was giggling. He takes more time to get ready than a Twelve Oaks debutante, but he's another dialogue wiz and a spark plug to every scene he's in. A joy to work with.

Josh Malina was another prankster. He never got me, but he and Brad would pants each other like twelve-year-olds. Josh couldn't work on Shabbat and never made any apologies about it. Something I felt he and I had in common was a commitment to faith, which isn't always easy to combine with the working world of Hollywood.

Martin Sheen might actually think that he is president. It wouldn't surprise me if he showed up to give the State of the Union. He's another good dad, who loves his kids even if they step in it, and he extended that dadly warmth to everyone on the set. One day I was bumming about having to fly somewhere. He went to his dressing room and came back with a rosary blessed by the Pope John Paul II.

"Carry this with you when you travel," he told me. "You'll be all right."

He's a mighty good man, Martin Sheen. Never wavered in his life or his craft.

I first met John Spencer while I was doing *Wicked*. He came backstage, and we immediately knew we were kindred spirits. I always wrangled to sit next to him at table readings and became his right-hand man on *The West Wing*.

"Oh, John," I said one morning, "we have a good scene together this week."

"Get used to it," the director said.

The two of us had done a scene in an elevator, and it popped, I guess. Producers said, "We want more of that." We both felt a little awkward about a romantic interest between our characters because we had such a brother-sister thing going in real life.

"I don't know," John teased. "If I was a little older, and you were a little younger . . ."

During an interview with Charlie Rose early on in the series, John said, "*The West Wing* is all about language. That makes it like stage work."

My first scene was a perfect example: Annabeth Schott (me) thinks she's coming in to interview for the job of deputy press secretary, only to discover that they're interviewing for press secretary, while the communications director, Toby Ziegler (Richard Schiff), thinks he's interviewing a fairly dim blonde, only to discover that she's pretty quick on the uptake. I went to the set wearing only a little makeup, a plain ponytail, conservative tweeds, and a pair of smart-girl glasses, prepared to do anything they asked. I knew the words inside out. My lines, Richard's lines, Janel Moloney's lines, everyone's blocking. You know how I am about doing my homework, and that was a good thing because until I looked it up as part of my research for this scene, I'd always thought Uzbekistan was a kind of leather. (Who knew?)

Richard was the opposite of warm and fuzzy while we were shooting, so I never really got a read on what he was thinking, but at the end of the day he said the nicest thing anyone could possibly have said: "You're going to fit right in."

❧

I was on what turned out to be the last two seasons of *The West Wing*, and during the hiatus in between, John Spencer came to see me in a workshop performance of *The Apple Tree*.

"This is your show," he told me. "You have to do this show."

I'm so sad that he didn't get to see it.

John's health issues were ongoing and not small, so I got mad at him one day when I found him out behind the building smoking a cigarette between takes. He sucked on Jolly Ranchers all the time, trying not to smoke, but sometimes that just didn't do it for him.

"*John,*" I scolded. "What are you thinking? What is in your head? Put that down."

"Sorry, kid. Every day without a cigarette is hell. No, make that every day without a drink and a cigarette—that's hell."

"Well, it's better than chemotherapy," I said, plucking the butt from between his fingers.

"Geez, yeah. I wouldn't want to go slow like that. I want to go quick."

"Me, too. Except I wouldn't want to be murdered. I'd love to be murdered in a slasher movie. But not in real life. And I don't want to drown. I hear that's horrible."

"Hear from who?" He laughed, unwrapping a Jolly Rancher.

"Well, you know. People get revived sometimes."

"Then they ain't dead! What the hell do they know?"

He offered me a Jolly Rancher, and I sucked on it while we debated that for a while, discussed the forensics of brain death, speculating on the soul, and that segued into speculating about what was being filmed on a lot down the street, then moved on to my various love-life issues and his various life-love issues, and one thing and another. Our hurry-up-and-wait conversations always climbed around like kudzu on a telephone pole.

On a rare night off, I went with Lippa to sing at a fund-raising gala for a small group of very rich, very drunk people, who basically treated me like a little canary chirping in the background. I came home from the miserable affair and crawled into pj's. Mom sent me a soft white pair with little red cherries. I love lingerie, but I keep that hidden. I wear either a tank and boxers or the style of pajamas you'd expect to see on Wally and the Beaver. Crazy, sexy, cool, huh? But that's how exciting my life is. I do my thing, go home, take a bath. I pray and read the Bible. (I love Psalms and Proverbs, and also the adventuresome Daniel and his kin.) Eventually, I plug my face into the TV. I try to avoid infomercials, but I do get talked into buying something once in a while—Slim n Lifts (I know! I know!), a hideous brooch for Mom, some crazy kitchen gadget for a friend. Sometimes I'll order a workout DVD. I was on the Tae Bo train for a while. And of course there's always good old Richard Simmons.

But on that particular night, I was rescued from home shopping by one of my favorite *West Wing* episodes: "Bartlet for America," in which Leo McGarry falls off the wagon.

"It's the one that got you the Emmy," I told John on the phone as soon as it was over. "I had to call you and tell you what a genius you are."

"That's what you're doing with your night off?" he said. "Watching reruns?"

"Well, look what you're doing with your night off. Listening to someone talk about watching reruns."

"Geezes. I don't know who to feel sorrier for in this scenario."

I told him about the evening festivities, and he laughed.

"Oh, honey, that's not about you. Just take the money and run. Screw them."

He shared a few good war stories with me. (Did you know he was on the *Patty Duke Show* back in the day?) He'd been around the block a time or two and was glad to share what he'd learned, and I was glad to receive the benefit of his hard-knock education.

That was the last time we talked. I received word a few days later that he'd died of a heart attack. He went quick, and I was glad for that, but, oh, so very sad to see him go. They asked me to sing "For Good," a song he particularly loved from *Wicked,* at his memorial service, and I summoned every scrap of self-control inside me so I could sing it the way he would have wanted people to hear it.

Who can say if I've been changed for the better? Because I knew you, I have been changed for good.

Our first day back on the set, Jimmy Smits and I ended up shooting outside late at night, exchanging hurried dialogue, striding across the tarmac toward Air Force One. Between takes, someone came and put a coat around my shoulders, and I gratefully huddled into it, pushing my hands deep in the pockets.

I started to cry, and Jimmy put his arm around me. "Hey . . . hey . . . are you okay?"

I pulled my fist from my coat pocket and showed him the handful of Jolly Ranchers.

There was really no choice but to write Leo's death into the show, and it made sense for Annabeth, who loved him, to discover his body. But that was a hard scene to shoot. The episode that featured Leo's memorial service gathered almost all the actors who'd appeared in the series over the years, and the shoot was like a family reunion. The new kids—Mary McCormack, Janeane Garofalo, and I—sat there watching the tearful hellos and hugs and feeling lucky to be a part of this company. An old gospel song asks, *Will the circle be unbroken, by and by, Lord, by and by?* This made me think about that place, that day, when I'd be gathered in with all the people from all my seasons.

Everyone felt that full circle, I think. Most everyone agreed that it was time for the show to end. Shows end. That's the way of it. You go on to the next thing. But some people you take with you, and NiCole is one of those people for me.

The night of her 3 Angels Fund benefit, she raised a walloping lot of money for research, and I hope that it brings her some peace, knowing that she's making a profound difference in the life of another family, a mother who reached out. NiCole was the mother who was forced to let go. When she found a way to go forward from that, she passed King Solomon's ultimate test. That night, I put my arms around her and said, "You did a good thing." This is the magic bubble of celebrity, it turns out: a gift becomes a song, which becomes a gift again, changed for the better, changed for good.

Toward the end of the evening, in the live auction, one of the items up for bids was "the opportunity to come up onstage and have Kristin Chenoweth sing a song just for you."

"Let's start the bidding at five hundred," I said. "Do I hear five? C'mon, let's give five hundred dollars to this worthy cause. I'll make it worth your while."

"Two thousand dollars."

Heads swiveled toward the corner of the ballroom. Mr. Writer stood with his arms folded in front of him, smiling one of my favorite smiles from his extensive repertoire of facial expressions. The one that reminds me what a good heart he has. A light round of applause and an audible *Awww* acknowledged the moment had definitely tested closer to eHarmony commercial than "Falls on Ass." Aaron's smile widened to a grin. The one that triggers something like champagne pouring down my spine. There are times when I ask God to please, *please* make me stop loving this man, but at that moment I could not for the life of me remember why. At that moment, all I could feel was the song inside me.

I held out my hand and said, "Sold."

❦

chapter fourteen

TILL THERE WAS YOU

My BlackBerry buzzes in my pocket. Another message from Aaron.

The people sitting near my table at Cosi must think I'm either on Ritalin or very easily amused. He keeps making me laugh out loud. This is how he wins my favor, skins my resolve, does a double-buffalo-time-step around every meltdown and blowup. How am I supposed to argue with a man whose words strike as true as *you can't handle the truth?* Nothing is more cranium-cooking sexy than a guy who gives good text.

I'd done a couple of TV movies, the dozen or so eps of *Kristin,* and a handful of series guest shots, but I didn't get the full workout until *The West Wing.* You get shot out of a cannon at 7 a.m. and drag home exhausted at eleven that night. It took me a while to learn to pace myself; sometimes it was six hours before I got on camera, and after all that hurry-up-and-wait, my skirt was wrinkled, I'd had a nap, food was all over my shirt, and I'd have to start the whole journey over. Part of what made it so exhausting—and so exhilarating—was how much I learned in between. Not just about television (though this was definitely the boot camp that prepared me for *Pushing Daisies*); my role on *The West Wing* required me to read about, learn about, and *care* about the world in a way I never had. Aaron has said that writing *The West Wing* during the two years before and the two years after 9/11, he felt as if he had "a front-row seat to the tectonic cultural shift in America." His gift is the way he challenges us to think while making us laugh.

No one else can pull words out of the universe and settle them into a jet stream of meaning like Aaron Sorkin. His writing is beyond musical; it's operatic. Which makes it just my thing. He was no longer writing the show when I was hired, but during the first four seasons, he'd set the tone that carried the series to the end. Everyone on the show had tremendous respect for him, and he couldn't stay out of *Variety,* so I felt as if I knew him. But of course I didn't.

Oddly enough, in 2001—three years before we met—a *New York Observer* gossip column ran an item about my purchasing an apartment on the Upper West Side, and directly below that was an item about writer/producer Aaron Sorkin being arrested for possession in the Burbank airport. What made me laugh a little about that at the time was that this big-shot executive producer was not in possession of the stylish sort of drugs you would expect from a Hollywood hedonist on his way to an orgy. He was packing 'shrooms, the navel-contemplating drug of a spiritual seeker on his way to a poetry reading. What makes me laugh about it now is how terribly insulted Aaron is that my apartment purchase outranked his arrest in the litany of celebrity gossip.

"How is 'Cheno purchases apartment' more newsworthy than 'Sorkin arrested'? Come on!" Using both his hands and his lanky arms, he makes a wide gesture of outrage that's only half-joking. "You were in a 'quaint one-bedroom with stellar view'; I was in *jail.*"

Aaron has a totally logical explanation about how the incriminating items came to be in his bag, but his struggles with substance abuse were well-documented, and, honey, I don't touch that with a vaccinated cattle prod. So I have to assume that had I taken that first job on *The West Wing*, it would have been the wrong time and place for us to meet, and things would have been very different.

Three years later, I was in an entirely different place professionally; he was in an entirely different place personally. Shortly after I signed on to do *The West Wing*, he called and asked me out to dinner, and on the phone, the guy everyone talked about as if he were the Great and Powerful Oz was genuine, funny, and sweet and seemed to have gotten a leash on his demons. He sounded like someone I wanted to know.

At the right time on the right day, I walked out the front door of my hotel and looked around the parking lot. Across the way, I saw a quiet man in khaki pants and a blue shirt. Leaning on the door of his car, he raked his fingers through his hair, and for a moment he looked like a boy watching a jet plane pass over, squinting up at the sky through his smart-kid glasses.

When he saw me, he smiled, and I said, "God, please, let that be Aaron Sorkin."

He Said (Special Guest Appearance by Aaron Sorkin)

I don't have a lot of cool. If you looked in my closet, you'd see a half dozen pairs of Gap khakis, a half dozen blue button-down shirts, and a half dozen dark sport jackets. For my first date with Kristin I boldly chose a dark sport jacket, blue button-down shirt, and a pair of Gap khakis. I picked her up in front of the Beverly Wilshire at the appointed time looking like I'd just been elected cocaptain of the Andover debating team.

When she walked out the door, the first thing I noticed was that she didn't look short. Kristin is famously short. I defy anyone to find anything written about her that doesn't mention her height. I'm six feet tall, so any-one who doesn't play for the Duke Blue Devils looks a little short to me, but she didn't. And the only reason I was thinking about this was that she was still about fifty yards away and I hadn't seen her eyes yet.

∞

I'd fallen for Kristin two years earlier, on a Sunday night in February 2003—two years before I met her. I was living at the Four Seasons Hotel on Doheny Drive, my five-year marriage having ended in the summer of 2001. ABC was broadcasting its production of The Music Man *with Matthew Broderick and Kris in the leads. I'm crazy about musicals, and* The Music Man *is one of my favorites, so I settled in with a sixteen-ounce bottle of Yoo-Hoo and a bag of Ruffles.*

    I'd heard of Kristin but somehow I'd managed to miss everything she'd been in on and off Broadway. The year she won the Tony Award was the first year since I was fourteen that I'd missed the Tony Awards. The sum-mer her sitcom was aired, I was spending a lot of late nights at my office at Warner Bros. working on the new season of The West Wing, *so I'd missed her on TV, too.*

    I'd written a new character onto the show—Ainsley Hayes, a lawyer with the Republican National Committee who was drafted into service by Jed Bartlet's lefty White House. Our casting director said, "You have to go to Kristin Chenoweth for this. Her series didn't get picked up and I think she'd do TV again." I told him to get me some tapes and check on I&A (interest and availability), but we quickly heard back that Kris was in San Francisco doing a pre-Broadway tryout of a new Stephen Schwartz musical. Something about witches, they said.

    So I sat down in front of The Music Man, *ready to see what all the fuss was about. Her character, Marion Paroo, Marian the Librarian, makes her entrance about eight minutes into the piece. Eight minutes and twenty seconds into the piece I understood what all the fuss was about. She was charming and beautiful. Confident and effortless. (Effortless is hard—*

effortless in a period piece is a lot harder.) She was funny and feminine and irresistible.

And we hadn't even gotten to the footbridge.

It's called "The Eleven O'Clock Number" in the theater (because it's the second-to-last song, which, back when curtain time was eight thirty on Broadway, would come at around eleven o'clock). Evening. A small Iowa town's Fourth of July picnic going on in the distance. Matthew and Kristin standing on a footbridge and Kris starts singing "Till There Was You." She modulates up a halftone for the final verse . . .

. . . and the Ruffles slipped out of my hand. I put down my Yoo-Hoo, and I fell for her.

The next day at the office, I faxed her manager a note saying how much I liked her performance. The next day I got a fax back from Kristin saying she'd never heard of me but thank you.

After four years of writing The West Wing, *I'd left the show. It was 2005 now and I'd moved from the Four Seasons into a rental in the Hollywood Hills that had once been owned by one of the Mamas and the Papas and then Sam Kinison. Exactly the right place for someone who needs to concentrate every day on not using cocaine. Whoever was renting the house before me had home subscriptions to* Variety *and the* Hollywood Reporter, *and the trade papers were still coming to the front door every day. Flipping through* Variety *one morning, I saw that—incredibly—Kristin was now joining the cast of* The West Wing.

I started slowly banging my head against the polished granite kitchen counter.

And it turns out that if you bang your brains against something hard for long enough, something good might happen. Because that's when it occurred to me that I'd been both single and clean for quite some time. I couldn't stand that I was missing the chance to work with her, but didn't that also mean I wasn't her boss? In other words, couldn't I, without any undertone of creepiness . . . hit on her?

You bet.

I sent flowers to her trailer on The West Wing set with a note that read, "Just my luck—I stop writing the show and you come to work. Knock 'em dead. Aaron Sorkin."

My assistant, the long-suffering Lauren Lohman, called me that night and said, "There's a message on the voice mail at the office I think you're going to like." It was Kristin singing eight bars of "Till There Was You." Then she thanked me for the flowers and told me she was staying at the Beverly Wilshire while she was looking for a place in L.A. I spiked the phone. Then I started bothering Lauren.

> ME: Do you think she wants me to call her?
>
> LAUREN: Yes.
>
> ME: She didn't say in the message that she wanted me to call her.
>
> LAUREN: But she said she was staying at the Beverly Wilshire.
>
> ME: That means she wants me to call her?
>
> LAUREN: Why else would she tell you where she was staying?
>
> ME: What is it with you people that these messages need to be encrypted? Why can't she just say, "Call me sometime" or "Would you like to meet for a drink?" Is she afraid the Russians are gonna intercept it? [Pause] Well?
>
> LAUREN: I stopped listening. Do you want the number of the Beverly Wilshire?
>
> ME: Yes, please.

As she walked toward me on this October night in front of the Beverly Wilshire, I gave her a half wave that said, "Hi. I'm grown man and I don't know how to dress myself."

As she got a little closer, her eyes were all I could see. She has eyes the

color of the water off Bermuda. Her eyes are so diverting that it takes another moment to notice that she has, as Jerry Seinfeld would say, many of
the other qualities prized by the superficial male. (Our first fight would
come when I was schooling her on how Jews invented Broadway—from
the Shubert brothers to Irving Berlin, Rodgers and Hammerstein, Kauf-
man and Hart, Leonard Bernstein, Stephen Sondheim, Hal Prince, Mike
Nichols, Elia Kazan, Arthur Miller and Neil Simon—and I said that if
it weren't for Jews, she'd be working at the Hooters in Tulsa. You want a
reading on just how dumb I am? I meant it as a compliment.)

The date had been under way for about twenty minutes and I hadn't
yet spilled something on myself or said anything stupid—the rough equivalent of being in a boxing ring with Evander Holyfield for twenty minutes
and not being dead yet. My hot streak would come to end when the waiter
came by to tell us the specials, ending with "Anybody have any questions?"

Silence.

"Sir?"

"Uhh, I'm so sorry," I blurted, "I wasn't paying attention. I was—I
can't stop looking at her eyes. I mean, look at her eyes! You see what I'm
talking about, right?" The waiter smiled in agreement, then gave Kristin
the pitiful look reserved for women who are on first dates with complete
schmoes.

After dinner I took her back to her hotel and she invited me in to the
bar to have a drink. I took this as a good sign. At the end of the night she
told me to call her again sometime. So I called her as soon as I got home.

Date number two was at Mr. Chow, a trendy Chinese restaurant
about a block from her hotel. I mention that it's a block from the hotel
because on the way there I got lost. Kris's face isn't something you want in
your head when you're trying to do something hard like driving one block
to a restaurant. The place was jammed and rowdy and great. I made her
laugh a few times. She made me laugh a lot more. She asked me if I
minded that she loved Jesus. I said no and asked her if she minded that I
thought she was crazy for thinking a magical wizard walked the earth two

thousand years ago. And then I did a rewind in my head to see if there was a way I could have said that without insulting her entire family. I didn't wait to get home before I asked her out for a third date.

I took her to a place on Melrose called the Little Door, where they don't like you unless you were born in Europe, so you know it has to be good. We sat down at the bar and either I said something right or I'd picked the right jacket and pants combination because right there at the bar Kristin leaned in and kissed me.

It was so much better than the footbridge and the Yoo-Hoo.

Monday morning my press rep sent me an item in Page Six that said that Kristin and I had been spotted making out at the Little Door, and the blurb went on to suggest that Kris had poor taste in men. I was stunned because it was the first time I'd seen something in the New York Post that might be true. We saw each other steadily until New Year's Eve rolled around. Kristin was singing with the San Francisco Symphony that night and asked if I'd like to come up for it.

New Year's Eve, sold-out house in San Francisco. I'm standing in front of Symphony Hall at about ten minutes before eight when a well-dressed couple step up to me. The man says, "We're big fans of yours." I assume they think I'm somebody else but thank them for the compliment anyway. Then the woman asks, "What's it like seeing your girlfriend perform live?"— which is when I realized that I hadn't. I'd watched tapes of the Kristin *series, I'd seen her in the PBS production of* Candide *and of course* The Music Man, *but I still hadn't seen her perform live. I went inside and sat down in my seat.*

On the first day of the first week of Playwriting 101 we learn what that's called: the Fatal Error. Because by the end of the concert I knew two things that I didn't know two hours earlier: (1) I'd never been in love before, and (2) I was now.

Kris's manager, the hilarious Dannielle Thomas, came to my seat at the end of the third and final encore and took me back to Kristin's dressing room, which was stuffed with dozens of vases of flowers from friends, fam-

ily, agents, and fans. (Somewhere in there were the ones I'd sent.) I saw her and took her to a quieter corner of the room. When I put my hand on her arm, I saw that it was shaking a little. (My hand, not her arm—she was fine.)

I said, "Kristin, that was unbelievable. There's nobody like you. I'm so proud of you."

It came out sounding like this: "Grrrglplelmphfranglerhmphhh . . . God." Pause. "I mean it."

I was in trouble deep now because I needed to make her fall in love with me, and just being me wasn't going to do the trick. Most guys need to show off for the girls they like, and certainly when, like me, they have an ego the size of Butte, Montana. It's not likely I'm going to score the winning touchdown in the Fiesta Bowl, land an F-16 on the deck of the USS Nimitz, *or perform a miracle. But I'm an above-average writer, so my only hope was to be able to write something that would do to her what she'd just done to me.*

I'd made my Broadway playwriting debut at twenty-eight with A Few Good Men, *which was a hit, and I'd followed that six months later with an off-Broadway flop and I hadn't written a new play since. But I had an idea for a new one. The true story of a kind of epic battle that took place between Philo Farnsworth, who invented television, and David Sarnoff, who was the young president of RCA at the time. (Note to the men: if you want to really turn a girl's head, write a play about U.S. patent law in the 1930s.) It took two years to research and write the play, and after a brief, scaled-down workshop production at the La Jolla Playhouse in San Diego, commercial producers were attached for a move to New York. The Broadway production would be capitalized at $4 million. The most expensive pickup line in history.*

Kristin and I have had our ups and downs, and while the ups more than make up for them, the downs have been sad. We'd broken up by the time The Farnsworth Invention *opened on Broadway in the fall of 2007.*

And I have no idea if we'll be together or not on the day this book is published. But for certain I know I'll always love her, I'll always miss her if she's not there, and I'll always be trying to show off for her.

Is it too late for me to take up ski jumping?

Aaron Sorkin
June 11, 2008
Los Angeles

chapter fifteen

MY NEW PHILOSOPHY

It irks the daylights out of me when I see it printed or blogged in a "romantically linked with Hungadunga Hungadunga" sort of way that Aaron dumped me because I went on *The 700 Club*. As if he's really that sanctimonious, and I'm really that . . . dumpable. (I mean, really, what man in his right mind dumps a woman with a singing, weather-predicting hoo hoo? What else am I supposed to do, dispense Gummi Bears?) The notion persists because during an "on-again" period, Aaron was developing his show *Studio 60 on the Sunset Strip* and asked if it would be all right with me if he borrowed certain elements from my life, including my *700 Club* debacle (which I'll get to in a moment) and other events surrounding the release of my second album with Sony Classical. Some time had passed. The welts had settled to a sting. So I said, "Go for it."

Aaron was on fire for this show, which everyone (including him) assumed would be a hit. He'd get up at night and pace and make notes, then lie down next to me again, coiled like a spring, trying not to wake me but fairly vibrating with creative energy as lines and ideas struck him like a tuning fork.

"I spent a lot of time and big chunks of my flesh on *Studio 60*," he says now, and he's raw about it, wound tight the moment it comes up in conversation. If someone calls it *Studio 60 on Sunset Strip*, he stolidly reminds them, "There's a *the* in there. It's *Studio 60 on the Sunset Strip*." That's how much he cared—still cares—about each word down to the smallest article. In any artistic endeavor, it's personal. You put yourself out there in a big way. Some bigger than others.

Studio 60 was a backstage drama about a *Saturday Night Live*–type comedy-sketch show. The protagonist is the show's embattled head writer, Matt Albie, who is still in love with his former girlfriend Harriet Hayes, one of the stars of the show within the show. Harriet is that rarest of mermaids, a devout, dyed-in-the-wool, "gimme that old-time religion" Christian in Hollywood. There's a big difference between "based on" and "inspired by," but Harriet's life does borrow heavily on the details of mine in many of the same big and small ways that the Kristin Yancey character did. There's no Hum Dum Ditty, but Broken Arrow, Oklahoma, is in there. (I guess it has that says-it-all quality without being quite as blatantly South-sploitative as "Marry Your Cousin, Arkansas" or "Squeal Like a Pig, Kentucky.") There's pageant stuff, a baseball-player beau, a scantily clad photo shoot, theatre things, and I don't remember what all.

Harriet is a great character, but Aaron is quick to remind people (and I'm just as quick to agree), she's not me.

Like Harriet, I'm comfortable saying, "I don't know." In fact, I'm keeping a list of "Questions for God When I Meet Him" (a list that gained a few inches after I was on the *700 Club*). I don't recall being pinned with a Junior Deputy Jesus badge that authorizes me to police what others do in this life or the next; Harriet is likewise unwilling to judge. But unlike Harriet, I'm not on the fence about certain old-school fundamentalist beliefs. I do not believe that Jews automatically go to hell or that being gay is a sin. I'm not a strict constructionist where the Bible is concerned. It's like my grandma used to say: "I eat the fish without choking on the bones."

Harriet is far more serious than I am, more of an intellectual, less of a happy-go-plucky, hey-darlin' power shopper.

Once when Aaron and I were bantering back and forth, he made some unanswerable point, and I said, "Honey, I'm so tired of debating. Either accept Jesus Christ as your personal savior, make me laugh, or get the f#%k out."

It feels like a soaring personal victory to crack up someone as smart and funny as Aaron Sorkin, and that cracked him up big-time, probably because it's pretty rare for me to drop an F-bomb. (I keep it on reserve to maximize effect.)

In the show, one of Harriet's castmates needles her about praying before the show, and she says, "You know what, Rook? When you start making a contribution to this show, you can talk to me any way you want, but you had two lines tonight, and you stepped on one of 'em, so until you either accept Jesus Christ as your personal savior or make somebody laugh, why don't you talk to somebody else?"

Obviously, the line had to be work-safe and Sanitized for Your Protection, but the flippant spirit of what I said got buried in scathing . . . osity . . . ness. I don't do much scathing. Not a big scather. So that line pretty well illustrates the Kristin-to-Harriet correlation. As righteously tight-lipped as she needs to be for dramatic effect, she's grown staunch and a bit angry after years of being constantly challenged about her beliefs while she is consistently respectful of the beliefs of others. Good scripts are all about conflict, and Harriet's got the spirit and vocabulary for effective smack-down. I, on the other hand, enjoy a good fight about as much as I enjoy a good intestinal parasite. Jesus told us to extend our peace to others, and if they don't accept it, to keep that peace within ourselves. I try to do that.

Sarah Paulson, the actress cast in the role, is a knockout and terrifically talented, but Harriet was supposed to be a big Broadway musical star with a concert and recording career, and Sarah doesn't really sing. (I love that she knows this about herself and celebrates her other gifts, which are formidable and include the uncanny ability to whinny like a dolphin.) Her wit is dry and sly, while mine is *Animal Crackers* and sight gags.

Aaron and his producing partner, Tommy Schlamme, originally thought about casting me in the role of Harriet, but understandably they had concerns about how that was going to work personally, professionally, and creatively. Meanwhile, I wasn't crazy about the idea of being the boss's girlfriend. That doesn't even play well on a sitcom. I said I'd have to think about it. A week or so later, we were lying in bed reading, and Aaron said, "Just to let you know—we've moved on."

I looked up from the script I was studying. "What?"

"Since you rejected the idea of playing Harriet. We moved on."

"I didn't reject it, Aaron. You guys never made me an actual offer."

"Kris, there's nobody I'd rather have in that role. You'd be funny and terrific, and I would love spending long days and nights in the trenches with you, but it needed a conversation before we could offer—"

"I was supposed to come in and sell myself to you and Tommy?"

"I didn't say that."

"Aaron, I'm not going to *audition* to play *myself* on TV."

"I wasn't asking you to audition *or* to play yourself! I just wanted to talk about how this was going to work."

"Well, either way, it's good that you've moved on."

"Well . . . we did," he said, his nose back in some obnoxiously thick book.

"Good." I returned to my script. "Keep on movin', pal."

"What?"

"Nothing."

"You said something."

"No, I didn't."

"Yes, I believe you did."

Cue the word-tornado.

We broke up again a short time later, but not over that. It's just this dance we do. Aaron did what he always does when I break up with him: he got me back. And I did what I always do when he gets me back: I broke up with him again. Once I broke up with him twice in less than twenty-four hours. Seriously. I broke up with him because I thought he lied to me about something, but then I discovered I was mistaken, so I called him to deactivate the breakup and apologize for wrongly accusing him. But he wasn't as gracious about it as I thought he should be, so I stewed on that for a while, called him back, and said we were through.

(Oh, shut up. Ya think I don't know?)

We're like the *Green Eggs and Ham* of breakers-up: in a box. With a fox. On a train. In the rain. Down at Mel's. On our cells. Over a martini. In a Lamborghini. But never once did *The 700 Club* have beans to do with it. The real issues of our relationship are private. He didn't write about them on that show, and I'm not writing about them here. Suffice it to say that Aaron and I don't struggle over TV; we have far more important things to be petty and vicious about. On *Studio 60*, however, the Matt character does dump the Harriet character, directly or indirectly, because he finds her appearance on a right-wing Christian television show unconscionable.

"It was three minutes," Aaron said in dismay. "Three minutes out of twenty-two hours of television."

But because we live in Sound Bite Nation, celebrity gossip scroungers drew their own conclusions, and the story stuck to the soles of our shoes like a wad of Super Bubble.

We were "off-again" by the time the first episode of *Studio 60* was aired, which made me horribly sad because it left him alone as the show foundered and sank, and while most ill-fated shows are allowed to slip quietly beneath the surface—well, this was the great Aaron Sorkin. It's like Jesus said in the Gospel of Luke, "From the one to whom much has been given, much more will be required." *Studio 60* wasn't initially a flop, but Aaron was supposed to deliver another *West Wing*. When that didn't happen, the *not!* vortex opened up, and bloggers swarmed like bandicoots. As detractors descended, the fun factor evaporated, and the lifeblood drained from the creative heart of the show. *Studio 60* was canceled after a single season, and Aaron took a horse-whipping. It broke my heart that I wasn't there to hold his hand, the way he'd held mine when I took my horse-whipping over *The 700 Club*.

∽

My first album for Sony Classical was *Let Yourself Go,* a collection of Broadway show tunes with the Coffee Club Orchestra. Best band in town, for my money, honey. Peter Gelb was running the record label at the time, and producer Paul Cremo brought me in and hooked up the six-record deal. (I called them the disciples of music, St. Peter and St. Paul.) Rob Fisher, whom I knew from City Center Encores! was brought in to conduct because he knows my voice so well. We wanted some original material that stayed in that 1930s vibe, so Dick Scanlan and Jeanine Tesori wrote "The Girl in 14G", which riffs on a real-life experience from my first New York apartment. A guy who played cello lived directly below me, and a warbling soprano was directly above. When we all practiced, we'd bang on the ceiling or floor, trying to get the others to shut up. "I'll Tell the Man in the Street" was my homage to Barbra Streisand. Of course, I had to do "My Funny Valentine" for Ms. Birdwell. Kurt Weill's wordy "I'm a Stranger Here Myself" brought a tasty little acting challenge. Jason Alexander, whom I knew from when he and Marc Kudisch did *Bye Bye Birdie*, joined me on "Hangin' Around with You." The last song we recorded was Duke Ellington's "On a Turquoise Cloud." Incredibly hard, long, *high*, and requires a squinch more finesse than I was able to summon at the end of a grueling four-day recording blitz. So it's not perfect. But it's close. The whole project was a joy from start to finish.

When it came time to do the second album, I wanted to draw from the music that started me singing. Sandi Patty, Amy Grant, a few traditional spiritual songs, and some all-purpose feel-good numbers that weren't Christian or "inspirational" per se but expressed my goodwill toward the weary world in an inclusive, Miss Congeniality, I'd-like-to-buy-the-world-a-Coke sort of way. The furthest thing from my mind was to stir up any sort of controversy. Saints Peter and Paul were not entirely on board with this idea, but I felt strongly about responding to the strife and war in the world with this gesture of peace and hope.

The CD was a joy to plan and record; every song was filled with love, including the funny little bonus track, "Taylor, the Latte Boy." I dedicated the first song, "It Will Be Me," to my dear pals Denny Downs and Erin Dilly. "There Will Never Be Another" is my shout-out to Amy Grant, who inspired me so. "Upon This Rock" is a kick-butt, uplifting Gaither number. "Poor, Wayfaring Stranger" took me all the way back to my grandma's lap. And "Abide in Me" eloquently states what faith—for me—is all about: *If you abide in me, then I'll abide in you, my words in your heart. Child, believe that when you seek my face and make me your first love, then all the rest will be taken care of.*

I thought I'd seen the worst of what any promotional junket could throw at me when I was doing the rounds promoting my TV show. I found myself on *Politically Incorrect* with Bill Maher, mired in a series of tortured topics: Charlton Heston–caliber gun control, the use of *Vogue* fashion models to illustrate a book of Bible stories, and whether Andrea Yates—the tragically mentally ill mother who drowned her children—should be put to death. I was the token Christian on the panel. The other guests were a model, a Texas senator, and a stand-up comic who was about as hilarious as that *Dr. G* episode about inexplicable itching. Thinking back on it, I'm reminded of a great line Aaron later gave to Christine Lahti in *Studio 60:* "It's like seasickness. You think you're going to die. Everyone else just thinks it's funny."

The promotional junket for the CD included all the usual suspects—Letterman, Leno, the daytime talkers. That's all good. But the PR genius's pièce de résistance was booking me to appear on *The 700 Club.* I wasn't familiar with the show (no handheld coroner-cam), but I was told that these were my people: folks who love music and love the Lord.

"Kris, don't do it," Aaron told me. "That is a bad idea."

"Don't be silly." I waved him off. "It's a nice Christian show. They won't be mean."

"No, but—have you ever seen *The 700 Club?*"

"No," I said. "Have you?"

"No."

"Well, then you're hardly qualified to tell me what to think about it."

"Kris, you have no idea who you're getting in bed with there."

Oh, yeah? That's what YOU think.

"Excuse me, Mr. Sorkin, I can handle my own media, thank you."

Why are you telling ME?

"You know very well I'm not part of that hard-line hate stuff."

No!

"I refuse to hide my faith under a bushel. I am a Christian. I'm proud to be a Christian. But I'm not allowed to say that, am I? No, I'm supposed to be politically correct and smile and agree because Jews invented theatre and Christians invented Hooters."

I can't stand it!

"I'm sick of people who've never been to church telling me that church is full of hypocrites, and people who've never read the Bible telling me that it's baloney."

Yes, I covered all the philosophical bases, plus one of my very own:

"I did this project purely with the loving spirit of Jesus in my heart, and anybody who doesn't like it can suck it!"

And off I went to . . . Lynchburg?

Yeah. That's where the show is taped. I saw the sign on my way from the airport—WELCOME TO LYNCHBURG!—and you'd think that would have been my first clue. But no. The interview was brief and uneventful. Pat Robertson wasn't even there. I was with the former–Miss America chick. I sang "Abide in Me," talked up my album, pluggy-plug-plug, gave Miss America a Hollywood kiss, huggy-hug-hug, everybody happy, home I went.

The next day, a howl went up, from the East Village to San Francisco.

Even the most moderate members of the gay community were astonished to see me perched on the Pat Robertson Couch of Homo-Hate. It didn't matter that Pat Robertson wasn't there. Or that I used this opportunity to urge the Christian community to be more open-minded, loving, and inclusive. The blogosphere exploded with rants about what a skinny, rotten, hateful hating hater I was.

Meanwhile, I'd been booked to join the Women of Faith tour for a series of concerts, and all nine of the events in which I was included were sold-out. I'd already done the first concert, and it went fantastically well. But when a few of my gay fans tried to stick up for me, pointing out how obviously not homophobic I am, folks in some conservative Christian circles caught wind of it and decided that I was a liberal, gay-loving whore of Babylon and called for me to be fired.

Lynch. Burg.

"All Christians are gay-haters," shrilled the überhomos. "Anyone who believes in freedom should boycott Kristin Chenoweth's albums, shows, and concert performances!"

"All gays are going to hell," shrilled the fundies. "Anyone who believes in Jesus should boycott Kristin Chenoweth's albums, shows, and concert performances!"

Somewhere in the middle, where the vast but less vocal majority of both Christians and gays reside—a tiny town I like to call *reality*—I struggled to make nice with everybody while refusing to say anything I didn't mean. So apparently, though it's famously impossible to *please* all of the people all of the time, it is quite possible to simultaneously piss everyone off.

"Ah, Kris," Aaron said when he found me sobbing over it. "If you would have listened to . . . c'mere."

He stopped himself just short of "I told you so" and pulled me into the place I most needed to be, with my arms around his middle inside his suit jacket, his chin touching the crown of my head. From the moment Aaron saw that I was about to take a beating from both sides, he did nothing but embrace and support me. He's had plenty of experience corralling the media centipedes, and he gave me sound advice on how to move forward. I heard him barking on the phone later. Didn't catch exactly what he said. Just heard him say my name and then a bunch of words that ended with "and anybody who doesn't like it can suck it!"

Michael Musto, a columnist for *Out*, invited me to talk about all this, probably thinking I'd take the opportunity to apologize, but I told him, "I'm not going to spend my life apologizing to the gay community or anyone else for what I do. There's always someone pissed off. Would I do the show again now that I know what it's about? Probably not, but that's up to me. Anyone who knows me knows I don't agree with all that antigay stuff. They could just as easily say it's a sin to be short. Well, I guess it is in the Miss Oklahoma pageant—but you know what I mean."

I was on location shooting the movie *RV* with Robin Williams, Cheryl Hines, and Jeff Daniels when the head of Women of Faith came to see me on the set.

"You need to know that my best friend is gay," I told her. "And in a few months I'm going to play a gay woman in a major-release movie. I'm not going to pretend to be something I'm not. I'm sorry if that's a problem for you."

It was a problem for her. I thought about suggesting more fiber in her diet, but the handwriting was on the wall.

I wasn't surprised when they asked me to quietly withdraw from the concert series. That would make it easy for everyone. They'd save face; I'd avoid any more adverse publicity. Dannielle and I discussed it for hours as the series organizers pressured me to quit. My fan club had gotten buses together. People who believed in me were counting on me to be there. But what about other people? Now that such a big deal was being made of all this, I didn't know how Christian audiences were going to respond to me. At the end of the day, after weighing all the apples and oranges—professional, personal, financial, and spiritual—I decided I'd rather stand up and get booed off the stage than sit down and backpedal my beliefs. I'd never watered down my message of faith for Hollywood, and I wasn't going to water down my message of acceptance for these folks now. It's no picnic to be where you're not wanted, but I was determined to fulfill my contract, sing my heart out, and do a great job for them.

"Kristin will not quit," Dannielle told organizers. "If you want her out, you'll have to fire her."

They fired me.

A bunch more blather ensued with CNN and all the gang covering the whole thing. I got a heartbreaking letter from a woman who'd come to see me at my first and only Women of Faith concert: "I wanted to rededicate my life to Christ after that night, but I've changed my mind. This has reminded me why I hate church people."

It was the single saddest moment in my professional life.

"I don't understand," I cried on Aaron's shoulder. "It was so—so hearts and flowers—the little personal note about each song—the happy little extra track. How the heck does anybody read something malicious into Taylor the freaking Latte Boy?"

There was really nothing I could do but wait for time to distance me from the stench. When I tried to think what possible good God could draw from this experience, all I could come up with is that it really required me to ask myself, "What am I willing to fight for?"

Not long ago, I sat in the corner of the sink-into-it sectional on Aaron's lanai overlooking L.A., listening to him talk about *Studio 60* with a writer friend. She chalked the show's failure up to casting and circumstances, but Aaron wouldn't have it. He's never allowed one stripe of the horse-whipping to fall anywhere but on his own back, and I admire him a lot for that. He's a stand-up guy.

"Look, I screwed up *Studio 60* nine ways from Sunday," he told her. "I made storytelling mistakes. I wrote angry. And anger is good fuel for the tank when you're writing, but not over the course of twenty-two episodes."

It occurred to me that the same is true of life in general. At times you have to get your Harriet up, but it's corrosive to be constantly embattled. Life requires peace. Peace requires balance. And balance requires a certain amount of get-over-yourself.

No more struggle, no more strife, with my faith I see the light. I am free in the Spirit. Yes, I'm only here for God.

Every time I go to church with Denny, I can't help but notice how nicely our singing voices blend. I usually go to a grand old United Methodist church with soaring architecture and sturdy rituals, but Denny's discovered this new place, and the integrated message appeals to every part of my soul. I'm not sure if the service is nondenominational or all-denominational, but I feel the same spirit that inhabits the more traditional churches I've attended throughout my life—the same spirit that surrounds me during my strongest moments onstage and quietest moments of contemplation.

One aspect of *The 700 Club* thing that tore me up for a long time was the idea that I'd inadvertently done something to embarrass or hurt Denny. He didn't tell me not to go on the show and never said a word about it after. I never apologized about it to anyone, but standing beside Denny in church today, I make my elbow touch his arm when we speak the prayer:

"For those we have harmed, knowingly or unknowingly, we are truly sorry. Forgive us and set us free."

Religion and politics. Dicey territory. I try to steer clear. I don't beef with people like Mel Gibson. I don't need to agree with his religion to like his movies. Not my pig, not my farm, as Grandpa used to say. And I don't need Gibson or Tom Cruise or the Women of Faith to agree with me.

When Jerry Zaks (who calls me his "shiksa goddess") directed me in *Stairway to Paradise* in the City Center Encores! series, he and I were sitting backstage, shooting the bull one day. Jerry stuck a cigar in the side of his mouth and said, "So, kid, tell me about that Rapture."

"Well, it's when Jesus comes and takes all his followers up into Heaven."

"You mean, we'll be sitting here and you'll just disappear?"

"That's what I believe."

"What's left after you disappear?"

"I don't know. A pile of clothes, I guess."

He pondered that a moment. "Will your panties still be here?"

"Yes, Jerry," I said with the loving spirit of Jesus in my heart. "My panties will still be here. And you may have them."

I'm looking forward to Heaven, where I suspect Mel Gibson and Marc Kudisch's dad will sit around with me, Molière, Emily Dickinson, and Grandma Chenoweth, sharing a good laugh about that. All these years on earth, I've lived by the motto "Drink more coffee and sleep when you're dead," so I'll be ready to take a nice long nap as soon as I get there, but before I do that, there are a few things I really need to know . . .

Questions for God When I Meet Him

- Who killed JonBenét? And does she pretty much own the pageant circuit up here?
- Did Marilyn kill herself or was it a Kennedy?
- Did Lee Harvey Oswald really act alone?
- Seriously . . . was it the cookies?
- Why is forgiveness so dang hard?
- Why is slapstick so dang funny?
- *Who* is the sadistic genius behind cellulite? Lord, please tell me you did not have anything to do with that.
- Does restless legs syndrome actually exist? And is there something about it that compels the person to sit in the front row?
- How on earth (or elsewhere) do you keep track of everyone?
- Why would someone go to all the trouble it takes to be a serial killer? Is there always some kind of *Sweeney Todd* backstory?
- Where are the mates to most of my socks?
- Why did Mom have to battle cancer twice? Seriously. Once was more than enough.
- Does sugar cause cancer? And if not, *what does*?
- Does sugar cure cancer? And if not, *what does*?
- Why do so many people find homosexuality scarier than war?
- What if you made it so that hate would cause hemorrhoids? Just an idea.
- Do you have Leonard Bernstein's cell number? I need to talk to him right away. Also, Puccini. And Ethel Merman.
- And one more thing, Heavenly Father. Are you proud of me?

chapter sixteen

THE LORD NEVER GIVES US MORE THAN WE CAN BARE

"**I** know you're going to say no," Dannielle said when *FHM* came calling in 2006, "but we should talk about it."

I'd been asked to bare all for *Playboy* and turned them down flat (having evolved past the simple criterion of "What would a bunny do?"), but *For Him Magazine* wasn't asking me to bare all. Just bare . . . most. And you have to understand that actors are used to getting stripped naked by costumers and crew. There's not a lot of room for modesty when two dressers are cinching you into a corset and a soundman is spelunking up your skirt to artificially inseminate you with your microphone pack. You get used to the idea that your body is the canvas on which another artist works her craft.

I weighed the risks and benefits of the *FHM* thing, but in the wake of the whole "As I Am" rodeo of danged-if-you-do-danged-if-you-don't, I wasn't in the mood to kowtow to anyone's idea of who I was supposed to be.

It fits, I decided.

But for some reason . . . nothing else fit. Helping me prep my wardrobe for a concert at Walt Disney Hall, Denny and Kay, the dresser, tugged at an obstinate zipper. They finally managed to wrench it all the way up, but the Betsey Johnson dress I'd worn just a month or two earlier now fit me like a latex glove fits a football.

Denny looked at me dolefully. "You're Fatty McFatterson."

I tugged at the muffin-puffed bodice. "I guess I'm retaining a little water."

"Like Hoover Dam retains a little water?"

"I was looking at a *West Wing* forum last night," said Kay. "People were saying you're preggers."

"*What?* Oh, my gosh. I can't be fat right now. This is not a good time for fat."

I don't often step on the scale, but it was time for a reality check.

"You're up nine pounds," said Kay. "Hard to distribute on a four-foot-eleven-inch frame. And every little dimple is going to show in that *FHM* thing you've got coming up."

"Thanks, Kay, for that important message from our sponsors."

"*FMH?*" Denny coughed. "You're kidding."

"They said I could wear my own bikinis. You've seen my bikinis, Denny. They don't give up much. I'm not Miss Noodle. I'm a woman."

"With a nice rack," Denny nodded.

"I have nothing to prove to anyone."

"But if you did want to prove that you're a woman with a nice rack, this would do it."

"Yes, it would. And I won't be displaying anything you don't see sashaying down the catwalk in the Miss USA pageant. What's the difference?" I heard myself protesting too much, but felt compelled to add, "I told them no nipples. Strictly Barbie breasts."

"What did your mom and dad say about it?"

"My parents love me unconditionally . . . so there's no reason for them to know."

"Kristi, they're going to know sooner or later."

"I'll take the second one."

"Maybe the Ambien is making you fat," said Kay. "I've hear it causes night eating."

This made sense in conjunction with the fact that I'd recently awakened with a Pop-Tart in one hand and a chicken leg in the other. I thought maybe Denny was playing a joke on me. But a few days later, he was out of town, and I opened my eyes to find several of those little red Hot Tamales candies stuck to my leg.

I asked my mom, "Have you heard of people night-eating on Ambien?"

"Oh, it's possible," she said. "I heard someone bought a car."

"Oh, no . . ."

A chasm of crap yawned on each side of me. Take the Ambien and be a well-rested fat girl. Or skip the Ambien and be a skinny insomniac. Tipping the scales as it were, was the *FHM* photo shoot. But I certainly wasn't going to tell my mom about that. Better to break it to my parents as a fait accompli, I figured. A done deal. A fleeing horse after which there is no point closing the barn door.

First things first. I had to whittle down to bikini weight in time for the shoot. The best body I'd seen on camera in quite some time was Jessica Simpson's in the movie *The Dukes of Hazzard*. Dannielle and I did some homework and came up with the name of her trainer: Mike Alexander. A personal trainer has to be the right combination of technical expertise (that's the trainer) and motivation (that's the personal).

Mike's standard greeting is "Who wants to get hotter than they are?"

He begins and ends his fitness philosophy with the idea that every woman has reason to celebrate her body exactly as it is because if you don't love this body, what could possibly motivate you to invest the time and energy it takes to make it stronger? Yes, we do our share of "curls for the girls" and "flies for the thighs"; self-improvement is always possible, but it has to spring from an appreciation for what's already there. Maybe I'm not as tall as most women, but there's a lot goin' on with what I got. My skin's not perfect, and neither is my hair, but I have a simple choice when I look at myself in the mirror each morning: be happy. Or not. Happiness requires less raw cookie dough.

I'm not going to sit here and make any pretenses about it. Those *FHM* pictures are pure, all-American, tape-it-to-the-bottom-of-the-top-bunk, razzleberry-swirl cheesecake. The accompanying Q&A asked loaded questions to which I gave coquettish answers. The photo shoot was a lot of fun, and I felt the finished product successfully accomplished the Gypsy Rose Lee thing—leave 'em wanting more. I was proud of the results of the hard work I'd put into it, but I waited to tell Mom and Dad until just before the photos were published.

Kaboom.

"I'll never be able to go to church or 7-Eleven again," Mom mourned.

Dad was . . . unhappy. Let's just draw the curtain there because I have to give them credit; a year later, I did a completely nude photo shoot for *Allure* magazine, and they were completely cool about it.

"These are more tasteful," said Mom. "With the nature and everything."

The pictures were softly focused and posed to shield my most private privates. (But I can't really recommend the whole concept of tree bark as underwear.) The text that went with the photos was about body image, how women struggle with it no matter how big or small or short or tall they are. A good message.

"Howard Stern says you're definitely the hotter witch," Dannielle told me after the photos came out. "He wants you on the show."

That was not hard to turn down. Howard Stern and I don't fit. But I wish him all the blessings in the world.

"So Miss High-and-Mighty is too good for the show," Howard Stern railed after I turned him down. "I just want to know how you do this Christian-music CD and then you do the T-and-A thing in nude photographs?"

It's funny—the fundamentalist Christians said the same thing. And so did Joy Behar one morning on *The View*. Who would have thought that just by showing a little skin, I could bring together such disparate groups, uniting them in a common cause. See, I really am promoting world peace. One pink bikini at a time.

Lord, make me an instrument of Thy peace.

I say it daily in my heart. I sing in concert, in the shower, and wherever else the spirit moves me. At first blush, it sounds like a rather pageantastic ambition, and sometimes it's hardest to extend that peace to those closest to me, those I've hurt and been hurt by, knowingly and unknowingly, including my parents and Denny and Mr. Hello I Must Be Going.

But there's the beauty of life beyond the bubble. It's possible for someone to see your wicked bits and still love you.

∞

curtain call

New York, New York
May 2008

It's a beautiful day on the Upper West Side, and my cooter is predicting continued spring sunshine with a 10 percent chance of late-evening precipitation.

One of the loveliest things about living in Manhattan is seeing three people I know on every block. Sometimes it takes us a moment to remember which show we did together, but then it's hugs and remembrances. Theatre is like a barbershop that way, I guess. Full of unfinished conversations. Grandpa used to sweep the customer's shoulders with a wooden-handled brush, whisk away the barber smock and say, "To be continued." Show people part and come together again with that same ease.

Every once in a while, I'll see someone and shriek her name in the middle of the street, and it's not actually her. That can be embarrassing. Worse yet is when I see someone I don't feel like talking to and I dodge into a doorway. I always feel horrible about it later and obsess over whether the person saw me give him or her the slip. (Even worse is when the *other* person dodges into a doorway.)

I see a friend and her teenage daughter peering into a shop window, and I call to them.

"Joy! Isabelle!"

They don't dodge. Hugs all around.

"Come to Starbucks," says Isabelle. "Allison's waiting for us. She's going to have a spaz attack when she sees you."

As we walk up the street, Joy can't resist the mandatory love-life pulse check.

"What's up with the battling sunfish? Is Chenorkin on-again or off-again?"

"Off-again," I tell her. "He's being a putz."

She sighs something about wanting to slap the both of us upside our heads.

"How's Griz?" I ask, hoping to change the subject.

"He's taken up home winemaking. We're going to France this fall for our twenty-fifth anniversary, and it seemed like a good idea to start drinking now."

"Congratulations." I squeeze her hand. "Twenty-five years with the same person. I want to know what that feels like."

"I know you do, sweetie," says Joy. "But I'll give you my standard line: it's not possible to be married to the same person for twenty-five years because it is not possible to *be* the same person for twenty-five years. My old man and I are lucky. We keep falling in love with each other's inner stranger."

"But how is that done?"

"We make each other laugh. That's essential. We work well in the sack. And we're both willing to do what it takes to be married. We're willing to compromise. Marriage as an institution doesn't fare well in the hands of perfectionists. Life's too short."

"So the key to longevity is a mutual willingness to lower your standards?"

"Exactly!" Joy holds out her hand. "Five cents, please."

When we arrive at Starbucks, Isabelle pulls the door open and spots her friend, and I can see the history between them as they rush to hug each other. Allison Rihn, it turns out, is one of the zillion aspiring actors in New York, and she does have a little bit of a spaz attack when she sees me, but she handles it like a pro. She's six feet tall, willowy, and blonde. Her face is wonderfully quirky. She's different. She'll have to look a little harder to find what fits, but she'll work. When we come to the front of the line, I order my soy chai latte and hand over a Starbucks card personalized for me by a friend. The barista looks at it and laughs.

"Hey, 'Taylor, the Latte Boy.' That's a song about Starbucks," he explains.

"Yes, I think I heard that." I tuck a few bucks in the tip jar, enjoying the fresh giggles from Allison and Isabelle.

"Allison, you should watch for Susan Stroman auditions," I tell her as we settle in at our table. "She's always casting your look. And the dancers love her. She's so inspiring, you'll want to follow her off the edge of a cliff. I mean, if Susan says, 'Dance,' it wouldn't matter if you had no feet. You'd get up and dance on the bloody stumps."

Allison finds this statement not one bit over-the-top, so I know she's going to fit in nicely here. Rummaging her purse for a pen and paper, she judiciously jots down Susan's name, eager to learn, hungry to grow as the conversation dwells and circles around all things theatrical. I love engaging in energized conversation with the new blood on Broadway. I want to take them by the hand and lead them through the turnstiles, the way I was adopted by my *Animal Crackers* cohorts and so many others. Our lattes last through a quick coverage of the basics:

Cool Aunt Kristin's Advice for Young Actors

- It's been said a thousand times, and it's true: if there's anything else you could be happy doing, you should do it.
- Run with the big dogs or stay on the porch with the puppies, but

let your ambition be about who you want to be, not what you want to get.

• Awards are on the outside. Rewards are on the inside. That means rewards don't have to be dusted.

• Do unto others as you would have them do unto you.

• Never, *never* forget the fun factor.

"Good advice for theatre and life," Joy concurs.

As Allison and Isabelle depart for an afternoon of shopping, I ponder that fun factor.

"Joy, let me ask you . . . *hypothetically* . . . if a woman in her late thirties is being pursued by a guy is in his mid twenties—"

"I'd better hypothetically hear every gory detail."

"He's smart. *So* cute. Kind of like a young Manfred Mann. If Manfred Mann was funny. And had a gym membership."

"Well, speaking in the abstract, a smart, funny forty-five-year-old man is hot, while a smart, funny twenty-five-year-old man is just getting warmed up. But for the purposes of practical application . . ." Joy considers it for a moment, then shrugs. "*Eph'phatha.*"

"What?"

"It's Aramaic. Means 'be open.' In the Bible, Jesus put mud in a deaf man's ear and said, '*Eph'phatha*' and the guy was healed."

"*Eph'phatha.* I like it." The word fits nicely between my tongue and hard palate. "I asked him to be my date for the Tony's."

"Mr. Hypothetical?"

"No, Joy, I meant Jesus. He's wearing Armani and Birkenstocks."

"Funny girl." She dips a finger in Isabelle's cup, and flicks an ice cube at me.

"Am I crazy?"

"Yes, but I love that about you." She raises her latte in a toast. "Here's mud in your ear."

After a warm hug, we part ways, and I head up the street toward home, hoofing it instead of hailing a cab. I need to soak in all the

Manhattan I can before I leave for L.A., where I'll spend the summer living on the same coast as Mr. Writer and a host of hypotheticals.

In the first season of *Pushing Daisies*, Chad Gomez Creasey and Dara Resnik Creasey wrote a wonderful episode entitled "Bitches." (The dog kind!) Olive Snook and Ned the Pie Maker have shared a kiss that means everything to her and confusion to him, so he says something mean and breaks her heart. As they close down the Pie Hole for the night, Ned is stiff, but Olive is done struggling with it and simply says, "See you tomorrow."

"Olive?" says Ned.

"I'm still here."

"I'm sorry I've been avoiding you. And I'm sorry I said our saliva wasn't compatible."

"I'm a big girl," says Olive. "I'll be okay."

It felt good to speak those words. *I'm a big girl. I'll be okay.* With each take, I felt it becoming more and more true. Before Olive leaves, she tells Ned something she could have just as well been telling me: "I hope you two make it work. I really do. And if you can't make it work, I hope it doesn't take forever to figure that out. I just want you to be happy."

She squeezes Ned's hand as she walks out the door, and the narrator says something about the different forms love can take, each one precious in its own way.

I want to love somebody now. Lippa's lyrics drift down the back of my mind. *Is it you? Is it me?*

The song ends in a tantalizing nonresolve, poised on the dominant chord instead of coming to rest on the obvious tonic, the musical equivalent of *to be continued*, the thrilling and terrifying act of asking a question. Maybe the answer is in L.A., maybe not, but whatever happens next, I'll be open to the love and happiness God wants for each of us.

Life's too short. I'm not.

why i oughta . . .

(BONUS UPDATE)

Los Angeles, Summer 2009

A year later, things were not panning out quite the way I'd expected.

I sat on the curb outside the foreclosed house, duffle bag by my side, contemplating the vagaries of life and showbiz.

"What happened?" asked the man sitting beside me.

"I hitched my wagon to the wrong star," I sighed, helping myself to a plastic cup from my box of wine. I laid out the whole sordid chain of events, and he listened sympathetically, smiling in all the right places with his wide, boyish smile.

"It's not too late for you," he told me.

I looked up into his eyes, trying to feel a surge of hope, trying to balance everything that had gone wrong with all the good I know is in the world.

"You're an amazing singer," he said gently. "We'll get you sobered up . . . buy you some underwear . . ."

That line slays me.

There was a time when writing like that made it very hard to stay in the moment, in the scene, keeping a straight face, but I've been blessed with such great scripts in the past few years—from *Running with Scissors* to *Pushing Daisies*—I've learned to give myself over to those moments. Writing like that takes you for a ride, whether you're speaking the lines or listening to them and every episode of *Glee* is a-fizz with it. The talented cast is capable of delivering serious song and dance action along with the story. As a guest star on the show, I was showered with love and got to sing one of my favorite old bonbons from *Cabaret* ("Maybe This Time," not the "tweedly-deet-dee-dee" ditty.) Matthew Morrison and I did a power ballad in a bowling alley and I went cowgirl for a big production number with the cast.

So. Much. Fun.

I was cast as April, a down on her luck diva, who returns to the scene of her former glory—high school glee club—bedraggled and boozy, but still dreaming big Broadway dreams. It was easy to connect with her shop-worn chutzpah; things hadn't gone super-smoothly for me over the preceding year.

Rewinding for the short version:

That bright and beautiful first season of *Pushing Daisies* didn't generate huge ratings, but the people who loved it—viewers and critics— really *really* loved it. The show had a great buzz going and received an astonishing twelve Emmy nominations, including Lee Pace for Outstanding Lead Actor, Bryan Fuller for his wildly brilliant writing, Barry Sonnenfeld for his insightful *Who thinks like that?* direction, a raft of technical nods for the eye-popping spectacle and transcendent music—and then there was little ol' me, nominated for Outstanding Supporting Actress.

I believe the term we're searching for here is, "*TAWANDA!*" Only because I'm not totally comfortable saying "Hells-to-the-YEAH!"

Jean Smart whooped me on the Emmy, but I was fine with that. I was genuinely surprised to be nominated at all, and losing to someone as fabulous as Jean Smart doesn't sting so bad. All that really mattered was that the show got picked up for a second season. The network ordered thirteen eps, and we all exhaled for the first time in months.

But it was one of those natural wonders that just isn't meant to last. Like those amazing lightning storms that roll across the plains in Oklahoma. Or the first rush of feeling when you're smitten stupid in love. Enjoy it while it lasts, sweet things, because life and work roll on like a river. Unstoppable.

A few episodes into its second season, *Pushing Daisies* was canceled. We knew in our hearts it was coming, but it was heartbreaking nonetheless. Every member of the cast and crew loved and believed in this extraordinary work of art. We loved and believed in each other. It was a devastating gut-check for all concerned.

I was up to my false eyelashes in concert performances and movie projects, but the loss of this work—this family—opened up a sucking black hole of sadness, and I tumbled in headfirst.

The winter was a mixed bag.

The suicidal hooker movie I'd dug deep for was shown at the Newport Beach International Film Festival. People loved it, and Jeremy Sisto won Best Actor. The film didn't get the Full Monty distribution deal we'd hoped for, but just when it seemed like it was going to slide over to Netflix in less time than it takes to make the popcorn, it was picked up by a few more festivals and achieved a limited but respectable release. I was cast as a brilliant but psychotic attorney in a David E. Kelly show called *Legally Mad* and was stunned—along with the rest of the world—when the pilot wasn't picked up. As the economy went south (and not in a good way), belts were tightened all around the industry from craft services to city symphonies. I'd been hired to do Samira in *The Ghosts of Versailles* at the Metropolitan Opera, but the production was canceled due to budget concerns. Frugal was the new black.

All I could do was keep working and hold fast to my friends. Fireball Dannielle Thomas brooked no BS and kept me in extensions. My assistant Marcy wrangled everything I just couldn't wrap my head around. Dear Erin Dilly was that Voice on the Phone when I needed her to be. Denny was madly in love with a wonderful man, but still made time to keep tabs on me, and it was good to be reminded that mad love still exists.

My own love life was on hiatus.

With early spring came new hope. I decided I kinda liked being a single girl. My little book came out in hardcover, and people came out—rain or shine—in New York, Oklahoma, and everywhere else I went on the book tour. I spent the summer in Canada shooting a movie, and in July, the Emmy nominations were announced. *Pushing Daisies* was nominated in five categories, including Best Supporting Actress.

I was surprised the first time. The second time, I was flabbergasted. Flat out flabber-drop-jaw-gasted. The show had been canceled. All thirteen episodes of the season had been aired, but the last three had been tossed out without advertising in late spring like that leftover Easter candy you see piled in the bargain cart three weeks into May. Obviously, I had zero chance of actually winning—being an expired marshmallow PEEP next to four fresh tomatoes—but it was a thrill to be nominated. Seriously. It *was*. Embrace the cliché. I was terrifically thrilled, and not knowing if I'd ever make it to the Emmys again, I was determined to enjoy myself.

For starters, Erin Dilly was my date, ensuring there'd be plenty of giggles and zero drama. We were planning to cruise the after parties and storm that gift lounge like the Valkyrie. Instead of wearing some overblown big name parade float of a gown on the red carpet, I decided to go with an adorable short cocktail dress by Lebanese designer Zuhair Murad. My hair would be pulled back in a simple, sleek ponytail. No fuss, no muss. The dress was encrusted with little clear crystals which provided plenty of shine, so instead of belaboring myself with borrowed jewelry, I'd wear my favorite little Tiffany earrings and a trusty pair of Manolo Blahniks—perfect for sprinting between press pods and avoiding anyone we don't like.

This was all about the fun factor.

The night before the Emmys, there's a big party where everyone gets together to go over the logistics, schmooze, air kiss, photo op, all that. I'd come down with a killer cold and flu a few days earlier, but I was determined to shake it off and squeeze in every moment of Emmy joy I could, so I was there with my little red nose shining.

We were told the Best Supporting Actress in a Comedy Series award would be the very first one, which made my life even easier. Amy Poehler and Kristen Wiig were both nominated for *Saturday Night Live*, Elizabeth Perkins for *Weeds*, Vanessa Williams for *Ugly Betty*, and Jane Krakowski for *30 Rock*. Tina Fey would be presenting along with Jon Hamm, the star of my Sunday night obsession, *Mad Men*. I'd be sitting right there in the front row where I could gaze up at him.

"My secret dream is to be stranded on a desert island with Jon Hamm, George Clooney, and a freezer full of Neapolitan Dippin' Dots," I told Amy Poehler at the night-before party.

"Never mind that," she said. "I have an idea, and I really want us all to do it. We're the first award. We're the funny girls. We have to do something great. I was wondering if you'd be willing to—"

"*Yes*. I'm in. Whatever it is," I said. "Quack like a duck, stand on my head, wear a pig nose. Name it."

"Mustaches."

"Yes! I want a big one. A crazy one. Handlebar! No—twirly! Snidely Whiplash."

"Okay, they go in alphabetical order, so the first one to—"

"*Me!* I'm first!" Sweet child of God! This was way too good to be true. "And Vanessa is last. How hilarious would it be if they cut to her, and she's like *no, huh-uh*. Like this prima donna who's completely above it?"

"That's perfect," Amy laughed. "The thing is, I don't really know her. Will she do it, you think? Kristen Wiig is into it, and now you're on board, but Jane's on the fence."

"I can't help you with Jane, but Vanessa's a Broadway girl. She'll do it," I said with certainty.

"No one can know, okay?" said Amy. "Top secret."

I crossed my heart and she gave me a quick hug.

"I loved you before," she said seriously. "But now I really love you."

And I loved her for coming up with this. It was so back-to-basics Commedia dell'arte: "No laugh too small, no bit too cheap." The funny girls. Dang right we are. Five of the six of us would be going home second-runner-up-style, but in that moment, we were all in it together.

The next day, I got into my adorable crystal-encrusted cocktail dress and stood in front of the mirror with Jill, the stylist. The crystals shone and sparkled like mirrors, reflecting sunshine from an open window. They were a little heavier than I remembered—the dress probably weighs about fifteen pounds—but it was worth it. Plain and simply gorgeous.

"I feel pretty," I told Jill.

"You look pretty," she said. "Although . . . that's really sheer on the sides."

"Hmm. You're right. What does one wear underneath—"

"One doesn't."

"Oh." I pondered that for a moment, then shrugged. "Okay. I mean, it's not like I'm going to have to go up on stage or anything.

And as hot as it is outside, this is actually really comfortable. I'll be the only one there who's not melting into the red carpet."

Really, the whole fashion police thing was way down my list. I'd been practicing twirling my mustache, obsessing about exactly how I'd time my little sliver of the funny girl bit.

Then disaster struck. While I was getting my makeup done, Amy called.

"I heard through the grapevine," she said, "Sarah Silverman is doing a mustache."

"What? No! Are you kidding? Wait—it doesn't matter. We're first."

"Yeah, but I heard she's been planning it. I don't want to wreck it for her."

"Dang. Well, now I don't even want to go."

"Oh, c'mon. We have to do something else. Help me think of something."

"No one's going to want to do hats or anything that would mess up hair or makeup," I said. Although, I would have in a heartbeat. "Remember when somebody . . . oh, who was it that wore the 2004 glasses that year? You know, the kind you wear on New Year's and the zeros are like the eyes? I wonder if we could come up with—"

"Hang on. I think I have a pair." She clanked and rummaged on the other end of the line. "Ha! 2009 glasses! I'm looking at them right now."

"Me! Mine! Dibs! What else have you got?"

"Pirate eye patch . . . nerd glasses . . . are we sensing a theme?"

"You're a magician, girlfriend."

Showbiz people always have the best junk drawers. Amy scavenged accessories for the crew and charged her publicist with the task of delivering them to us via top secret spy methodology.

My date, Erin Dilly showed up looking delightful-de-lovely in a scoop-necked royal blue dress, but she had her doubts about the whole Lebanese thing.

"You're going commando to the Emmys?"

"I prefer to think of it as air-conditioning," I said. She started to say something else, but I held up my hand. "We're here. We're sheer. Get used to it."

"Did Denny approve of this?"

"Absolutely. He says I'm like the anti-Cher."

As I suspected, the brightest stars in television were all dying hot and sweating to death as we worked our way through the gauntlet of fans, photographers, and press people. I started out feeling pretty breezy, but that fifteen-pound dress had gained some weight in the hot sun. Looking around at the men in their tuxedos and women in their wowee getups, I worried that we'd all pass out from dehydration before we got to the actual awards. I moved from mark to mark, smiling for the cameras, chatting up my appearance on *Glee*, answering questions about Broadway and being adopted, and a few other issues that came up in my book. By the time Erin and I got to the theater doors, I swear that dress weighed a solid twenty pounds.

"Kristi," Erin said just before we went in, "I just got the strangest feeling . . ."

"Are you okay? Do you need water?"

"You're going to win." She gripped my hand and pulled me close to her side. "I mean it. This feeling just—it washed over me. You're going to win. I know it."

"That's sweet," I laughed. "But no. Sorry. Not gonna happen."

"*You're going to win.* Do you have a speech prepared?"

"Why would I do that?"

"You'd better write something down. Make a quick list of—"

"Would you stop? I have to concentrate on my glasses moment. When they cut to me, I'm going to do my tongue like this—like give it a little rock nod, right? Very '80s MTV hair band zoom shot."

Neil Patrick Harris blew the doors off with a great opening number, there was a little of this and a little of that, and then Jon Hamm and Tina Fey did their opening patter and got a few nervous laughs. This whole time, I was consumed with hiding my 2009 glasses, plotting the exact timing, visualizing the goofy Kiss tongue action.

"The women nominated tonight for Supporting Actress in a Comedy are the finest in their field," Jon intoned. "Smart, Funny, Beautiful, Crazy, Big Eyes, and Pee Wee. Those aren't adjectives, those are my nicknames for them."

A good little laugh. I readied my glasses and squeezed Erin's hand. "Here we go."

"The nominees are . . ." Tina Fey leaned into the mike. "Kristin Chenoweth, *Pushing Daisies* . . ."

Oh, yeah. I was so there. I wasn't looking at the monitor, but I heard startled laughter ripple through the seatbanks, and it grew as the bit played out—spot on—one funny girl at a time.

"Jane Krakowski, *30 Rock* . . ."

She raised a pair of opera glasses with a coquettish smile.

"Elizabeth Perkins, *Weeds* . . ."

She gave it a hundred-twelve percent and slayed everybody, beaming earnestly from behind her Coke-bottle-bottom nerd spectacles.

"Amy Poehler, *Saturday Night Live* . . ."

Pirate vamp! She flipped up her eye patch for a quick wink.

"Kristen Wiig, *Saturday Night Live* . . ."

Talk about timing. First she does the monocle, then in comes the pipe. Elementary, my dear Watson. And then. In for the kill. The *pièce de résistance* . . .

"Vanessa Williams, *Ugly Betty* . . ."

Full-on in character, Vanessa pursed her perfect lips and delivered the goods with a "we are not amused" shake of her head. "*No.*" And then she brought it home with this imperious diva smile.

Perfect. The whole thing. It could not have been more perfect.

I sat there basking in the sheer pleasure of working with such wonderful creatures as the people who filled this room. There are so many crazy-making moments in this business, a moment like this—a moment filled with love, community, laughter—that's to be enjoyed.

"And the Emmy goes to . . ."

There was nothing anyone could say to spoil this moment of—

"Kristin Chenoweth."

Jon Hamm said my name.

Not sure how to describe that feeling. A cross between staring directly into the sun and getting smacked upside the head with a croquet mallet. My heart traded places with my stomach. My mouth dropped open wider than my head. Seriously, check it out on YouTube. I look like a Chilean sea bass. I turned to Erin, who looked smugger than smug about her psychic abilities as she swept me into a warm, grounding hug.

Applause. Noise. A tornado inside my head.

"Are you okay?" Erin asked as I got unsteadily to my feet.

I nodded. Headed toward the stage. Climbed the steps. Wearing a million little mirrors. And no underwear. To get my Emmy. For my defunct show.

Neil Patrick Harris was offsides somewhere, his voice carrying through the thunder and lightning. "Kristin Chenoweth was raised in Broken Arrow, Oklahoma."

My heart filled up with Mom and Dad. I felt myself shining—a bright crystal reflecting their love and faith—and I started crying.

"She says if she were not on television, she would become a private detective, which in itself sounds like a pretty good TV show. This is the first Emmy win and second consecutive nomination for Kristin Chenoweth."

Tina Fey floated over and handed me the winged statue, which was heavier than my dress, and I stood weak-kneed in front of the microphone.

"Thank you. I'm totally surprised . . ."

Dang! My voice came out all weepy and even squeakier than usual.

Somebody told me later that garage doors went up all over the country.

"This is really heavy. Um . . ."

Oh, God . . . Jesus . . . please make words come out of my mouth . . .

"That was Amy Poehler's idea—the glasses and everything."

Yeah, you, Jesus. Talking to you here. Feel free to jump right in. Anytime now.

"I'd like to thank my parents . . . I'd like to thank Brian Fuller for trusting me . . . to create this part . . . I don't know why I'm crying . . ."

But of course, everyone in the room knew why. Anyone who's been in television long enough to make it to the Emmys knows the frequent agony of *almost* and the rare ecstasy of *enough*.

Funny girl, I reminded myself. *I'm one of the funny girls.*

"I'm unemployed now," I said, "so I'd like to be on *Mad Men*."

Big laugh. Thank you, God. *Why didn't I make a list?*

"I also like *The Office* . . . and *24* . . ."

Note to self: Always follow instructions of psychic BFF. *Think. Breathe.* I clutched the statue to the front of my sixty-seven pound dress.

"Um . . . Brian . . . the producers! Dan and Bruce. The whole cast—Ellen, Swoosie, Lee, Anna, Chi—I love you guys. My manager Dannielle Thomas who said that I could go into TV from Broadway . . ."

For some reason the camera cut to Erin Dilly, who looked quite startled to suddenly see herself up on the ol' Jumbotron. But I didn't know this at the time. Too busy bawling. Babbling. Being grateful. Someone behind a camera was wildly gesticulating.

"Oh—wrap it up? Okay. I'm wrapping it up. Um, thank you so much to the Academy for recognizing a show that's no longer on the air. Thank you so much. Bye!"

Thank God, I had the presence of mind on my way off to detour and throw my arms around Jon Hamm. That sort of opportunity doesn't come along every day of the week, and it was everything I hoped it would be. One Clooney and a handful of Dippin' Dots away from unblemished bliss. I was whisked off to the press room where I mugged and bubbled in front of a phalanx of flashing cameras until it was someone else's turn. Basically, the whole thing had come and gone like a freight train before I knew what hit me.

But when it hit me, it really hit me.

Back in my seat, I whispered to Erin, "I can't see out of my right eye. I'm getting a migraine. All those flashing lights . . ."

"Oh, no. We should go to the medics. Maybe they have Imitrex."

"No way," I said. "If I go to the medics, it'll be all over the tabloids that I passed out because I don't eat or threw up because I'm on drugs or broke water backstage and gave birth to Simon Cowell's baby."

"Kristi, you don't look so good."

She put her arm around me, and we staggered to the medics' station just outside the gift lounge. (Ah, my lovely Gift Lounge . . . so close and yet so far.)

"I'm fine. Really. I'm good," I told my mom on the phone. "I told Erin to tell them I just have to lie down for a few minutes, and then I'll be good to go."

"Kristi, maybe you should go home," she said.

"No. No way. I don't know if I'll ever get here again, Mom. We're not missing the parties. And I don't want Erin to miss out on the gifts. She's been so great. We going for the gifts, Mom. I don't care if my hair's on fire."

I kept insisting as the invading headache tied my frontal lobe in a knot and turned my large intestine inside out, but in the end, I slumped off to bed in my two-hundred-forty pound dress. When I woke up, it was four in the morning, and the migraine had passed. The parties were over, the gift lounge was a distant dream, and I was alone with my Emmy.

"Hi, Mommy. I'm sorry to wake you up."

"No, I'm glad you called. I've been worried."

"I'm okay. You know how it is."

Lying in the cool dark of just-before-dawn, I cupped the phone close to my ear, and Mom told me how funny the glasses bit played, how excited everyone was, how they loved my speech. She told me Dad got all choked up and sentimental and we laughed about all the everything that had brought us to this extraordinary moment. Dance lessons. Driving to churches around the state. School plays, Flo Bird, Broadway.

Best after party ever. Just me and Mom. I'm so grateful I didn't miss it.

The next day I headed back to New York to continue rehearsing a terrific show called *Minsky's*. I arrived at the gate in plenty of time to nail my first class seat, and all the way down the concourse at LAX, people offered congratulations and kind words.

"Welcome aboard, Ms. Chenoweth." A handsome flight attendant hoisted my bag into the overhead bin. "I thought you were terrific on *Pushing Daisies*. Congratulations."

"Oh, thank you," I beamed. "You're so sweet."

As he moved up the aisle, two tricked-out L.A. fabulistas pushed past him. Dressed head to toe in trunk sale must-haves, they'd clearly been abusing salesgirls in all the best places. Both of them had *Nip/Tuck* bodies, lips inflated like a flotation device.

"Kristin Chenoweth?" said one.

"Hi," I smiled. "How are you today?"

She wrinkled her nose and said, "STAR-F#%KER."

Stunned, I slumped into my seat, thinking, *STAR-F#%KER?* What does that even mean? I suppose it could be a compliment, like "star pupil" or "star athlete" . . . but probably not. I fished my cell phone from my bag and called Dannielle to report this travesty that had taken place.

"Congratulations," she said philosophically, "now you know you've really made it."

I speed dialed Mom, thinking she'd be a little more sympathetic, but instead of coddling, she firmly said, "Kristi. Let it go. That's just them."

"I know, but . . ."

I glanced over my shoulder at Blimp Lips and Can Can. They were already sucking down Bloody Marys and trashing someone else. That was just them. But an ugly remark like that gets me like a hole in the stage floor. One minute you're up there in the bright lights, doing your groove thang. The next minute, this trap door swings away, and you drop into the darkness.

"Kristi," said Mom. "Don't let them steal your joy. They didn't earn that joy. You did."

That's my mom. I ask you, what would have become of me if God hadn't seen to it that I got into the arms of the right parents?

The engines roared to life beneath us all: sinners, saints, and everyone between.

"I have to shut off the phone, Mom. I love you."

"I love you, too, Kristi."

So, my dears, we're right back where we started: an awards show and an airplane. A good metaphor for the ups and downs of life in general and showbiz in particular. I do what I do, I love who I love, and all the rest—well, I try to give that to God. My friend Joy says that when the jet engines roar to life, she always takes her daughter's hand and together they say what Isaiah said in the Bible:

Those who hope in the Lord
    will renew their strength.
They will soar on wings of eagles;
    they will run and not grow weary;
    they will run and not be faint.

That feels like a good a place to end this chapter and begin another.

⤜∞⤏

lovefest

A NOTE FROM THE AUTHOR

When I'm a grand old dame of the stage, I might get around to writing a proper "tell-all" autobiography. Right now, I'm offering this completely biased "tell-a-little" slice of life, which reflects my personal recollections and opinions and not the opinions of Simon & Schuster, ABC, Sony Classical, or any of the other wonderful organizations I've been privileged to work for. To make this book more of a tea party and less of a Wagnerian night at the opera, it was necessary to composite some events, conversations, and people. Some names have been changed in the interest of diplomacy and to protect my privacy. If you're not mentioned in these pages, please don't think that means I didn't appreciate your presence, friendship, or contribution. I'm probably saving you for the magnum opus.

Roll the Thank-You Cam!

Thanks to my family for loving and accepting me always. (And for continually upping that fun factor!) Mom and Dad, you gave me faith in Him, belief in myself, and the best life I can imagine. Mark, you're the man. Betsye, you're the *W-O-M-A-N*—more than my sister-in-law, you're my soul sister, best friend, and matchless shopping buddy. Zach and Emily, you're just plain adorable. Aunts, uncles, and cousins—love ya! To my dear friends Denny, Erin, Regina, and Anne, thank you for listening to me and for allowing me to listen to you. I'm grateful to all my teachers, good and bad, but I'm forever indebted to *my person,* Florence Birdwell at Oklahoma City University, who taught me to sing and be strong.

I deeply appreciate the encouragement and insight of my manager, Dannielle Thomas; my agent Tony Lipp and all my agents at CAA; and my publicists, Jill Fritzo (of the East) and Megan Proffitt (of the West). Thanks to James Adams. (I know you're not supposed to be friends with your lawyer, but I am.) And to Melody Young, my business manager, for her valiant (though ultimately futile) efforts to keep a lid on my shopping. I'm also very grateful to Mark Gompertz, who came to me with the idea to do this book, and to Michelle Howry, who expertly guided it from thought bubble to bookshelf.

Special thanks to Aaron Sorkin for reminding me to let the emotion come through. Come what may, A-so, you have my gratitude, respect, and love always.

∞

When Simon and Schuster talked to me about writing a book, they said it was because they thought I was a person of interest. I couldn't find myself less interesting or more dorky, so I knew I had to find a ghost writer, aka Casper, aka my vessel to help me say what I wanted to say clearly and honestly.

I met with many people. Because I am a God person, I believe Joni Rodgers was plopped into my lap on purpose. She has become a member of my family, someone I trust implicitly, and a woman I revere because of all she's gone through. She is so good at words, but there aren't words in the English dictionary for me to say how much I love her and thank her for her hard work. She never missed a deadline, she laughed at my jokes even when they weren't funny and she came with her great assistant/daughter who is now like a little sister. Joni, you survived cancer to give other people the gift of words. Thank you for giving me mine.

Kristin Chenoweth
June 2008

A Note from the Memoir Guru

Thanks to Kirby Kim and Kirsten Neuhaus at Vigliano Associates and to my literary agent, Wendy Sherman. Gratitude and love to Gary for keeping the Houston home fires burning while I was sucked into the Hollywood vortex, to my son, Malachi, for steady laughs, and to my daughter, Jerusha, the best research assistant anyone ever grew. J'ru, your hard work and hipster insights made this book (and the story of my life) many metaphors and a Gucci bag better. Huge thanks to Aaron Sorkin for invaluable research assistance and creative insights, in addition to the long-suffering good humor and ridiculous courage it took for him to participate in this project. (Peace be with you, Studs Mulligan.)

Most of all, I'd like to thank Kristin Chenoweth for inviting me into her life and allowing me to be her book Sherpa. Her astonishing generosity, boundless energy, and shining spirit made it a delight from cover to cover.

Joni Rodgers
July 2008

∞

KRISTIN CHENOWETH TIME LINE

1968 Born July 24 in Broken Arrow, Oklahoma
1986 Graduate Broken Arrow High School
      Miss Broken Arrow pageant (2nd runner-up)
1990 BA in Musical Theatre from Oklahoma City
      University
1991 Miss Oklahoma City University pageant (winner)
      Miss Oklahoma pageant (2nd runner-up)
1992 Miss State Capitol (winner)
      Miss Pennsylvania (2nd runner-up)
1993 *Animal Crackers*
      Little Me
      Zombie Prom (workshop)
1994 *The Box Office of the Damned*
      Dames at Sea
1995 *Phantom*
      The Fantasticks
      MFA in Opera Performance from OCU (finally!)

1996 *Scapin* (Broadway debut)
     Steel Pier (workshop)
1997 *Steel Pier* (Broadway)
     Theatre World Award
     Wild Party (Eugene O'Neill Theatre Center)
1998 *A New Brain*
     Strike Up the Band
     You're a Good Man, Charlie Brown (Broadway)
1999 *Epic Proportions* (Broadway)
     Lateline
     Paramour (series on AMC)
     Annie (TV movie with Kathy Bates)
     The Rosie O'Donnell Show
     Tony Award: Best Featured Actress in a Musical
     Drama Desk Award: Outstanding Featured Actress in
     a Musical
     Outer Critics Circle Award: Best Featured Actress
     Joseph Jefferson Award: Actress in a Supporting Role
     Clarence Derwent Award
2000 *On a Clear Day You Can See Forever*
     Wicked (workshop)
     54th Annual Tony Awards (presenter)
     Carnegie Hall Celebrates Lerner and Lowe
     Late Show with David Letterman
2001 *Wicked* (workshop)
     Kristin (Huge Hit Sitcom on NBC)
     The Kennedy Center Honors Julie Andrews
     "Let Yourself Go" (Broadway music CD)
     Sesame Street (Miss Noodle)
     Frasier
     55th Annual Tony Awards (presenter)
     The Rosie O'Donnell Show
     The Isaac Mizrahi Show

2002 *Strike Up the Band*
    Babes in Arms
    Funny Girl (Broadway)
    Wicked (workshop)
    Isn't It Romantic: The Love Songs of Rodgers and
    Hart (concert)
    The Rosie O'Donnell Show
    West Side Story in Central Park (Great Performances
    on PBS)

2003 *The Music Man* (TV movie with Matthew
    Broderick)
    Wicked (Broadway)
    The View
    Fillmore!
    Sesame Street
    Crossing Over with John Edward
    The *Today* show
    Macy's Thanksgiving Day Parade

2004 *Wicked* (Broadway)
    Wicked: The Road to Broadway
    58th Annual Tony Awards (performer)
    The West Wing (Season 6)
    Broadway: The American Musical
    The Late Show with Craig Kilborn

2005 *Bewitched* (movie with Nicole Kidman)
    Carnegie Hall Concert (sold out)
    Candide (Great Performances on PBS)
    The West Wing (Seasons 6 and 7)
    Bewitched: Star Shots
    Why I Love Bewitched
    Casting a Spell: Making Bewitched
    As I Am (inspirational music CD)
    The 700 Club

The *Today* show
Late Show with David Letterman
The Early Show
The Tony Danza Show
Breakfast with the Arts
Last Call with Carson Daly
The Late Show with Craig Ferguson
MAD TV
2006 *The Apple Tree* (Broadway)
The West Wing (Season 7)
A Sesame Street Christmas Carol
Sesame Street
Deck the Halls (movie with Danny DeVito)
Running with Scissors
    (movie with Annette Bening)
Stranger Than Fiction (movie with Will Ferrell)
RV (movie with Robin Williams)
The Pink Panther (movie with Steve Martin)
Barry Sonnenfeld: The Kosher Cowboy
RV Nation: A Culture of Road Warriors
Robin Williams: A Family Affair
The Late Show with Craig Ferguson
The View
Last Call with Carson Daly
The Tonight Show with Jay Leno
Ellen: The Ellen DeGeneres Show
A Night of Too Many Stars: An Overbooked Event
for Autism Education
Live with Regis and Kelly
The Martha Stewart Show
CMT Insider
The Megan Mullally Show
Late Night with Conan O'Brien

2007 *Ugly Betty*

Pushing Daisies

Robot Chicken (animated series by Seth Greene)

Elmo's World

Sesame Street

The View

Show Business: The Road to Broadway

Metropolitan Opera Concert

52nd Annual Drama Desk Awards (host)

Ellen: The Ellen DeGeneres Show

Late Show with David Letterman

The Tonight Show with Jay Leno

Late Night with Conan O'Brien

The Late Show with Craig Ferguson

Jimmy Kimmel Live!

The Red Dress Collection 2007 Fashion Show

2008 *Pushing Daisies* (series on ABC)

Space Chimps (animated movie with Jeff Daniels)

Tinker Bell (animated movie with Lucy Liu)

Four Christmases (movie with Reese Witherspoon)

62nd Annual Tony Awards (presenter)

80th Annual Academy Awards (performer)

Entertainment Tonight

The Tonight Show with Jay Leno

"Kristintervention" (Funny or Die Web feature)

Emmy nomination for *Pushing Daisies*

2009 *Into Temptation* (movie with Jeremy Sisto)

Publication of *A Little Bit Wicked*